The Taney Court

ABC-CLIO SUPREME COURT HANDBOOKS

The Burger Court, Tinsley E. Yarbrough
The Fuller Court, James W. Ely, Jr.
The Hughes Court, Michael E. Parrish
The Stone Court, Peter G. Renstrom
The Taft Court, Peter G. Renstrom
The Taney Court, Timothy S. Huebner
The Waite Court, Donald Grier Stephenson
The Warren Court, Melvin I. Urofsky

Forthcoming:
The Chase Court, Jonathan Lurie
The Jay/Ellsworth Court, Matthew P. Harrington
The Marshall Court, Robert L. Clinton
The Rehnquist Court, Thomas R. Hensley
The Vinson Court, Michal R. Belknap
The White Court, Rebecca S. Shoemaker

Peter G. Renstrom, Series Editor

ABC-CLIO SUPREME COURT HANDBOOKS

The Taney Court

Justices, Rulings, and Legacy

Timothy S. Huebner

ABC-CLIO
Santa Barbara, California • Denver, Colorado • Oxford, England

Library of Congress Cataloging-in-Publication Data

Huebner, Timothy S. , 1966–
The Taney Court: justices, rulings, and legacy / Timothy S. Huebner.
p. cm.—(ABC-CLIO Supreme Court handbooks)
Includes bibliographical references and index.
ISBN 1-57607-368-8 (hardcover: alk. paper) ISBN 1-57607-369-6 (e-book)
1. United States. Supreme Court—History—19th century. 2. Taney, Roger Brooke, 1777–1864. 3. Constitutional history—United States. I. Title. II. Series.
KF8742.H79 2003
347. 73'26'09—dc22
2003018224

07 06 05 04 03 10 9 8 7 6 5 4 3 2 1

ABC-CLIO, Inc.
130 Cremona Drive, P.O. Box 1911
Santa Barbara, California 93116-1911

This book is printed on acid-free paper ♾.
Manufactured in the United States of America

For Kristin,
who was there from beginning to end

Contents

Series Foreword

There is an extensive literature on the U.S. Supreme Court, but it contains discussion familiar largely to the academic community and the legal profession. The ABC-CLIO Supreme Court series is designed to have value to the academic and legal communities also, but each volume is intended as well for the general reader who does not possess an extensive background on the Court or American constitutional law. The series is intended to effectively represent each of fourteen periods in the history of the Supreme Court with each of these fourteen eras defined by the chief justice beginning with John Jay in 1789. Each Court confronted constitutional and statutory questions that were of major importance to and influenced by the historical period. The Court's decisions were also influenced by the values of each of the individual justices sitting at the time. The issues, the historical period, the justices, and the Supreme Court's decisions in the most significant cases will be examined in the volumes of this series.

ABC-CLIO's Supreme Court series provides scholarly examinations of the Court as it functioned in different historical periods and with different justices. Each volume contains information necessary to understand each particular Court and an interpretative analysis by the author of each Court's record and legacy. In addition to representing the major decisions of each Court, institutional linkages are examined as well—the political connections among the Court, Congress, and the president. These relationships are important for several reasons. Although the Court retains some institutional autonomy, all the Court's justices are selected by a process that involves the other two branches. Many of the significant decisions of the Court involve the review of actions of Congress or the president. In addition, the Court frequently depends on the other two branches to secure compliance with its rulings.

The authors of the volumes in the ABC-CLIO series were selected with great care. Each author has worked extensively with the Court, the period, and the personalities about which he or she has written. ABC-CLIO wanted each of the volumes to examine several common themes, and each author agreed to work within certain guidelines. Each author was free, however, to develop the content of each volume, and many of the volumes advance new or distinctive conclusions about the Court under examination.

Each volume will contain four substantive chapters. The first chapter will introduce the Court and the historical period in which it served. The second chapter will examine each of the justices who sat on the particular Court. The third chapter will represent the most significant decisions rendered by the particular Court. Among other things, the impact of the historical period and the value orientations of the individual justices will be developed. A fourth and final chapter will address the impact of each particular Court on American constitutional law—its doctrinal legacy.

Each volume will contain several features designed to make the volume more valuable to those whose previous exposure to the Supreme Court and American constitutional law is limited. Each volume will have a reference section that will contain brief entries on some of the people, statutes, events, and concepts introduced in the four substantive chapters. Entries in this section are arranged alphabetically. Each volume will also contain a glossary of selected legal terms used in the text. Following each of the four chapters, a list of sources used in the chapter and suggestions for further reading will appear. Each volume will also have a comprehensive annotated bibliography. A listing of Internet sources is presented at the end of the bibliography. Finally, there will be a comprehensive subject index and a list of cases (with citation numbers) discussed in each volume. ABC-CLIO is delighted with the quality of scholarship represented in each volume and is proud to offer this series to the reading public.

Permit me to conclude with a personal note. This project has been an extraordinarily rewarding undertaking for me as series editor. Misgivings about serving in this capacity were plentiful at the outset of the project. After tending to some administrative business pertaining to the series, securing authors for each volume was the first major task. I developed a list of possible authors after reviewing previous work and obtaining valuable counsel from several recognized experts in American constitutional history. In virtually every instance, the first person on my list agreed to participate in the project. The high quality of the series was ensured and enhanced as each author signed on. I could not have been more pleased. My interactions with each author have been most pleasant, and the excellence of their work will be immediately apparent to the reader. I sincerely thank each author.

Finally, a word about ABC-CLIO and its staff. ABC-CLIO was enthusiastic about the project from the beginning and has done everything necessary to make this series successful. I am very appreciative of the level of support I have received from ABC-CLIO. Alicia Merritt, senior acquisitions editor, deserves special recognition. She has held my hand throughout the project. She has facilitated making this project a reality in every conceivable way. She has encouraged me from the beginning, provided invaluable counsel, and given me latitude to operate as I wished while keeping me on track at the same time. This project would not have gotten off the ground without Alicia, and I cannot thank her enough.

—Peter G. Renstrom

Preface

From 1836 to 1864, perhaps the most difficult and tumultuous era in American history, Roger Brooke Taney of Maryland served as chief justice of the United States Supreme Court. Although well known for its infamous decision in *Dred Scott v. Sandford* (1857), in which the Court explicitly denied the rights of African Americans and implicitly affirmed the constitutional rights of slaveholders, the Court during this period has received relatively little scholarly attention. This fact is striking. During no other period in the Court's history has the tribunal come under such strain and been subject to so much criticism.

After the death of Chief Justice John Marshall, many Americans viewed Taney as a poor replacement for Marshall, who had already achieved the status of mythic greatness in some quarters. Taney, in contrast, seemed too much a product of the rough-and-tumble politics of the age and too closely tied to the president who appointed him. President Andrew Jackson, the self-proclaimed champion of the so-called common man, had elevated Taney to the bench after the lawyer had served extraordinarily controversial stints as U.S. attorney general and secretary of the treasury. In the latter post, Taney had carried out Jackson's desire to dismantle the Bank of the United States by withdrawing the deposits of the U.S. government and placing them in a variety of small state banks. By implementing Jackson's policy on the bank—Jackson's previous treasury secretary had resigned after refusing to do so—Taney earned the reputation as something of a political hack.

It would take a while for Taney to gain the respect of the legal community and to win over his colleagues on the Court, particularly Marshall's old friends and allies, but the chief justice eventually proved equal to the task. Universally acclaimed as a gentleman, Taney demonstrated a remarkable ability to charm even his most vociferous political opponents. Not merely an affable man, though, Taney proved able as both a constitutional theorist and judicial leader. Although he never forged the degree of unanimity on the Court that had been the hallmark of his predecessor, the Court with Taney at the helm maintained its prestige as an institution despite a sharp increase in the frequency of disagreements and dissents among the justices. Generally pragmatic in outlook, the Court skillfully navigated a number of potentially dangerous constitutional channels during the mid-nineteenth century. In the process, the Taney Court built on Marshall's work without either blindly adhering to precedent or needlessly overturning it. Instead, the Taney Court adjusted existing constitutional doctrine to the demands of the age—to the new, more open, and more enterprising society that began to emerge during Jackson's presidency. Had it not been for the slavery issue—which had practically never intruded itself into the work of the Court during the Marshall era—Taney and his colleagues might have attained reputations equal to those of their early-nineteenth-century predecessors.

Slavery, in some ways, came to define the Taney era. The issue lurked beneath many of the Commerce Clause decisions of the age, and it inserted itself directly into the Court's work beginning with the landmark case *Prigg v. Pennsylvania* (1842). An issue powerful enough to divide the nation had consequences nearly as catastrophic for the work of the Court. Almost immediately after the *Dred Scott* decision, Taney went from being perceived as a respected jurist and worthy heir to Marshall to being compared by some, literally, to Pontius Pilate. The Court that Taney led, in turn, became subject to all sorts of criticisms and proposals for reform. These ranged from abolishing the tribunal altogether, in order to give President Abraham Lincoln the opportunity to appoint a brand new set of justices, to rearranging the geographical regions represented by the circuits and the justices. The latter plan, implemented during the Civil War, promised to make the Court less "southern" and more reflective of the views of Lincoln and northern Republicans.

This book takes account of the Taney Court's successes as well as its failures. Although sensitive to the competing interpretations and emphases of those who have studied the Taney era, this general reference work is by no means comprehensive, either in its interpretation or its coverage. The justices heard numerous disputes during this period—particularly relating to property law and land titles, for example—that make no appearance here. The book focuses rather on the major constitutional opinions of the Taney period and the justices who wrote them. Implicit in this account is the assumption that the lives of the justices—their regional and religious backgrounds, families and education, party affiliations and judicial experience, to name but a few factors—influenced their work as Supreme Court justices. Also assumed in this text is the notion that American constitutional history is worthy of study on its own terms, not simply as a means of understanding current constitutional doctrine or debates. That is, not every case discussed here remains "good law" from the perspective of the lawyer. Still, from the standpoint of the historian, these decisions merit our attention and understanding because of what they tell us about their times and about our nation's historical experiences with the Constitution.

Many have helped make this book possible. I would like to acknowledge the generous support of Rhodes College, which provided me with a sabbatical year during which I researched and wrote much of the manuscript. The staffs of Burrow

Library at Rhodes, the University of Memphis Libraries, and the Memphis–Shelby County Public Library demonstrated their usual helpfulness and professionalism as they assisted in locating materials. Jim Gerencser and Bobby Reeves, of the Dickinson College Archives and Special Collections Department, meanwhile, helped make my visit to Taney's alma mater both productive and pleasant. Rhodes students Robert Edgecombe, Kathryn Barbour, Amanda Moshier, Elizabeth Porras, Amber Korb, and Elokin CaPece skillfully performed many research tasks along the way, and Nancy Hunt and Tonya Mosley provided expert secretarial assistance. Michael Nelson, a political scientist at Rhodes, read a portion of the manuscript and provided many thoughtful comments and stylistic suggestions. I am also indebted to my students and colleagues in the Department of History at Rhodes, who allowed me to discuss portions of this work with them in a variety of settings both formal and informal.

Finally, I owe my greatest debt to my wife Kristin, who never ceased to listen to me talk about this book and who never became frustrated with the many hours I devoted to working on it. She has always been my biggest fan and greatest supporter. To her I dedicate this volume.

Timothy S. Huebner
Memphis, Tennessee

PART ONE

Justices, Rulings, and Legacy

1

The Taney Court and the Period

The history of the United States Supreme Court under Chief Justice Roger Brooke Taney (pronounced "Tawny") coincided with the middle part of the nineteenth century. Born in 1777, the first chief justice to come of age after the American Revolution, Taney presided over the high court for twenty-eight years, from 1836 to 1864.

This was a period of extraordinary change that, in many respects, held great promise for the young republic. Factories producing everything from textiles to firearms sprang up, particularly in the Northeast. A new transportation and communication network, composed of roads, canals, and railroads, spanned the country. Steamboats, locomotives, and telegraph lines facilitated opportunities for business and connected Americans to each other more than ever before. As the population moved westward, new cities emerged—places such as Rochester, Cincinnati, St. Louis, and Chicago, where canals, rivers, or railroads converged to create bustling centers of commercial activity. Immigrants arrived from Europe, particularly Ireland and Germany, in search of better economic opportunities and greater political freedoms. In the southern states, the production of cotton and other cash crops yielded enormous profits for planters as well as for the region's expanding middle class. Across the country, a series of religious revivals generated evangelical fervor and spurred social reform movements to improve the lot of the poor and oppressed. And the United States acquired vast new territory west of the Mississippi River, largely the result of a brief and successful war with Mexico. During the middle of the nineteenth century, most Americans were on the move and on the rise. They viewed their country as far different from—and much superior to—the nations of Europe, where monarchs and aristocrats still held sway. Free from the constraints of nobility and the legacy of feudalism that still plagued the Old World, America offered its citizens boundless economic opportunities and extensive political liberties. In many ways, these middle years of the century were the heady days of American idealism, optimism, and nationalism.

Yet, the mid-nineteenth century was also the darkest and most devastating era in American history. For some, economic growth produced dislocation and alienation. Many skilled craftsmen and working-class Americans, while hoping to achieve the material benefits of prosperity, longed for greater stability than the ever-changing marketplace provided. The growth of banks and the advent of business corporations fed suspicion of concentrated wealth and special interests, giving rise to powerful antimonopoly sentiment. Meanwhile, in the South, slavery was a grim reality for 4 million African Americans. The foundation of the southern economy and an important part of the region's culture, slavery existed in thirteen of the twenty-five states in the Union in 1836, the year Taney became chief justice. Because slave property constituted most of the wealth in the South, slaveholders resolved to preserve their "peculiar institution," as they often referred to it. When slavery came under attack, first from religious abolitionists and later from political opponents of slavery's extension, eleven southern states eventually left the Union. The Civil War ensued. By the time the Taney era came to a close in 1864, the war was winding down, but only after four years of bloodshed that had resulted in more than 600,000 deaths. During this tumultuous time in the nation's history, Chief Justice Taney and his fellow justices wrestled with questions that no other Court, before or since, has had to confront. For this reason, the chief justiceship of Roger Taney remains one of the most controversial in Supreme Court history.

The Jacksonian Era and the Supreme Court

The Taney period may be said to have begun in 1828, with Andrew Jackson's election to the presidency, rather than in 1836 with Taney's actual appointment as chief justice. Jackson's ascension to the presidency further weakened John Marshall's Supreme Court, in which personnel changes had begun a few years earlier. Before 1823, the Court under Marshall had been characterized by a remarkable degree of stability, harmony, and unanimity. From 1811 to 1823 the Court's composition remained constant, and the justices resided in a common boardinghouse. The seven members of the Court ate together on a regular basis and discussed the cases before them over meals. During these years, Marshall built on his landmark decision in *Marbury v. Madison* (1803), in which the Court had asserted the power to decide the constitutionality of legislative acts, and issued a number of important decisions regarding contracts, commerce, and the proper relationship between the national government and the states. In the process, Marshall established the Court as a major player in national constitutional debates. By the 1820s, though, these nationalistic rulings aroused much opposition, particularly from the "Old Republicans" of Virginia, who clung tenaciously to a states' rights ideology and a limited view of national power. This challenge to the Court's authority, along with changes in its membership, marked the beginning of a decline in the Marshall Court's power and influence.

The rise of Andrew Jackson signaled a new era in U.S. constitutional and political history. As the last president to have fought in the American Revolution and the first with humble origins, Jackson held wide appeal as a presidential candidate. Born in 1767 in South Carolina, Jackson fought as a young man in the guerrilla warfare that came to the southern backcountry during the Revolution, and he was wounded and imprisoned. Already an orphan, by war's end he was only sixteen years old and had lost two brothers in the fighting. With little money, Jackson took up the study of law and then headed west to Tennessee, where he established a practice and married into a prominent family. During the next several years, he invested profitably in land and slaves, made a name for himself in state politics, and assumed the air of an aristocrat. Still, underneath, Jackson was a rough product of the frontier. He fought in several duels in Tennessee (once killing an opponent) and exhibited a fiery temperament. Severe and stern, Jackson earned the nickname "Old Hickory" during this period. His rise to national fame came during the War of 1812, when he and his men routed the British at the Battle of New Orleans, although the victory occurred after the Treaty of Ghent had brought an end to the war. Later, he fought the Seminole Indians in Florida and served as governor of that territory after the United States obtained it from Spain in 1821.

Jackson's military renown coincided with changes in the style of U.S. politics. By the middle of the 1820s, the westward expansion of the nation, along with the gradual disappearance of property qualifications for voting, made Jackson's common origins a political asset. As the number of voters increased in the United States, torchlight parades and mass political gatherings, where whiskey and political rhetoric were handed out in equal measure, came to characterize campaigning. Gradually, it seemed, having aristocratic origins began to work against candidates for high office. In 1824, in the midst of this changing political environment, Jackson entered the presidential race and received more popular votes than any of his three opponents, but remained short of the electoral vote majority he needed for victory. The election moved to the House of Representatives, where an apparent agreement between Henry Clay, the fourth-place finisher, and John Quincy Adams, the second-place candidate, allowed Adams to win the White House. Adams received Clay's support, and the new president then made Clay the secretary of state. Four years later, in 1828, Jackson defeated the incumbent Adams, who never fully recovered from the charges that a "corrupt bargain" had allowed him to assume office. Jackson took the oath in March 1829, after which an adoring mass of spectators pushed their way into the presidential mansion to see their new leader and continue the celebration. In the most raucous inaugural event in history, a horde of visitors jammed the place to capacity. Barrels of punch and pails of liquor spilled all over the fine carpets, while men with muddy boots stood on satin-covered chairs to get a better look at the president. The scene erupted into a near riot. Supreme Court Justice Joseph Story, Marshall's closest friend on the bench, reacted in horror to the mixing inside the presidential mansion of "the highest and most polished down to the most vulgar and gross in the nation." "The reign of KING MOB seemed triumphant," Story noted. "I was glad to escape from the scene as soon as possible" (Remini 1981, 177).

At the time of Jackson's inauguration, geography and party politics figured most prominently in the appointment of justices to the Supreme Court. From the origin of the Court until after the Civil War, the justices joined U.S. district judges in staffing the federal circuit courts throughout the country. This meant that justices spent most of the year outside the nation's capital, "riding the circuit." Justices typically logged hundreds, even thousands, of miles a year in travel, usually via horse and buggy, steamboat, and eventually rail. Familiarity with a particular state or region thus became a virtual requirement for nomination to the Court, and justices almost always came from the circuit that they were to represent. Political considerations, of course, also weighed heavily in the appointment process, and even more so by the middle of the 1820s with increased political participation and the new style of mass political campaigning. As politics came to involve public opinion more than ever before, presidents sought not only to reward party loyalists with appointments but also to win popular approval for their nominees.

Jackson made six appointments to the Court—more than any nineteenth-century president—and his appointees reflected these geographical and political considerations. The Senate's refusal to approve the nomination of John J. Crittenden to the Court by outgoing President John Quincy Adams in February 1829, to replace the recently deceased Robert Trimble, cleared the way for Jackson to select a justice immediately upon his inauguration. The new president needed a politically loyal, legally skilled, and well-known individual to fill the vacancy. In addition, because the new justice would have responsibility for what was at that time the western circuit, the nominee would have to come from that part of the country. John McLean, who had served as postmaster general under Presidents Monroe and Adams, fit the description. McLean had adroitly courted Jackson during the 1828 presidential campaign, even while he remained in Adams's cabinet. An Ohioan, the forty-three-year-old McLean had served six years on his state's supreme court. A leading Methodist layman who took an active role in church affairs and wrote articles for religious magazines, McLean had developed a popular national following. Indeed, he had presidential aspirations. Although Jackson had initially decided to keep McLean as postmaster general, McLean's boredom in the Post Office Department, along with Jackson's desire to eliminate a potential political rival, led to McLean's selection for the Court. The nomination aroused no opposition, and the Senate gave its approval the day after his appointment. McLean took the oath to become a justice in January 1830.

McLean's inaugural term on the Court coincided with Jackson's second appointment. The death of Justice Bushrod Washington in 1829 created a vacancy on the

Court, and the president nominated Henry Baldwin, a fifty-year-old Pennsylvanian. Baldwin's support of Jackson went back to 1818, when as a member of Congress he had supported General Jackson's questionable behavior during his assault against the Seminoles. (Jackson had invaded Florida without permission and nearly provoked an international incident when he executed two British subjects accused of inciting the Seminoles to rebellion.) Later, in 1823, Baldwin urged Jackson to run for the presidency and championed his candidacy in Pennsylvania. Despite Old Hickory's defeat in 1824, Baldwin remained in close contact with the Tennessean, and Jackson's eventual victory made Baldwin a prime candidate for a federal appointment. Although the new president nominated Baldwin to serve as secretary of the treasury, Vice President John C. Calhoun succeeded in blocking the appointment because of Baldwin's support for higher federal tariffs, which Calhoun and many southerners strongly opposed. When the position on the Court opened up, Jackson nominated Baldwin, despite protests from the vice president and his friends from South Carolina. Baldwin won confirmation easily, by a vote of 40–2.

If Jackson succeeded in gaining wide support for his early nominees to the Court, the ensuing years of his presidency presented more severe political challenges. Three episodes were particularly controversial. First, Jackson's plan to remove Native Americans from the southeastern states to new territory in the West (present-day Oklahoma) incurred the wrath of many northern evangelical Protestants, who hoped that missions to the southern Indians would help "civilize" them and incorporate them into U.S. society. The Supreme Court, still led by Marshall, attempted to halt Jackson's removal of the Indians in *Worcester v. Georgia* (1832), in which the Court upheld the rights of the Cherokee under treaties negotiated by the U.S. government. Jackson simply ignored the ruling. Second, an increase in the federal tariff in 1828, and another in 1832, provoked the ire of Vice President Calhoun and other southerners, who favored free trade and thought that tariff policy benefited northern industry at the expense of southern agriculture. Calhoun fought the high tariff by advocating the doctrine of nullification, the idea that states possessed the power to declare as void acts of Congress that they viewed as detrimental to their interests. Eventually Calhoun broke with Jackson, resigned the vice presidency, and returned to South Carolina to take up the fight against enforcement of the tariff. Third, Jackson's opposition to the rechartering of the national bank, the Bank of the United States, in 1832 constituted a major political showdown. The president vetoed a bill to extend the life of the bank, and he successfully used the issue in his reelection campaign that year. Although Old Hickory won each of these political fights, he did not emerge unscathed. Jackson's vigorous use of presidential power served to energize his opponents, and the opposition to "King Andrew I," as he was derisively labeled, coalesced in the form of the new Whig Party.

The bumpy political road Jackson had traveled during his first term made him more determined to shape the Supreme Court in his image during his second four years in office. The death of Justice William Johnson in the summer of 1834, followed by the passing of Justice Gabriel Duval that winter, presented the president with two more appointments to make in 1835. The lackluster performance of Jackson's first two nominees to the high court by that time may have had a role in his choices. McLean had yet to make a mark on the Court, despite nearly six years on the bench, and Baldwin had only irritated the president by strongly supporting the Bank of the United States in a circuit opinion in Pennsylvania. Jackson looked for a politically loyal southerner—either a South Carolinian or a Georgian—to fill Johnson's seat. Secretary of State John Forsythe, a Georgian, recommended James M. Wayne, a former superior court judge and congressmember from Georgia, for the position. Wayne had supported the Jackson administration on all the major issues of the day, but his relative obscurity and his gentlemanly qualities helped quell any opposition from the Whigs. As one observer noted, "The appointment caused great dissatisfaction, but the handsome person and the engaging manners of the appointee won the day" (Lawrence 1943, 79). Wayne easily won confirmation and took his seat almost immediately.

For the other opening, Jackson attempted to appoint Roger Taney, of Maryland. A very controversial figure within the administration, Taney had served as attorney general since 1831 and had drafted Jackson's bank veto message in 1832. Appointed by Jackson in 1833 as secretary of the treasury while the Senate was in recess, Taney had removed federal deposits from the national bank to ensure its demise, a move that was more politically controversial than the veto itself. When the Senate returned to session, Taney's nomination as treasury secretary was defeated. Disappointed and disgraced, Taney had returned to Baltimore to practice law. Jackson vowed revenge, though, and the vacancy on the Court created an opportunity for the president to reward his loyal friend. Senators promptly killed the Taney nomination by indefinitely postponing it on the last day of its session. The Senate even tried to reduce the Court's size to six and eliminate the seat altogether, although the House of Representatives refused to go along with that measure.

The death of Chief Justice John Marshall during the summer of 1835 heightened the drama over the future of the Supreme Court. Marshall had created the Court in his own image during his thirty-four years of judicial service. Now Jackson would have a chance to fill the Court's most important seat, in addition to the Duval vacancy. While the public waited to see whom the president would select for the two openings, Jackson plotted his strategy. After Democratic gains in the spring elections and the death of two Whig senators improved the likelihood that his nominees would win approval, the president made a bold move. At the end of 1835, he announced the appointment of Taney to the chief justiceship and Philip P. Barbour of Virginia to succeed Duval. Jackson had thrown down the gauntlet. He would force the Senate to reckon again with the Taney nomination. Barbour's selection, meanwhile, proved equally repulsive to Whigs. An Old Republican and advocate of states' rights and strict constitutional construction, Barbour opposed federally funded internal improvements, the protective tariff, and the national bank. Unlike Jackson's earlier choices for the Court, neither Taney nor Barbour enjoyed bipartisan support. But it mattered little. Despite vehement Whig protests, both men won confirmation. In March 1836, senators voted 29–15 in favor of Taney and 30–11 in support of Barbour. Jackson had now appointed five members to the Court, and he had placed his friend in the chief justice's chair. The Marshall Court was dead.

During the January term of 1837, when Taney first presided as chief justice, the Supreme Court met in its courtroom in the basement of the Capitol, directly beneath the Senate chamber. Since 1808, the basement chamber had served as the meeting place of the nation's highest judicial tribunal, except for the period from 1814 to 1816, when the Capitol had to be reconstructed after being burned by the British during the War of 1812. (The Supreme Court did not have its own building until 1935.) There the justices sat in high-backed chairs at individual desks on a platform only slightly higher than the floor. Although furnished with mahogany and adorned with fine carpets and silken draperies, the chamber was small, damp, and dark. Because the justices sat with their backs to the only set of windows that let light into the room, it was often difficult for lawyers to see the faces of those whom they addressed. The Supreme Court even had to share its courtroom with other, lesser courts in the District of Columbia. The justices occupied this basement chamber until 1860, when the expansion of the Capitol allowed the Court to move into a new courtroom in the former chamber of the Senate.

The Court's poor accommodations reflected the relatively primitive conditions in the nation's capital at the time. At the start of the Court's 1837 term, Washington, D.C.—or "Washington City," as it was referred to—bore faint resemblance to a grand national capital. With a population of about 20,000, the District of Columbia looked and felt more like a collection of villages than a city. Only the Capitol and the President's House (not yet commonly called the White House) stood out on the landscape, for the rest of town was made up of small, shabby-looking structures. What would later become the grand avenues of the city were only dusty—or at times, muddy—streets. The city had neither a sewage system nor streetlights. The large number of boardinghouses attested to the transient nature of the capital's population. During the winter, when Congress and the Court were in session, reporters, lobbyists, and others providing services poured into the city, and during the summer as many government officials as possible left the city to flee the oppressive heat.

The year 1837 proved significant for the Supreme Court in many respects. In addition to Taney's arrival, Justice Smith Thompson brought his wife to Washington, thus ending the tradition of common residence in a boardinghouse. Perhaps most significant was Congress's passage of the Judiciary Act of 1837, which added two new circuits to the federal court system and thus two new justices to the Supreme Court. Because the Constitution had not specified the number of judges who would sit on the Court, the Judiciary Act of 1789 had provided that the Court have six members, which Congress had increased to seven in 1807. Since that time, the Mississippi Valley states of the West and the Southwest had clamored for adequate representation in the federal judiciary. Easterners, fearing the West's support of debtor relief and other reforms, resisted calls to make the federal court system more reflective of the nation. Eventually, though, the West's growing population gave it a greater voice in Congress, and westerners succeeded in redrawing the lines of the federal circuits and in expanding the Court's membership to reflect geographic realities.

Passage of the Judiciary Act of 1837 gave Jackson the opportunity to make two more nominations to the Court, although one of those nominated declined to serve. On March 3, 1837, Old Hickory's last day in office, he appointed John Catron of Tennessee and William Smith of Alabama to the new positions. Catron, a friend and political supporter as well as a former chief justice of Tennessee, eagerly accepted the job. Catron had proved his loyalty to Jackson over the course of several years, even when it hurt his own career. In fact, Catron's support of Jackson's choice for president in 1836—Vice President Martin Van Buren—cost Catron his judicial post in Tennessee. Most Tennesseans and members of the state legislature rallied to the presidential candidacy of favorite son Hugh Lawson White, and a new state constitution afforded legislators the opportunity to punish Catron for his early and fervent support of Van Buren. When legislators elected members of the Tennessee Supreme Court at the end of 1835, Catron went down to defeat despite twelve years of judicial service to the state. Catron viewed his appointment to the U.S. Supreme Court as a victory over his Tennessee opponents. He won Senate approval on March 8, 1837, by a vote of 28–15. Smith won confirmation on the same day, but by a narrower margin, 23–18. Smith, seventy-five years old at the time of his appointment, was a former U.S. senator from South Carolina with a record of strong support for states' rights. He declined the seat, citing the low salary and his desire to continue to comment freely on political matters.

Smith's unwillingness to serve allowed President Martin Van Buren, who defeated four Whig opponents to win the presidency in 1836, to make his first appointment to the Court immediately upon taking office. Van Buren was Jackson's close friend and his chosen successor. A native of New York, Van Buren served as secretary of state under Jackson (1829–1831) and then as vice president (1833–1837) after the falling out between Jackson and Calhoun. Van Buren possessed tremendous political skills, which earned him the nickname "the Little Magician." There was nothing magical, however, about his selection of John McKinley to fill the vacancy on the Court. McKinley turned out to be one of the least effective justices in Supreme Court history. A group of congressmembers had originally suggested McKinley to President Jackson immediately after the enactment of the Judiciary Act of 1837. Van Buren picked up the idea mostly for political reasons—McKinley had helped secure his state's electoral votes for the new president. Geography also played a part in the nomination. The Judiciary Act had created two new circuits in the West, and McKinley hailed from Alabama.

President Van Buren spent most of his term preoccupied with pulling the nation out of the Panic of 1837, the worst economic downturn Americans had seen. Caused by credit restrictions implemented by the Bank of England, reckless lending practices by American banks, and Jackson's economic policies, the Panic hit the nation in the form of a series of bank failures during the first half of 1837. Prices fell, business activity declined, and many Americans lost their jobs. In the midst of the depression, Van Buren made it his priority to enact legislation creating an independent treasury system, one that would have no connection to the nation's banking system. Such a policy, he believed, would sever the ties between U.S. financial health and the actions of British banks. After years of political wrangling, Congress finally enacted such legislation in 1840, as Van Buren faced reelection. That year, the Whigs nominated William Henry Harrison, the former governor of Indiana Territory who had led U.S. soldiers against a confederation of Shawnee Indians at Tippecanoe Creek. Portrayed in a raucous campaign as a war hero and champion of the common folk, "Old Tippecanoe," along with his running mate John Tyler, of Virginia, won a decisive electoral victory. Van Buren, labeled an aristocrat by his opponents, fell victim to the new style of democratic campaigning that he and Jackson had perfected.

Despite Van Buren's defeat, the sudden death of Justice Barbour after less than five years on the bench and just a week before Harrison's inauguration gave the outgoing president a chance to cement the Jacksonian legacy on the Supreme Court. Before Barbour could be buried, Van Buren quickly nominated Peter V. Daniel, a fitting replacement for the deceased justice. Both were from Virginia, had held the same federal judgeship there, and strongly advocated states' rights. Both also proved to be controversial nominees. In the face of great opposition to Daniel, Senate Democrats outmaneuvered their Whig opponents and secured Daniel's confirmation. Late at night, with only a few Whig members present, the Democratic leadership of the Senate brought the issue of confirmation to the floor, where a quorum voted affirmatively, 22–5. Outraged, one Whig newspaper described the event this way: "The breath was hardly out of Judge Barbour's body before Van Buren hurries a successor into the Senate Chamber; and an approval of him is insisted upon, and carried at midnight by dragging Senators out of their bed. It is not an easy thing, one would think, to find a Judge fit for the Supreme Bench in 24 hours, but Mr. Van Buren found no difficulty in it. . . . Thus, in shame, and dishonor, injustice and disgrace ends the career of Mr. Van Buren" (Warren 1928, 81). Daniel took the oath to become a justice on March 2, 1841, two days before Harrison was sworn in as president.

Harrison's term in office lasted only a month before he died of pneumonia, after which Vice President Tyler assumed the presidency, the first vice president to succeed a president who died in office. From the beginning, when some objected even to his claim to the office of president, Tyler faced an extremely difficult political situation. Added to the Whig ticket in 1840 to give it regional and ideological balance, Tyler was a states' rights Virginian of the Old Republican school who had little in common with the nationally oriented party leadership. Senator Henry Clay, in particular, who had not gotten over his own failure to win the White House, came to despise the new president. Clay and Tyler clashed especially over the issue of a national bank, after Tyler vetoed legislation introduced by Clay that would have reestablished the institution that Jackson had dismantled. Eventually, congressional Whigs led by Clay passed resolutions that in effect expelled Tyler from the party.

Tyler's repeated and unsuccessful attempts to win confirmation for his nominees to the Supreme Court illustrate the problems he encountered in governing without party support. The president's troubles with the Senate began in December 1843, when Justice Smith Thompson, of New York, died. Tyler nominated his treasury secretary, John C. Spencer, also from New York, to fill the vacancy. Clay, who by this time deemed all members of Tyler's cabinet as disloyal to the Whig Party, opposed Spencer's appointment. Lacking Clay's crucial support, Spencer failed to gain confirmation, with the Senate voting 21–26. Tyler then nominated another capable New York attorney, Reuben H. Walworth. Before the Senate could act on this nomination, however, Justice Henry Baldwin died, in April 1844, thus creating a second vacancy. To this seat, Tyler hoped to appoint Pennsylvania's James Buchanan, but, in keeping with the president's fortunes, Buchanan refused the offer. Tyler then nominated Philadelphia lawyer Edward King to the second seat. By this time, Clay had again set his sights on the White House. Nominated as the Whig presidential candidate in 1844, Clay joined with his allies in June of that year to postpone the nominations of both Walworth and King. The senator from Kentucky presumed that he—as the next president—would have the chance to fill the two vacancies. Although Clay's defeat at the hands of Democrat James K. Polk that fall did nothing to strengthen Tyler's political position, the victory of a Democrat considerably weakened the Senate Whigs. In January 1845, with just a few months left in his term, Tyler withdrew both of the nominations that the Senate had postponed and on February 4, 1845, nominated Samuel Nelson, a respected New York judge, for the Thompson vacancy. Nelson won confirmation, thus bringing to an end a fourteen-month period during which the seat had been open. The president made one last attempt to fill the other vacancy by nominating John Read, a lawyer from Philadelphia, but the Senate adjourned without acting on the appointment.

Polk, who entered the White House in March 1845, had his own share of problems with Supreme Court nominations. A former Speaker of the House of Representatives and, also from Tennessee, a protégé of Andrew Jackson, "Young Hickory," as

Table 1.1 Taney Era Appointments*

Presidents/Justices	Appointed	Oath Taken	Term end
Jackson			
John McLean	Mar. 6, 1829	Jan. 11, 1830	Apr. 4, 1861, died
Henry Baldwin	Jan. 4, 1830	Jan. 18, 1830	Apr. 21, 1844, died
James M. Wayne	Jan. 6, 1835	Jan. 14, 1835	July 5, 1867, died
Roger B. Taney	Dec. 28, 1835	Mar. 28, 1836	Oct. 12, 1864, died
Philip P. Barbour	Dec. 28, 1835	May 12, 1836	Feb. 25, 1841, died
John Catron	Mar. 3, 1837	May 1, 1837	May 30, 1865, died
Van Buren			
John McKinley	Apr. 22, 1837	Jan. 9, 1838	July 19, 1852, died
Peter V. Daniel	Feb. 26, 1841	Jan. 10, 1842	May 31, 1860, died
Tyler			
Samuel Nelson	Feb. 4, 1845	Feb. 27, 1845	Nov. 28, 1872, retired
Polk			
Levi Woodbury	Sept. 20, 1845	Sept. 23, 1845	Sept. 4, 1851, died
Robert C. Grier	Aug. 3, 1846	Aug. 10, 1846	Jan. 31, 1870, retired
Fillmore			
Benjamin R. Curtis	Sept. 22, 1851	Oct. 10, 1851	Sept. 30, 1857, resigned
Pierce			
John A. Campbell	Mar. 22, 1853	Apr. 11, 1853	Apr. 30, 1861, resigned
Buchanan			
Nathan Clifford	Dec. 9, 1857	Jan. 21, 1858	July 25, 1881, died
Lincoln			
Noah H. Swayne	Jan. 22, 1862	Jan. 27, 1862	Jan. 24, 1881, retired
Samuel F. Miller	July 16, 1862	July 21, 1862	Oct. 13, 1890, died
David Davis	Oct. 17, 1862	Dec. 10, 1862	Mar. 4, 1877, resigned
Stephen J. Field	Mar. 6, 1863	May 20, 1863	Dec. 1, 1897, retired

*Two other members of the Taney Court were appointed before Andrew Jackson assumed the presidency. Justice Joseph Story was appointed by President James Madison on November 15, 1811, took the oath on February 3, 1812, and died on September 10, 1845. Justice Smith Thompson was appointed by James Monroe on December 8, 1823, took the oath on February 10, 1824, and died December 18, 1843. Their nominations are discussed in Chapter 2.

he was sometimes called, for the first six months in office ignored the Court vacancy he had inherited. Eventually, he selected Secretary of State James Buchanan, who had turned down Tyler's offer of the same seat a year before. This time the politically ambitious Buchanan took a few months to consider the offer before again deciding not to let his name go forward. Soon thereafter, Justice Joseph Story of Massachusetts died, after thirty-four years of distinguished service on the high court. Polk moved quickly to fill this seat—the "New England seat"—with Democratic Senator Levi Woodbury, of New Hampshire. Woodbury's appointment, made while Congress was in recess in September 1845, generated no controversy. Experienced and respected, Woodbury won praise from both parties, and the Senate unanimously confirmed him when it returned to session.

The selection and confirmation of a replacement for Baldwin proved more difficult. Buchanan, who despite his own refusal to serve insisted on choosing the new justice, pushed for John Read, the Philadelphian previously nominated by Tyler. Polk would have none of it. Read was a former Federalist, and the president feared that a lifetime appointment would permit Read to return to his previous habits of thought. "I resolved to appoint no man who was not an original Democrat and strict constructionist," Polk wrote in his diary, "and who would be less likely to relapse into the Broad Federal doctrines of Judge Marshall and Judge Story" (Quaife 1970, 138). In December 1845, more than a year and a half after Justice Baldwin's death, Polk nominated George Washington Woodward for the "Pennsylvania Seat" that Buchanan had twice refused. Although Woodward was a loyal Democrat from a distinguished family, intraparty divisions spelled his defeat. Senator Simon Cameron, a rival of Woodward's from Pennsylvania, led a group of Democratic opponents who, along with all the Whig senators, voted against confirmation. Polk waited another six months before making another attempt to fill the vacancy created by Baldwin's death. Once again, the president asked Buchanan to take the job, and, for the third time, Buchanan refused. The president then nominated Robert Cooper Grier, the president judge of the Allegheny County District Court in Pittsburgh. The Senate wasted little time before confirming Grier, and in August 1846 the seat that had been vacant for twenty-eight months finally gained a new occupant.

Polk's focus on foreign policy helps explain why he moved slowly in making his appointments to the Court. By 1846, the president, Congress, and the nation were preoccupied with territorial expansion. Newspapers trumpeted the notion of "Manifest Destiny," the idea that it was the duty and mission of the United States to fulfill its providential purpose and expand its borders. Rampant nationalism, a religious sense of mission, and greed for new lands fed the desires of many Americans to spread out across the continent. During the previous decade, thousands of Americans had crossed the Rocky Mountains to settle in Oregon Country, an area jointly occupied by British and American citizens. Although Polk initially hoped to assert U.S. control over all of Oregon, when threatened with the possibility of war with England, he negotiated a settlement that allowed the United States to acquire the southern portion of that area, up to the forty-ninth parallel. Around the same time, the United States declared war on Mexico. The U.S. annexation of Texas in 1845, which Mexico did not recognize, fed that country's hostility toward the United States and led to military skirmishes that culminated in a formal declaration of war by Congress in May 1846. Polk, who had campaigned for president as an expansionist who promised to extend the republic to the Pacific, welcomed the chance to acquire new territory. In roughly a year's time, U.S. forces arrived in Mexico City, and talk began of seizing all of Mexico. The eventual settlement, contained in the Treaty of Guadalupe Hidalgo of 1848, did not go that far, but it did give the United States vast new territory stretching from the Rio Grande River to the Pacific Ocean, including all of present-day California, Nevada, and Utah, most of New Mexico and Arizona, and portions of Wyoming and Colorado. Polk had succeeded in fulfilling the spirit of Manifest Destiny.

With Polk's pledge not to run for a second term and the subsequent election of Whig President Zachary Taylor in 1848, the Jacksonian Era—a period marked by increases in political participation and Democratic dominance in national politics—came to a close. Mass suffrage and the rise of a new style of campaigning significantly affected the Court, for the justices appointed by Jackson and his Democratic successors in many ways stood apart from their early counterparts. During the Marshall era, the justices had shared the common experiences of the American Revolution and the founding of the republic. Heavily influenced by eighteenth-century ideals such as deference, hierarchy, and public virtue, these justices had drawn a sharp distinction between law and politics and had viewed themselves as nonpolitical actors who expounded the law for the public good. By the 1820s, the new spirit of the age—the individualistic ethos of market capitalism, religious enthusiasm, and partisan involvement—legitimized political parties and made partisanship an acceptable component of the legal and judicial process. Justice John McLean spent much of his time on the Court running for president; Justice Catron frequently engaged in political gossip with presidents and often passed along information about how the justices were dealing with pending cases (most notoriously in the *Dred Scott* case); and Chief Justice Taney probably overstepped the bounds of propriety in offering personal advice to Presidents Jackson, Polk, and Buchanan on matters regarding the judiciary. Perhaps the fact that all of the justices appointed during this era were Democrats—members of the party that had ridden into power on the tide of egalitarianism—affected their attitudes toward partisanship and political maneuvering. In any event, the Supreme Court had taken on a distinctly different cast by the late 1840s. It was now avowedly partisan in its dealings, strongly Democratic in party affiliation, and—despite what the justices held in common—increasingly divided on the important issues facing the nation.

The Supreme Court and the Sectional Conflict

Polk's acquisition of new territories brought the issue of slavery to the forefront of American life. Slavery had taken root on North American soil soon after settlement by the first Europeans. In 1619, the same year that Virginians established self-government in the form of the Virginia House of Burgesses, the first Africans arrived in British North America. By the end of the seventeenth century, as Britain took an increasingly active part in the transatlantic slave trade, slaves rapidly replaced indentured servants as the primary source of bound labor in the colonies. Although many northern colonies abolished slavery during the American Revolutionary era, the framers of the Constitution promoted its continued existence in the South by writing it into that document. The Constitution provided, for example, for the return of fugitive slaves to their owners. Still, much ambiguity surrounded the constitutional provisions relating to slavery. Curiously, none of the constitutional references to the institution used the term "slavery" or "slave." In fact, all three clauses that were related to slavery described slaves as "persons," even though in most instances state law designated slaves as property.

Such paradoxes became more controversial as the southern states solidified their commitment to the "peculiar institution" after the advent of the cotton gin. Invented in 1793, this device made it faster and easier to separate cotton seeds from cotton fibers, thus revolutionizing agriculture in the South. As cotton became more lucrative, southerners became more committed to slavery. Although the proportion of white southern families who owned slaves never amounted to more than 25 percent, the vast majority of white southerners came to view slavery as an essential part of their society, economy, and culture. The South's increasing devotion to slavery portended serious political debate. In particular, the future of slavery in the massive Louisiana Territory, acquired in 1803, became a volatile question. Congress resolved the issue in 1820 by enacting the Missouri Compromise, which allowed the admission of Missouri as a slave state but prohibited slavery in the rest of Louisiana Territory, north of Missouri's southern border—at 36 degrees, 30 minutes north latitude. The Missouri Compromise solved for a time the political problem of the extension of slavery and for two and a half decades effectively prevented sectional antagonism. Still, slavery remained a compelling question, an issue viewed primarily in religious and economic terms by its advocates and opponents. In 1831, abolitionist minister William Lloyd Garrison began publishing *The Liberator*, an antislavery newspaper that took an unequivocal moral stance against the enslavement of human beings. That same year, a Virginia slave preacher named Nat Turner led a bloody slave uprising that resulted in the deaths of scores of blacks and whites. In response to abolitionism's steady rise in the North, during the 1830s white southerners, particularly clergymen, increasingly argued that slavery was a "positive good," an institution ordained by God to uplift, civilize, and Christianize heathen Africans.

The likelihood of territorial expansion arising out of the U.S. victory in the Mexican-American War brought the slavery question back into the realm of national politics. Barely two months after the war had begun, Congress took up an appropriations bill to finance diplomatic efforts to acquire territory from Mexico. Pennsylvania representative David Wilmot introduced an amendment to the bill to prohibit the spread of slavery to any such new acquisitions. Given that Polk and many Americans had their sights set on extensive new lands—more than 500,000 square miles—the introduction of the "Wilmot Proviso" had profound implications. Although the proviso failed to pass in 1846, its subsequent and continued reintroduction in Congress kept the slavery issue at the center of national debate. By again raising the issue of the extension of slavery, the Wilmot Proviso altered the U.S. political landscape, as sectional allegiances rather than party loyalty marked debate in Congress.

The politics of the presidency, meanwhile, took a different turn. Hoping to enlist national support for their candidacies, presidential aspirants avoided the pressing question of the future of slavery. In fact, during the 1848 campaign—while controversy over the Wilmot Proviso still raged—the Whig Party neglected even to write a platform. Thinking that silence on the issue would prove more successful at the polls, Whigs seemed content to let their candidate, Zachary Taylor—a career military officer who had never even voted—run on his popularity as a hero of the Mexican War. The gambit worked. Taylor defeated Democrat Lewis Cass as well as Martin Van Buren, who had been nominated by the newly formed antislavery Free-Soil Party. No one really knew Taylor's stance on the issue of slavery until he was in the White House; his many southern supporters were in for a surprise.

Taylor, a Louisiana planter and owner of more than a hundred slaves, believed in defending slavery in the South but seemed determined to halt its spread in the West. Perhaps at the behest of his party's antislavery wing, Taylor insisted on the admission of California and New Mexico to the Union as free states and proclaimed that if Congress passed the Wilmot Proviso he would not veto it. White southerners expressed shock. John C. Calhoun, the aging senator from South Carolina who had long dreamed of a southern confederacy, used Taylor's pronouncements to rally fellow southerners in support of a united front against the antislavery forces. With the threat of disunion looming, Senator Henry Clay stepped forward with a compromise proposal that contained provisions favorable to both sections. Both Calhoun and Taylor opposed the compromise, though, and the sections seemed on a collision course over the spread of slavery. The death of both men—Calhoun in March and Taylor, unexpectedly, in July—cleared the way for compromise. In the fall of that year, Congress enacted what came to be known as the Compromise of 1850, which provided for, among other things, a new fugitive slave law that would ensure the protection of slaveholders' rights. On Taylor's death, Vice President Millard Fillmore assumed the presidency, and although his brief term of service was undistinguished, he oversaw a period of relative peace between North and South.

Up to this time, the Supreme Court had not yet played much of a role in the sectional disputes. In 1842, the Court had rendered an important decision regarding slavery, *Prigg v. Pennsylvania*, which had upheld the constitutionality of the federal fugitive slave law of 1793 and invalidated a Pennsylvania law that granted legal protections to fugitive slaves. But that ruling came before the war with Mexico and the Wilmot Proviso. The political environment had changed by the time of the Fillmore administration, and the new brand of sectional politics affected the selection and confirmation of Supreme Court justices. Given that law and tradition had already linked certain seats on the Court to specific regions—even states, in some instances—the sectional conflict would not affect the geographical balance that had come to characterize the Court. A seat vacated by a New Englander, for example, would continue to be filled by a New Englander. But a nominee's political stance on slavery and its extension, as well as his personal experience with the institution, would figure more prominently than before in the appointment process.

President Fillmore had two opportunities to make nominations to the Court. The first chance came in 1851, when Justice Levi Woodbury passed away. Fillmore looked for a first-rate lawyer from New England, a Whig who would stand up to Democratic colleagues on the Court, and a man of "such age as gives a prospect of long service" (Gillette 1969, 900). On the recommendation of Daniel Webster, the president found such a person in Benjamin Robbins Curtis, a forty-one-year-old Boston attorney. Curtis's nomination sailed through the Senate, primarily because, in a series of fugitive slave cases in Massachusetts, he had defended the right of southerners to reclaim fugitive slaves in the North. In addition to the strong support he enjoyed from Whigs and New Englanders, Curtis's opposition to extreme abolitionism and his respect for the rule of law with regard to slavery made him acceptable to southern Democrats.

Fillmore's second attempt to nominate a member of the Court proved unsuccessful. During the summer of 1852, the death of Justice John McKinley, of Alabama, created a vacancy, and the president moved quickly to choose a successor. Aware of his party's slim chances of retaining the presidency that fall (Winfield Scott, rather than Fillmore, was the Whig nominee), the president hoped to fill the seat before leaving office. He appointed Edward Bradford, of Louisiana, in August 1852, but the Senate failed to act on the nomination before it adjourned. Early in 1853, after the Whig candidate had indeed lost the election and before Democrat Franklin Pierce was inaugurated, Fillmore attempted twice more to fill the vacancy. The Senate postponed the nomination of George Badger, of North Carolina, and then failed to act on that of William Micou, of Louisiana, whose name Fillmore sent to the Senate less than two weeks before leaving office. Although lame-duck presidents had previously succeeded in winning confirmation of their nominees to the Court (even Tyler had done so with his appointment of Nelson in February 1845), Fillmore's efforts proved futile. The vacancy would be left to the new president to fill.

Pierce, a former U.S. senator from New Hampshire and a brigadier general in the Mexican-American War, assumed the presidency in 1853 and swiftly appointed

John Archibald Campbell, of Alabama, to the Supreme Court. A celebrated lawyer who had argued many cases before the Court, Campbell was a popular choice among the justices. In fact, Justices John Catron and Benjamin Curtis, at the behest of Chief Justice Taney, personally urged the president to nominate Campbell. During this brief period of sectional peace, most senators also looked favorably on the appointment. Despite his support of slavery and states' rights, Campbell had sold five slaves during the winter of 1852–1853, thus reducing the number of slaves he owned to six. The Alabaman might have taken this step, his biographer asserts, to blunt whatever criticism of the nomination would come from northern abolitionists. In any event, Campbell won confirmation easily and took his seat among the justices in April 1853.

Campbell's appointment proved to be one of the few uncontroversial events of Pierce's presidency. In 1854, the introduction of the Kansas-Nebraska bill in Congress again set off a sectional controversy that rivaled that over the Wilmot Proviso eight years before. The bill organized separate Kansas and Nebraska Territories and provided that the residents of those territories would decide for themselves whether or not to allow slavery. This policy on the extension of slavery, known as "popular sovereignty," originated in the Compromise of 1850, which had lain down similar terms for the territories of Utah and New Mexico. Popular sovereignty allowed the people of the territories—rather than Congress—to determine the fate of slavery in their territories. More controversial, though, was the fact that both Kansas and Nebraska Territories lay north of the Missouri Compromise line, where slavery had been banned since 1820. In addition to support from proslavery southerners, Illinois Senator Stephen Douglas, the prime advocate of the bill, secured its passage with the help of entrepreneurial-minded members of Congress, who hoped that the establishment of the new territories would speed the development of a transcontinental railway. Meanwhile, at the height of the controversy over Kansas and Nebraska, three diplomats in the Pierce administration issued a statement calling for the purchase of Cuba from Spain. The Ostend Manifesto, as the proclamation was known, bluntly stated that if Spain would not sell the island, the United States would be justified in taking it. Presumably, Cuba would eventually enter the Union as a slave state. Such a bold pronouncement provoked an avalanche of criticism. Combined, the Kansas-Nebraska Act and the Ostend Manifesto discredited not only the Pierce administration but also the basic ideals on which these policies claimed to rest. Popular sovereignty and Manifest Destiny, both previously respectable notions with broad national support, now became closely identified with the extension of slavery.

By the late 1850s, as the sectional crisis grew worse, the Supreme Court assumed a significant role in the slavery debate. In the aftermath of the Kansas-Nebraska Act, the Whig Party, torn apart by conflict over the slavery issue, all but disappeared from the American political landscape. A new party—the Republicans—emerged in 1854 as the primary opponents of the Democrats. Founded on opposition to the Kansas-Nebraska Act as well as on a general belief in "free soil" principles, the Republican Party appealed almost exclusively to residents of the northern free states. Although their first presidential nominee lost in 1856 to Democrat James Buchanan, violence in Kansas over the future of slavery in that territory and the Supreme Court's decision in *Dred Scott v. Sandford* (1857) pushed more northerners into the Republican ranks. *Dred Scott* involved a Missouri slave whose master had taken him into free territory to live temporarily. Scott sued for his freedom on the basis of his residency on free soil, but the Court ruled that he remained a slave. In one of the most controversial Supreme Court decisions in U.S. history, Chief Justice Taney wrote that because blacks had long been considered "so far inferior that they had no rights which the white man was bound to respect," Scott could not claim the rights of citizenship (60 U.S. 393, 407). The majority of the justices contended, moreover, that Congress could not legislate on the question of slavery in the new territories. The Missouri Compromise and any other attempts by Congress to dictate the fate of slavery in new lands violated the Constitution, in that such legislation posed a threat to the property rights of slaveholders.

The effects of the *Dred Scott* decision were immediate. Justice Benjamin Curtis, of Massachusetts, one of two dissenters in the case, resigned his seat on the Court. Curtis's general unhappiness on the bench, combined with a heated exchange he had with the chief justice over the timing of the public release of his dissent, prompted the resignation. After considering a number of individuals for the vacancy, including the extremely proslavery William L. Yancey of Alabama, President Buchanan settled on Nathan Clifford of Maine, an old friend and political ally of the president who had served with Buchanan in President Polk's cabinet. An able lawyer and a former member of the House of Representatives, Clifford was a reasonable choice, and not an unexpected one. But in the poisonous political climate growing out of the *Dred Scott* decision and Curtis's abrupt resignation, antislavery advocates went on the attack. The *New York Tribune* described the selection of Clifford as part of "the process of deterioration" of the Court. "[T]he Supreme Court is gradually becoming a mere party machine," the article continued, "to do the bidding of the dominant faction and to supply places to reward party hacks" (Warren 1928, 323). From the perspective of abolitionists, Clifford's experience as attorney general of the state of Maine and as U.S. attorney general under Polk mattered little. Clifford was a "doughface" (someone easily molded)—a northern apologist for the South and slavery—just like the president who appointed him. In the face of great opposition, it took the Senate nearly five weeks to confirm the appointment, and by a narrow margin, with a vote of 26–23. Had it not been for the absence of a few crucial senators, the Senate would have rejected the nominee. Clifford was sworn in as a justice on January 21, 1858.

The *Dred Scott* decision not only contributed to the resignation of one justice and to a confirmation battle over another, the infamous ruling also transformed the political landscape. Republicans vilified Taney's opinion and warned that by guaranteeing the rights of slaveholders and ruling that a territory could not prohibit the introduction of slavery, the Court came close to nationalizing the institution of slavery. Many antislavery northern newspapers condemned the decision as tainting the pure administration of justice and undermining the legitimacy of the Court. "The moment the Supreme Judicial Court becomes a Court of injustice," the *New York Independent* charged, "a Court to carry schemes of oppression against classes of men, by forced constructions of the Constitution, that moment its claim to obedience ceases" (Warren 1928, 307).

By far the most famous criticisms of the opinion came from a relatively unknown former U.S. representative from Illinois named Abraham Lincoln. Born in Kentucky in 1809, the young Lincoln had moved with his family to Indiana and later to Illinois, where he had worked a variety of odd jobs, including as a store clerk, a postmaster, and a surveyor. Drawn to politics, Lincoln had served four terms in the Illinois legislature before retiring to practice law in Springfield. He had won election to Congress in 1846, and during his single term of service there became unpopular back home for his vocal opposition to the war with Mexico. Returning to Springfield somewhat disillusioned with politics, he devoted the next several years to his law practice. But when Congress transformed the political landscape with the passage of the Kansas-Nebraska Act, Lincoln emerged as a leading antislavery spokesman in Illinois, and in 1858 he was selected by the newly formed Republican Party as a candidate for the U.S. Senate. Lincoln placed the *Dred Scott* ruling at the center of his campaign against incumbent Democrat Stephen Douglas. In seven debates across the state, Lincoln challenged Douglas to defend the Court's decision, particularly Taney's assertion that the Constitution protected the right to own slaves and thus territories could not exclude slave property. The Court's holding clashed with Douglas's commitment to the notion of popular sovereignty, and Lincoln attempted to make much of this contradiction. Although he lost the race to Douglas, Lincoln won nationwide acclaim for his pointed attacks on the Court and his eloquent articulation of the antislavery position. After his election as president two years later, Lincoln would have more of an opportunity to shape the Supreme Court than any president since Andrew Jackson.

Secession, Civil War, and Lincoln's Supreme Court

By 1860, sectional tensions had reached the level of hysteria. A year before, white abolitionist and religious zealot John Brown had led an unsuccessful armed slave revolt at Harper's Ferry, Virginia (later West Virginia), the site of a federal arsenal. Although convicted and hanged for the offense, Brown's crime convinced many white southerners of the utter fanaticism of abolitionists. It was in this atmosphere that

Americans voted in the presidential election in 1860. Abraham Lincoln, Stephen Douglas, John Bell (of Tennessee), and John C. Breckinridge (of Kentucky) all sought the office, but given the sectional affiliations and regional appeals of the candidates, it was as though two distinct presidential elections took place that year. In the North, voters essentially chose between the Republican Lincoln and the Democrat Douglas; in the South, citizens cast their ballots either for Bell, the candidate of the Constitutional Union Party, or Breckinridge, the southern Democrat. (Lincoln's name was not even on the ballot in most of the slave states.) Although he garnered less than 40 percent of the popular vote nationwide, Lincoln won the electoral votes of every free state in the Union—enough for victory. A little more than a month later, out of fear that the new Republican administration threatened the existence of slavery, South Carolina became the first state to secede from the Union. By February 1861, the Deep South states of Mississippi, Florida, Georgia, Alabama, Louisiana, and Texas had all followed suit.

The Supreme Court, in the meantime, was facing a crisis of its own. Although the justices had moved into a new and larger courtroom in the old chamber of the Senate in 1860, the position and reputation of the Court in the U.S. constitutional system was more precarious than ever. In July 1860, Justice Peter V. Daniel of Virginia had died, and President James Buchanan had begun searching for a replacement. By the time of Lincoln's election, Buchanan still had not settled on a choice, although Attorney General Jeremiah Black of Pennsylvania was the most frequently mentioned nominee. The architect of Buchanan's policy on secession, Black had contended that the president could neither recognize the independence of a seceded state nor take any steps to punish a state for its actions. The appointment of Black, officially announced on February 5, 1861, a month before Lincoln's inauguration, met with much Republican hostility. By that time, because twelve southern senators had already resigned their seats and headed home, support for Buchanan's nominee lay almost exclusively with northern Democrats. On February 21, the Senate voted 26–25 against confirming Black. At the same time, while the seven seceded states met to elect a president and draft a constitution for the Confederate States of America, rumors circulated about the southern members of the Supreme Court. Justices Wayne, Catron, and Campbell all came from states that had seceded or were considering secession, and Chief Justice Taney's well-known sympathy for the South also made him a potential candidate for resignation. The future of the Court hung in the balance.

On March 4, 1861, all the members of the high court, including the southern justices, filed onto the inaugural platform at the Capitol for the swearing in of the sixteenth president of the United States. They were eager to hear what Lincoln would say. His inaugural speech, conciliatory toward the South, made specific mention of the Court. Although the incoming president acknowledged that its decisions were "binding . . . upon the parties to a suit" and "entitled to very high respect and consideration,"

Lincoln asserted that a powerful Court posed a threat to popular self-government: "[T]he candid citizen must confess that if the policy of the government, upon vital questions, affecting the whole people, is to be irrevocably fixed by decisions of the Supreme Court, the instant they are made, in ordinary litigation between parties, in personal actions, the people will have ceased to be their own rulers, having, to that extent, practically resigned their government into the hands of that eminent tribunal" (Delbanco 1992, 201).

Still, Lincoln chose not to take as harsh a tone toward the Court as some of his fellow Republicans. He emphasized that his words did not constitute "any assault upon the Court, or the judges." Rather, he argued, "it is a duty, from which they may not shrink, to decide cases properly brought before them; and it is no fault of theirs, if others seek to turn their decisions to political purposes." Here Lincoln seemed to say that the Court had decided the *Dred Scott* case in accordance with its constitutional authority and that the decision needed to be observed. He implied, moreover, that partisans on both sides had exaggerated the practical effects of the ruling, which, after all, had decided the fate of only a single slave and had overturned a law—the Missouri Compromise—that had already been superseded by the Kansas-Nebraska Act. It was an odd assertion, coming from one who had earned a national political reputation for attacking the Court's ruling. After the speech, Chief Justice Taney, the author of the *Dred Scott* opinion, administered the oath of office to the new president.

Despite the moderate tone of Lincoln's address, the ensuing weeks and months proved calamitous for both the Union and the Court. At the time of Lincoln's inauguration, many expected the president to nominate John J. Crittenden, an aging Kentucky Whig, to replace the deceased Justice Daniel. Lincoln needed to ensure that Kentucky, a slave state, remained in the Union, and Crittenden seemed the perfect political choice. As a senator, Crittenden had achieved national prominence during the period between Lincoln's election and his inauguration for proposing an amendment to the Constitution that would extend the old Missouri Compromise line to the Pacific. This plan, Crittenden thought, would resolve the issue of slavery's extension. But the Crittenden Compromise came under fire from both northerners and southerners, and so did the idea of his being nominated to the Court. Lincoln never made the appointment. Adding to the confusion over the Court's future, a month after Lincoln's inauguration, Justice John McLean died, after more than thirty years on the bench, thus creating a second vacancy.

The president had little time for such matters, however, for the nation was breaking apart. On April 14, 1861, when Confederate forces fired on Fort Sumter, a Union-occupied garrison in the middle of Charleston Harbor, South Carolina, the Civil War began. Lincoln issued a nationwide call for 75,000 troops to put down the secessionist rebellion, and he announced a naval blockade of southern ports. A week later, on April 25, 1861, despite playing an active role in peace negotiations between the administration and the Confederacy, Justice John A. Campbell chose to resign his seat and go home to Alabama. By June, four more slaveholding states from the upper South—Virginia, Arkansas, North Carolina, and Tennessee—had followed the seven states that had already left the Union. Although Justice Campbell's fellow southern justices remained on the bench and professed loyalty to the Union cause, their circuits now lay within enemy territory. In fact, when Justice Catron attempted to hold federal circuit court in Tennessee that summer, a group of Nashville citizens threatened his life and insisted that he leave town at once.

The situation of the beleaguered Court, now composed of just six members, would worsen before it would improve. Immediately after the war began, in addition to ordering a blockade of southern ports, President Lincoln suspended the writ of habeas corpus throughout most of Maryland, a slaveholding border state essential to Union military victory. This measure gave the Union Army the authority to arrest and to imprison any individuals it believed sympathetic to the Confederacy. A month later, Chief Justice Taney ruled on circuit that Lincoln's actions constituted a gross abuse of presidential power and a violation of civil liberties. Viewing Taney's ruling as a treasonous pronouncement, the Court's critics again took the offensive. Republican newspapers led the charge. The *New York Tribune* put forth a plan to increase the number of Supreme Court justices from nine to thirteen. Because the Court still had three vacancies at the time, the newspaper's proposal would allow Lincoln to appoint seven new justices—a majority of the Court. Taking such reforms a step further, in December 1861 Republican Senator John P. Hale, of New Hampshire, introduced a resolution proposing that the Supreme Court be abolished and that another Supreme Court, presumably made up entirely of Republican appointees, be created in its place. Hale justified the dubious constitutionality of his plan by engaging in an extremely loose—perhaps wholly incorrect—reading of Article III, Section 1 of the Constitution. That section states that "[t]he judicial power of the United States shall be vested in one Supreme Court and in such inferior courts as the Congress, may, from time to time, ordain and establish." Hale interpreted the phrase as allowing Congress to "ordain and establish" a Supreme Court whenever it chose to do so. "My idea is that the time has come," Hale argued. "[T]hat this is one of the very times the framers of the Constitution contemplated" (Silver 1957, 44). The Taney Court, the senator contended, functioned as a mere political organ of the Democratic Party; the Court's recent decisions proved that politics, rather than law, governed the justices' decision-making process.

Although Hale's resolution received some support, most congressional Republicans turned their attention instead to the reorganization of the federal circuits. Lincoln had previously urged action on this issue and hesitated to make appointments to the Court until Congress had enacted changes. Twenty years had passed since Congress had last taken up the matter, and the states that had entered the Union since that time were not included in any circuit. Proposals to redraw circuit lines focused on redistributing the nation's population into nine relatively equal circuits based on the results of the 1860 census. Such a plan would also, not coincidentally, increase the number of northern circuits and reduce the number in the South. Under the 1837 legislation, the slave states were spread among five circuits. Because one Supreme Court justice was appointed from each circuit, southerners usually had held a majority of seats on the Supreme Court. Under reorganization, the southern states would most likely be consolidated into three circuits. As debate dragged on for months about the exact groupings of the states, Lincoln proceeded to nominate his first justice. The Court's reduced membership, in addition to the uncertain futures of Taney and Catron—who were both aged and in ill health—prompted the president to act before circuit reorganization was enacted. On January 22, 1862, Lincoln appointed Noah H. Swayne, of Ohio, a prominent lawyer in the state, to take the seat that had been held by the deceased McLean, another Ohio native. Swayne's nomination encountered virtually no opposition (most of the senators from slaveholding states had resigned), and he won confirmation two days after his appointment with just one dissenting vote.

Over the next several months, as Congress continued to wrangle over the rearranging of circuits, the question of who would fill the remaining two seats on the Court became closely connected to how those circuit lines would be drawn. Iowans in particular wanted to place their state in a different circuit from neighboring Illinois. Because Iowans hoped for the nomination of Samuel F. Miller, a respected lawyer and Republican leader in the state, they wanted to avoid being connected to Illinois, the home state of David Davis, a close Lincoln associate and another much-discussed possible nominee. Such disputes among various states containing aspirants for Supreme Court seats caused the debate over circuit reorganization to continue for more than seven months.

On July 15, 1862, Congress finally enacted legislation settling the matter. Under the new law, the first three circuits, covering New England and the Mid-Atlantic states, remained the same. The other six circuits, however, looked vastly different, with all of the slaveholding states consolidated into the Fourth, Fifth, and Sixth Circuits. Iowa was added to the Ninth Circuit, along with Missouri, Kansas, and Minnesota. This paved the way for the appointment of Miller. For months, Miller's friends and allies had not only played a critical role in the debate over circuit reorganization, they had also flooded the White House with letters recommending their favorite son. The state's governor, U.S. senators, and representatives, the Iowa bar, the state legislature, and the state supreme court made a concerted effort to keep Miller's name at the top of the list. The massive campaign paid off. On July 16, 1862, the day after circuit reorganization passed, Lincoln appointed Miller, who was confirmed unanimously the same day. Rearranging the federal circuits had allowed the president fill the seat of Justice Daniel, a Virginian, with an Iowan.

Table 1.2 Circuit Reorganization and the Rise of the Lincoln Court

1860	1864
First Circuit Nathan Clifford (Dem., Maine) Maine, New Hampshire, Massachusetts, Rhode Island	**First Circuit** Nathan Clifford Maine, New Hampshire, Massachusetts, Rhode Island
Second Circuit Samuel Nelson (Dem., New York) Vermont, Connecticut, New York	**Second Circuit** Samuel Nelson Vermont, Connecticut, New York
Third Circuit Robert C. Grier (Dem., Pennsylvania) New Jersey, Pennsylvania	**Third Circuit** Robert C. Grier New Jersey, Pennsylvania
Fourth Circuit Roger B. Taney (Dem., Maryland) Delaware, Maryland, Virginia	**Fourth Circuit** Salmon P. Chase (Rep., Ohio) Delaware, Maryland, Virginia, North Carolina, West Virginia
Fifth Circuit John A. Campbell (Dem., Alabama) Alabama, Louisiana	**Fifth Circuit** James M. Wayne South Carolina, Georgia, Florida, Alabama, Mississippi
Sixth Circuit James M. Wayne (Dem., Georgia) North Carolina, South Carolina, Georgia	**Sixth Circuit** John Catron Louisiana, Arkansas, Kentucky, Texas, Tennessee
Seventh Circuit John McLean (Rep., Ohio) Ohio, Indiana, Illinois, Michigan	**Seventh Circuit** Noah H. Swayne (Rep., Ohio) Ohio, Michigan
Eighth Circuit John Catron (Dem., Tennessee) Kentucky, Tennessee, Missouri	**Eighth Circuit** David Davis (Rep., Illinois) Indiana, Illinois
Ninth Circuit Peter V. Daniel (Dem., Virginia) Mississippi, Arkansas	**Ninth Circuit** Samuel Miller (Rep., Iowa) Iowa, Missouri, Kansas, Minnesota, Wisconsin
	Tenth Circuit Stephen J. Field (Dem., California) California, Oregon

After Miller's appointment, two major candidates emerged for the final vacancy on the Court, the seat previously held by Justice Campbell and associated with the newly drawn Eighth Circuit. Orville H. Browning, a U.S. senator from Illinois, and David Davis, judge of the Illinois Circuit Court, both had close ties to Lincoln and eagerly sought the position. Appointed to the Senate seat held by Stephen Douglas after his death in 1861, Browning sought nomination to the Court early in the Lincoln administration. The senator frequently sent long letters to the president relating political gossip and expressing his interest in a seat on the Court. Davis, for his part, had known the president for many years and had worked tirelessly on his behalf both during his 1858 Senate race and during the presidential campaign. More than anyone else, Davis was responsible for Lincoln's receiving the Republican Party's nomination for the presidency in 1860. Although Lincoln had announced Miller's appointment immediately after the reorganization of the circuits, he delayed for many weeks a decision on the Eighth Circuit seat. Finally, on August 27, 1862, the president informed Davis of his decision to appoint him, although Congress had already adjourned. The Senate received formal word of Davis's nomination on December 1 and confirmed him a week later. With this appointment, the Supreme Court again was composed of nine justices, three of whom owed their seats to President Lincoln.

During congressional debate about the circuits, lawmakers generally assumed that the western states, California and Oregon, would continue to be served by a circuit judge who did not sit on the U.S. Supreme Court. An independent federal circuit judge had served California since 1855. But by the end of 1862, concerns arose about whether that judge, Matthew McAllister, was performing his duties, and congressional Republicans realized that elevating the western circuit to a status equal to that of the others offered an opportunity for Lincoln to appoint an extra justice to the Supreme Court. With important cases related to Lincoln's prosecution of the war looming on the docket, Republicans in Congress knew that adding another seat to the tribunal would help solidify their party's grip on the Court. It made sense, moreover, to add a justice who was familiar with the complicated cases involving land titles that were coming from California to the Supreme Court at the time. During the month of February 1863, at the same time that the Court began considering the *Prize Cases*, a series of disputes involving the constitutionality of the president's blockade of the South, Congress initiated the process of adding a tenth justice to the Court. The action reminded the Court that Congress, under the Constitution, controlled the size of the Court and signaled that lawmakers were prepared to take such steps to ensure the successful prosecution of the war. Congress passed the measure creating the Tenth Circuit on March 3, 1863, and Lincoln signed the bill into law the same day. Immediately thereafter the president appointed Stephen J. Field, California's leading lawyer and a member of the California Supreme Court since 1857, to fill the new seat. A native of Connecticut who had gone to California in 1849, Field was a Democrat but a staunch advocate of the Union. His appointment made good political sense and greatly pleased President Lincoln. Field's selection marked the first time a president had appointed a justice who belonged to a political party other than his own. The tenth justice of the Court joined his colleagues on March 10, 1863.

As Lincoln filled these vacancies on the Supreme Court, the Civil War raged, thousands of young men died, and the nation's wounds became ever deeper. During the first two years of the conflict, the Confederacy won a series of victories that cast a pall over the northern states. Superior military leadership and strategy accounted in part for the South's early victories, and Lincoln looked in vain for an effective general to lead the Union Army. By the end of 1862, after a costly victory at Antietam, also known as the Battle of Sharpsburg, Maryland, Lincoln made the crucial decision to issue a proclamation freeing the slaves in Confederate-held territory. On January 1, 1863, the Emancipation Proclamation announced that slaves in those areas of the country were "forever free." Although the order excluded the slaveholding border states as well as Union-occupied areas of the South, the Emancipation Proclamation nevertheless served as a powerful symbol of the Union's commitment to abolish slavery. For nearly the first two years of the war, Lincoln had maintained that preserving the federal Union was the only goal of the northern army. Emancipation proved to be an effective instrument of war. The proclamation allowed for the use of black troops in the Union Army and helped prevent recognition of the Confederacy by foreign governments, most of which wanted to refrain from siding with slaveholders. Subsequent turning points in the conflict came during the summer of 1863, with Union victories at the battles of Vicksburg, Mississippi, and Gettysburg, Pennsylvania. By 1864, the Union Army, although suffering heavy casualties in a series of campaigns, seemed on its way to eventual victory. Northern superiority in numbers of troops and in materiel, as well as improved military leadership, proved important to success on the battlefield. When the war began, the region was home to almost three and a half times the number of white men of fighting age as the South, and the northern states far exceeded the Confederate states in every manufacturing category. These inherent advantages gave Union military leaders more time to implement a successful strategy—and more room to commit mistakes—than their Confederate counterparts.

As the war began to wind down in the closing months of 1864, Chief Justice Taney's health progressively worsened. When the Court ended its March 1862 term, the decrepit Marylander had asked each of his fellow justices to visit him before they left Washington, as he did not expect to see them again. Although Taney lived for another two and a half years, attending to his duties when he could, chronic intestinal troubles made his last years difficult. With the appointments of Swayne, Miller, Davis, and Field, the Court shaped by Andrew Jackson and his Democratic successors had ceased to exist. It was now Lincoln's Court—solidly Republican, antislavery, and pro-Union. Although all were qualified, Lincoln's judicial nominees, like those of the Jacksonian era presidents, had been selected more for their political leanings than for their legal learning. Lincoln wanted a Court that would uphold his controversial and unprecedented prosecution of the war. Congressional Republicans obliged by speedily confirming all of his appointments and even adding an extra justice to the bench. On October 12, 1864, as discussion of the Union Army's march through Georgia, the probable reelection of Lincoln, and plans for postwar reconstruction dominated the news, Chief Justice Taney died. President Lincoln, who himself did not live much longer, appointed Salmon P. Chase, of Ohio, an early abolitionist and Lincoln's secretary of the treasury, to assume the chief justiceship. Within six months, the Civil War came to an end.

Roger Brooke Taney presided over the Court during some of the most tumultuous years in U.S. history. The advent of mass political participation, the rapid economic and territorial expansion of the American republic, and the rise of the slavery issue during the late 1840s exerted tremendous political pressures on the nation's highest court. Although the era of Taney's predecessor, Chief Justice John Marshall, had been marked by the widely held belief that law existed apart from politics, the politically charged environment of the mid–nineteenth century forced presidents, senators, and justices to acknowledge that the legal and political realms often overlapped.

References and Further Reading

Abraham, Henry J. *Justices, Presidents, and Senators: A History of the U.S. Supreme Court Appointments from Washington to Clinton.* Lanham, MD: Rowman and Littlefield, 1999.

Bergeron, Paul. *The Presidency of James K. Polk.* Lawrence: University Press of Kansas, 1987.

Delbanco, Andrew, ed. *The Portable Abraham Lincoln.* New York: Viking, 1992.

Gillette, William. "Benjamin R. Curtis," in Leon Friedman and Fred L. Israel, eds., *The Justices of the Supreme Court of the United States, 1789–1969: Their Lives and Major Opinions*, vol. 2. New York: Chelsea House Publishers, 1969.

Hall, Kermit L. *The Oxford Companion to the Supreme Court of the United States.* New York: Oxford University Press, 1991.

Kahn, Michael A. "The Appointment of John McLean to the Supreme Court: Practical Presidential Politics in the Jacksonian Era." *Journal of Supreme Court History* (1993): 59–72.

Lawrence, Alexander A. *James Moore Wayne, Southern Unionist.* Chapel Hill: University of North Carolina Press, 1943.

Longaker, Richard. "Andrew Jackson and the Judiciary." *Political Science Quarterly* 71 (1956): 341–364.

McPherson, James M. *Ordeal by Fire: The Civil War and Reconstruction*, 3rd ed. New York: McGraw-Hill, 2001.

Newmyer, R. Kent. *Supreme Court Justice Joseph Story: Statesman of the Old Republic.* Chapel Hill: University of North Carolina Press, 1985.

Peterson, Norma Lois. *The Presidencies of William Henry Harrison and John Tyler.* Lawrence: University Press of Kansas, 1989.

Potter, David M. *The Impending Crisis, 1848–1861.* New York: Harper and Row, 1976.

Quaife, Milo Milton, ed. *The Diary of James K. Polk, During His Presidency, 1845 to 1849.* Chicago: A. C. McClurg and Co., 1910; reprint edition, 1970.

Remini, Robert V. *Andrew Jackson and the Course of American Freedom*, vol. 2, *1822–1832.* New York: Harper and Row, 1981.

———. *Andrew Jackson and the Course of American Democracy*, vol. 3, *1833–1845.* New York: Harper and Row, 1984.

Saunders, Robert. *John Archibald Campbell: Southern Moderate, 1811–1889.* Tuscaloosa: University of Alabama Press, 1997.

Silver, David M. *Lincoln's Supreme Court.* Urbana: University of Illinois Press, 1957.

Swisher, Carl B. *History of the Supreme Court of the United States*, vol. 2, *The Taney Period, 1836–1824.* New York: Macmillan, 1974.

———. *Roger B. Taney.* New York: Macmillan, 1936.

Warren, Charles. *The Supreme Court in United States History*, vol. 2, *1836–1918.* Boston: Little, Brown, 1928.

Watson, Harry L. *Liberty and Power: The Politics of Jacksonian America.* New York: Hill and Wang, 1990.

Wiebe, Robert H. *The Opening of American Society, From the Adoption of the Constitution to the Eve of Disunion.* New York: Vintage Books, 1984.

Wilson, Major L. *The Presidency of Martin Van Buren.* Lawrence: University Press of Kansas, 1984.

2

The Justices

The Taney Court spanned twenty-eight years, and its membership included twenty justices. Taken as a whole, their years of judicial service stretched across almost the entire nineteenth century. Justice Joseph Story, the senior associate justice at the time of Taney's arrival, began his service on the Court in 1811, and Justice Stephen J. Field, appointed in 1863, just a year before Taney's death, concluded his Supreme Court career in 1897. Indeed, the Taney years cut through the middle of the nineteenth century. Some of the Court's members grew up during the American revolutionary era, and others helped usher in the industrial age of the late nineteenth century.

In terms of their periods of service, two significant groups of justices made up the Taney Court. One cohort served together through nearly all of Taney's chief justiceship: Taney, along with fellow Jackson appointees John McLean, James Wayne, and John Catron. McLean and Wayne had recently arrived when Taney assumed his post in 1836, and Catron joined them the following year. The tenures of these justices overlapped almost perfectly, and all died during or immediately after the Civil War. The tenures of a second cluster of justices—Peter V. Daniel, Robert Cooper Grier, Benjamin Curtis, and John Archibald Campbell—coincided during the 1850s. All except Curtis were Democratic in party affiliation and served during the most controversial portion of the Taney era, when issues of slavery and states' rights dominated national political and constitutional debate. One more justice deserves mention. Justice Story, the most potent symbol of the Marshall Court, served only eight years alongside Taney. Nevertheless, Story led the Court's nationalist wing during the early years of the Taney era and played a profoundly significant role in U.S. constitutional and legal development right up to his sudden death in 1844. These nine justices—Taney, McLean, Wayne, Catron, Daniel, Grier, Curtis, Campbell, and Story—dominated the Supreme Court during this era. The other eleven justices during those years either had a relatively minor impact on U.S. legal and constitutional development or served the majority of their terms of service after the Taney period.

The Chief Justice

Roger B. Taney

President Andrew Jackson's appointment of Roger Brooke Taney to the chief justiceship held out the possibility of dramatically transforming the Supreme Court and the contours of constitutional interpretation. Jacksonians cheered the appointment of Taney because of his loyalty to the president and his apparent commitment to an egalitarian economic vision for the young republic. Jackson's political opponents, however, feared that Taney would threaten the interests of property holders, undermine the strength of the Union, and weaken the authority of the Supreme Court. Typical of the fatalistic reaction to the Taney appointment in some quarters was Senator Daniel Webster's statement to a friend: "Judge [Joseph] Story thinks the Supreme Court is gone, and I think so too" (Warren 1928, 10). From this perspective, Taney's selection threatened to undo all of the work accomplished by the great Chief Justice John Marshall.

Despite political rhetoric that drew a sharp contrast between the two chief justices, Taney's aristocratic background resembled Marshall's. Born in 1777 in Calvert County, Maryland, in the southern tobacco-growing part of the state, Taney had come from a family of planters. His father, Michael Taney, who was a descendant of an indentured servant who had arrived in Maryland in 1660 and later acquired land and slaves, married the wealthy Monica Brooke. The couple had seven children, of whom Roger was the third. During the eighteenth century, the Taney family had left the Anglican Church for the Catholic faith, a move that made them subject to religious persecution but at the same time gave them social prestige among the colony's Catholic elite. The Taney family placed a great emphasis on educational achievement, and young Roger studied in local schools and under the direction of a tutor. In 1795, he graduated from Dickinson College in Pennsylvania. As he was the second son in the family, the young Taney would not inherit the family's plantation, so he pursued a legal career. After studying with Judge Jeremiah Townley Chase of the Maryland General Court in Annapolis, Taney was admitted to the bar in 1799.

Over the next several years, Taney's rise within the legal profession coincided with his entrance into the political arena. Early in his career he embraced the Federalist Party of John Adams and Alexander Hamilton, and in 1799 Taney won election to the Maryland House of Delegates. His tenure in office lasted only a year, however, for he lost his seat in 1800 when Federalists all over the country suffered defeat at the hands of Thomas Jefferson and the Democratic-Republicans. In 1801 Taney moved to Frederick, Maryland, where he began to build up a successful law practice while taking an active role in the state's Federalist Party, and in 1806 he married Anne Phoebe Charlton Key, sister of Francis Scott Key. From 1810 to 1815, Taney served as director of a branch of a state bank in Frederick, and as a Federalist he expressed strong

Roger B. Taney (James King, for Charles Barmore Publishers, Collection of the Supreme Court of the United States)

support for the national bank, the Bank of the United States. He did not always adhere to party orthodoxy, however. His support for President James Madison's waging war against England in 1812 set him against many of his party's New England elite, and at the conclusion of the war his patriotic, popular stance made his faction within the party the most powerful. A year after the war ended, Taney won election to the state senate for a five-year term, during which he took an interest in banking and currency issues and advocated for the rights of slaves and free blacks.

Taney's moderation on the slavery issue typified southern opinion during the early nineteenth century, particularly in a border state such as Maryland, where slaves constituted only a small percentage of the population. Taney, in fact, freed his own slaves and supported colonization, a popular national movement at the time to send American slaves to Africa. In keeping with this moderate antislavery stance, in 1819 he successfully defended Jacob Gruber, a Methodist minister accused of inciting slaves to rebellion in an antislavery sermon. Appealing for Gruber's acquittal during the trial, Taney described slavery as "a blot on our national character." "Every real lover of freedom confidently hopes that it will be effectually, though it must be gradually, wiped away," he announced to the jury in the case, "and earnestly looks for the means by which this necessary object may be best attained." The jurors heeded the passionate appeal of the young lawyer and voted to acquit (Strickland 1860, 168). Such statements by the young Taney seemed to indicate that he was no friend of slavery.

After Taney moved to Baltimore in 1823, his political views began to evolve toward a more southern and Democratic-Republican position. By that time the Democratic-Republican Party had emerged as the dominant political party in the United States and had come to be known simply as the "Republican" party. A victim of its own success, the party had split into factions by the 1820s, and the 1824 presidential race revolved more around personalities and political rivalries than ideological differences. In the four-way election campaign that year, Taney supported Tennessean Andrew Jackson. "He is honest, he is independent, is not brought forward by any particular class of politicians, or any sectional interest," Taney wrote to a friend. "He is not one of the [Cabinet] Secretaries. He is taken up spontaneously by the people, and if he is elected will owe obligations to no particular persons" (Swisher 1974, 121). Although Jackson lost that election to John Quincy Adams, Taney helped deliver Maryland's electoral votes to Jackson four years later as chair of the state party's central committee. At the time of Jackson's election in 1828, the fifty-one-year-old Taney seemed destined to remain a fixture in Maryland's legal and political circles for the rest of his life. He had built up a substantial law practice in the state and had received an appointment as Maryland's attorney general in 1827. But Taney's loyalty to Jackson paved the way for new opportunities. In 1831, when the president reorganized his cabinet, he appointed Taney to the position of U.S. attorney general. Although Taney disliked his "laborious" new job and its meager salary, he soon emerged as a key player within the administration.

Taney's unpublished opinion in a dispute over state power to regulate slavery demonstrated how his political views had changed by the 1830s. In 1831, controversy erupted over the constitutionality of laws in South Carolina and North Carolina that mandated the imprisonment of free blacks who entered the state's ports on foreign ships. When British officials protested against these measures, Secretary of State Edward Livingston asked Taney for his official opinion on the constitutionality of such regulations. Taney affirmed the power of a state to protect itself from the potential dangers posed by the introduction of free blacks. Even if such a law violated a federal treaty—as in this case—the power of a state was paramount, he argued. Blacks, in such instances, had no rights, according to Taney, for they were "a separate and degraded people," who "were not looked upon as citizens by the contracting parties who formed the Constitution" (Swisher 1936, 154). Far from criticizing slavery as he had done in the *Gruber* case, Taney clearly stated his belief that neither the Declaration of Independence nor the Constitution granted any rights to African Americans. Taney's vigorous defense of slavery coincided with the development of the South's proslavery argument at the time, which emerged largely in response to abolitionism. The opinion, in its explicit denial of black citizenship, also foreshadowed Taney's infamous decision in *Dred Scott v. Sandford* twenty-five years later.

Taney's important role in the controversy over the continued existence of the Second Bank of the United States also showed the evolution of his political views. To many Jacksonians, the national bank symbolized the privilege and power of a monopoly and operated to the detriment of the laboring masses. Jackson's National Republican opponents in Congress, led by Henry Clay, attempted to embarrass the president politically by passing a bill to recharter the bank in 1832, four years before its charter was set to expire. Knowing that Jackson disliked the national bank, National Republicans hoped to turn the bank into an issue against the incumbent president, who was seeking a second term. Taney advised the president to veto the bill rechartering the bank, and, at Jackson's request, he helped draft a veto message for Jackson to deliver to Congress. Bank supporters failed to muster enough votes to override the president's veto, and Jackson won both the bank war and the presidential election of 1832. In some ways, Taney's actions in the struggle over the bank represented the Marylander's first attempt to dismantle the work of John Marshall. In a sweeping decision in *McCulloch v. Maryland* (1819), the Marshall Court had upheld the constitutionality of the national bank, and the veto message took aim directly at Marshall's justification for the bank's existence. Because its charter did not expire until 1836, the bank remained an issue in national politics even after Jackson and Taney had ensured its demise. Taney recommended to Jackson that he withdraw the $10 million in U.S. government deposits in the bank, but Secretary of the Treasury William J. Duane refused to take such action. Jackson promptly fired Duane and appointed Taney as secretary of the treasury to carry out the task. On September 23, 1833, Taney assumed his new post and began depositing the federal government's money in a series of state banks. When the U.S. Senate returned to session a few months later, senators rejected Taney's appointment to the cabinet and passed a resolution condemning his transfer of the deposits. The first cabinet member ever to have his nomination defeated by the Senate, the disgraced Taney returned home to Baltimore to practice law.

Before long, however, Taney found himself again on the national stage. The resignation of U.S. Supreme Court Justice Gabriel Duval, who had become deaf to the point that he could not hear anything during oral arguments, prompted Jackson to turn again to his friend from Maryland. On January 15, 1835, the President nominated Taney for the vacancy on the Court, whereupon the Senate promptly rejected the appointment by indefinite postponement. That summer, Chief Justice Marshall died, thus creating a second vacancy on the bench. At the end of 1835, Jackson resubmitted Taney's name to the Senate, this time to fill the vacant chief justiceship, while the President nominated Philip Pendleton Barbour to take Duval's place. By the spring of 1836, when the nominations were considered, Jacksonian Democrats controlled the Senate, and on March 16, the Senate confirmed both appointments. Taney took the oath as chief justice on March 28, 1836, and heard circuit cases that year, although he did not actually preside over the Supreme Court until the opening of its term on January 2, 1837.

The selection of Taney—to the delight of Democrats and the horror of Whigs—seemed to mark the dawn of a new era in the history of the Supreme Court. Perhaps the most provocative symbol of the change of leadership was evident when Taney opened the Court's January 1837 term wearing long trousers, rather than the traditional knee breeches that the justices had always worn. Unlike Marshall, who had grown up during the American Revolution, Taney had come of age during the early nineteenth century—a period of commercial expansion, democratic impulses, territorial growth, and social reform. Taney's closeness to Jackson, in particular, who himself symbolized the spirit of the expanding republic, seemed to foreshadow a revolutionary shift in the Supreme Court's interpretation of the Constitution. Critics of the new chief justice warned that the rights of property holders, the strength of the federal Union, and the authority of the Supreme Court were all at stake.

Taney's first major decision seemed to confirm opponents' fears about the future of property rights and provided the most striking contrast with the decisions of his predecessor. In *Charles River Bridge v. Warren Bridge* (1837), a case decided during his first term as chief justice, the Court confronted the issue of whether a corporation charter issued by a state contained an implied monopoly. In 1785 the Massachusetts legislature had chartered the Charles River Bridge Company to construct a bridge connecting Boston and Charlestown and to collect tolls from bridge passengers. By 1828, rapid growth of the two cities prompted the legislature to charter the Warren Bridge Company, which was to construct an adjacent toll-free bridge across the river. The Charles River Bridge Company, faced with the threat of losing much of its bridge's traffic, brought suit against the rival bridge company and charged that the granting of the Warren Bridge charter violated the Contract Clause of the U.S. Constitution. Although not explicitly stated, the Charles River Bridge Company argued, their state-granted charter implied that they possessed exclusive rights to operate a bridge over the Charles.

Writing for the majority, Taney rejected the notion of an implied monopoly and held in favor of the Warren Bridge. He viewed the case as a contest between the rights of corporations and the rights of the community, between an economic order that protected private property for the few and an enterprising economy that gave states the power to promote internal improvements in the public interest. "The object and end of all government is to promote the happiness and prosperity of the community by which it is established," Taney declared, "and it can never be assumed that the government intended to diminish its power of accomplishing the end for which it was created" (36 U.S. 420, 547). The state legislature, Taney held, thus maintained the power to grant the new charter. Though private property rights needed protection, he argued, "we must not forget that the community also have rights, and that the happiness and well being of every citizen depends on their faithful preservation" (36 U.S. 420, 548). Were the Court to decide otherwise, Taney believed, the entire nation's economic progress would come to a halt. Railroad companies that had been established along the same lines as turnpikes would be subject to lawsuits challenging their right to interfere with these supposedly implied contracts. If all such charters implied monopoly rights, "we shall be thrown back to the improvements of the last century, and obliged to stand still," Taney wrote (36 U.S. 420, 553). The chief justice's opinion thus exhibited his opposition to monopoly power, his support for new investment and technological advancement, and his commitment to promoting the welfare of "the community."

Although his *Charles River Bridge* opinion signaled a departure from the Marshall Court's protection of established property owners, Taney's other decisions regarding corporations and contracts demonstrated the chief justice's pragmatic commitment to property rights and economic progress. In *Bank of Augusta v. Earle* (1839), for example, Taney wrote for an eight-justice majority in overturning a circuit court ruling in favor of Alabama businessmen who refused to pay bills of exchange to out-of-state banks on the grounds that the state had banned out-of-state corporations from doing business within its borders. Allaying the concerns of the commercial community, Taney ruled in favor of the banks. The principles of "the comity of nations and between these states," he argued, made the contracts valid and enforceable (38 U.S. 519, 589). A state could exclude a foreign corporation from doing business or could impose reasonable restrictions on that corporation, he held, but only if those terms were clearly stated. Since Alabama had not expressly forbidden such transactions, Taney concluded, the contracts in question needed to be honored. In

Bronson v. Kinzie (1843), moreover, Taney struck down an Illinois debtor relief statute regulating mortgage transactions, which had been enacted to deal with the economic crisis growing out of the Panic of 1837. Virtually ignoring the plight of debtors all over the country, Taney held that any regulation of contracts enacted by states could not go so far as to "impair the obligation of the contract." Adopting economic nationalist language reminiscent of Chief Justice Marshall, Taney praised the virtues of the Contract Clause: "It was undoubtedly adopted as a part of the Constitution for a great and useful purpose. It was to maintain the integrity of contracts, and to secure their faithful execution throughout this Union" (42 U.S. 311, 318). Clearly, Taney's view of the Contract Clause proved no threat to commercial interests.

On matters relating to state power versus national power, Taney gave greater authority to states to regulate commerce than did his predecessor. As the nation's economy expanded, Taney and his colleagues struggled to define the specific parameters of national and state regulatory authority. Taney believed that states possessed a concurrent power to regulate commerce—even if that commerce passed beyond a state's borders—provided that the regulation did not conflict with existing federal law. He voted with the majority in *New York v. Miln* (1837), in which the Court upheld an ordinance requiring information about the income and occupation of passengers entering the port of New York as a valid exercise of a state's police power. The law, he and the majority believed, presented no conflict with the federal commerce power. In the *License Cases* (1847), a series of disputes involving state taxation and regulation of spirituous liquors, Taney made his first significant statement about the relationship of national and state power under the Commerce Clause. Because the state laws in question did not conflict with any congressional legislation on the issue, Taney believed, no grounds existed on which to invalidate them. "The mere grant of power to the general government cannot, upon any just principles of construction, be construed to be an absolute prohibition to the exercise of any power over the same subject by the States," he wrote. States retained the powers, Taney argued, to make regulations "for the safety or convenience of trade, or for the protection of the health of its citizens" (46 U.S. 504, 579). A few years later, in the *Passenger Cases* (1849), which involved state taxes on incoming passengers, including immigrants, Taney reiterated his view of the states' power to regulate. This time he found himself in dissent. Arguing that no existing federal statutes prescribed the character or condition of immigrants to the United States, Taney insisted that the state measures passed constitutional muster. Eventually, Taney and his colleagues adopted a compromise on the issue of the boundary between federal and state powers over commerce in *Cooley v. Board of Wardens* (1852), in which the Court held that areas requiring national uniformity would be the exclusive domain of Congress, while other matters of commercial regulation would be the purview of states. Overall, Taney placed greater faith in the states' police powers than had Marshall.

On other matters relating to the proper relationship between the state and national governments, though, Taney proved surprisingly nationalistic. He sided with nationalist Justices Story, McLean, and Wayne, for example, in *Holmes v. Jennison* (1840), in which he held that the governor of a state had no power to surrender fugitives to a foreign government. By doing so, Taney affirmed that only the national government possessed authority over foreign relations. In *Swift v. Tyson* (1842), he joined all of his colleagues in establishing that federal courts could follow general principles of commercial law without having to yield to state court decisions in the states in which they sat. This assisted national commercial development without the interference of state and local court rulings. And in *Genesee Chief v. Fitzhugh* (1852), Taney went even further than Marshall in expanding the admiralty jurisdiction of the federal courts. Upholding an act of Congress that had extended federal court jurisdiction to include certain cases arising on the Great Lakes, Taney brought navigable fresh water lakes and rivers within the scope of federal judicial authority. By discarding the English common law rule that admiralty law pertained only to those waters subject to the ebb and flow of the tide, Taney accommodated the development of steamboat technology and aided the growth of federal judicial power.

On the slavery issue, however, Taney consistently trumpeted the need for state control. In a number of slavery cases, he argued that states, rather than Congress, possessed the constitutional power to govern the "peculiar institution." In *Groves v. Slaughter* (1841), a case involving the sale of slaves in Mississippi, Taney wrote a concurring opinion affirming his commitment to slavery. Although the majority opinion addressed only the narrow issue of the validity of the commercial transaction in question, Taney went beyond the scope of the question at hand and argued that the power to regulate interstate slave trading lay exclusively with the states. "The action of the several States upon this subject, cannot be controlled by Congress," he wrote, "either by virtue of its power to regulate commerce, or by virtue of any other power conferred by the Constitution of the United States" (40 U.S. 449, 508). In *Prigg v. Pennsylvania* (1842), Taney elaborated further his views on the subject. He concurred with the majority opinion invalidating Pennsylvania's personal liberty law of 1826 as a violation of both the Constitution and the federal Fugitive Slave Law of 1793. The Pennsylvania statute required slave catchers to obtain a proper writ from a state judge before removing any African American from the state. In the majority opinion, Justice Joseph Story struck down the Pennsylvania law on the grounds that regulation of the slaveholder's right of recovery lay exclusively with Congress. Taney rejected Story's reasoning. He insisted that the Constitution prohibited states only from *interfering* with a slaveholder's right to recover his property, not from *supporting* or *enforcing* the rights of slaveholders. Therefore, he concluded, states could regulate slavery, so long as they did not threaten the constitutional guarantees of slaveholders.

As time passed and the sectional rift widened, Taney became increasingly sensitive to the slavery question. His opinion in the *Passenger Cases* (1849) revealed the extent to which he injected the slavery issue into disputes where it was not immediately relevant. Although the case itself dealt with laws regulating immigrants to the North, Taney interpreted the dispute in light of its implications for black immigrants to the South. Criticizing an attorney's argument about the meaning of a federal statute, Taney speculated that, if the lawyer were correct in his interpretation, "the emancipated slaves of the West Indies have at this hour the absolute right to reside, hire houses, and traffic and trade throughout the Southern States, in spite of any state law to the contrary; inevitably producing the most serious discontent, and ultimately leading to the most painful consequences" (48 U.S. 283, 474). In *Strader v. Graham* (1851), Taney again argued for state power to protect slavery, this time by dismissing a suit for damages involving a group of slaves who had been taken briefly into Ohio and later fled from Kentucky into Canada. When the owner of the slaves sued a group of men who had allegedly aided their escape, defense counsel argued that the Northwest Ordinance, which had banned slavery in the Old Northwest in 1787, freed the slaves upon their stepping foot on Ohio soil. The Kentucky Court of Appeals rejected this argument, and the case went to the U.S. Supreme Court. Writing for a unanimous majority, Taney dismissed the case for lack of jurisdiction by claiming that the laws of Kentucky superseded the Northwest Ordinance.

The pinnacle of Taney's proslavery jurisprudence came in *Dred Scott v. Sandford* (1857), in which he attempted to resolve once and for all the constitutional questions surrounding slavery that had bedeviled the nation for decades. Scott, a Missouri slave, accompanied his owner, an army surgeon named John Emerson, to Illinois and Wisconsin Territory during the 1830s. Several years later, after the death of Emerson, Scott initiated a suit claiming that, by virtue of his residence in free territory, he had gained his freedom. Instead of confining himself to the specific question of Scott's status and standing to sue, Taney delivered a proslavery diatribe that revealed his deep devotion to slavery and the values of southern society. The chief justice held that the lower federal court should have dismissed the case for lack of jurisdiction. Because Scott was black, according to Taney, he could not be a citizen and had no right to sue. Even if he were a free black man, he was not a citizen under the U.S. Constitution. Blacks had long been considered, according to Taney, "so far inferior that they had no rights which the white man was bound to respect" (60 U.S. 393, 407). Thus, Taney not only ruled that Scott lacked standing to sue, the chief justice also held, on the basis of his interpretation of the framers' intentions, that no African American could claim the privileges of citizenship under the Constitution.

The second part of Taney's opinion attacked congressional authority over slavery. Although the Court had no grounds for deciding this issue, Taney attempted to steer the discussion of Scott's status to the larger question of slavery in the territories. According to Taney, Scott's sojourn in Wisconsin Territory did not make him a free man, because Congress lacked the power to exclude slavery from the territories. Taney suggested that the Fifth Amendment's Due Process Clause prohibited Congress from interfering with slavery in these areas, because to do so would violate the property rights of the slaveholders who settled there. Slaves, he contended, were no different from any other form of property, and the rights of such property holders required constitutional protection. In arguing that the right to hold slave property was firmly grounded in the Constitution, Taney proved his unflagging support for the rights of slaveholders as well as his willingness to use federal judicial power to uphold those rights.

Taney remained committed to proslavery principles throughout his judicial career. Having positioned the Court squarely on the side of slaveholders in *Dred Scott*, Taney asserted the unqualified power of the federal judiciary to protect slaveholders' rights in *Ableman v. Booth* (1859). The case involved an abolitionist who had helped a fugitive slave escape into Wisconsin, in violation of the Fugitive Slave Law of 1850. Waging a battle with the U.S. Supreme Court over jurisdiction, the Wisconsin judges challenged federal authority to prosecute the alleged criminal. In response, Taney issued a sweeping statement of national judicial authority based on the Supremacy Clause of the Constitution—an opinion every bit as nationalistic as the most far-reaching of Marshall's decisions—and upheld the controversial law of 1850. "Without such a tribunal [as the U.S. Supreme Court]," Taney argued, "it is obvious that there would be no uniformity of judicial decision; and that the supremacy . . . so carefully provided in the [Supremacy] clause of the Constitution . . . could not possibly be maintained peacefully, unless it was associated with this paramount judicial authority" (62 U.S. 506, 518). Taney's opinion in *Ableman*, on the eve of the Civil War, clearly showed that the chief justice believed more deeply in slaveholders' rights than in states' rights.

When the war came, Taney retained his seat as chief justice of the U.S. Supreme Court, despite his vocal opposition to President Lincoln and his overt sympathy for the Confederate cause. From the bench, the aging Marylander railed against Lincoln's suspension of the writ of habeas corpus and attempted, in his view, to preserve liberty in the face of military despotism. In his circuit opinion in *Ex parte Merryman* (1861), a case involving an active Maryland secessionist who had been arrested upon Lincoln's order, Taney sharply criticized the president's action as unconstitutional. The chief justice argued that only Congress had the power to suspend the writ of habeas corpus and that any person arrested by a military officer should be turned over to civil authorities rather than be subject to military trial. Taney boldly sent a copy of his opinion to Lincoln, arguing that the chief executive needed "to take care that the laws be faithfully executed." In another circuit opinion, *Carpenter v. United States* (1863), Taney again strongly criticized the Lincoln administration, this time for attempting to halt trade between Baltimore and the Confederacy. "A civil war or any other war," Taney wrote, "does not enlarge the powers of the federal government over the states or the people beyond what the compact has given to it in time of war" (Swisher 1936, 553, 567). Perhaps the greatest evidence of Taney's bitter opposition to Lincoln's policies is the fact that the chief justice composed an opinion declaring the federal draft law unconstitutional, even though such a case never came before the Supreme Court. This measure, too, Taney believed, struck at the heart of Americans' freedoms.

That such impassioned defenses of the liberties of the people came from the Court's staunchest defender of slavery was not at all surprising, given the remarkable tensions and paradoxes that marked Taney's career. According to historian R. Kent Newmyer, Taney embodied the contradictions of the mid–nineteenth century United States: "He was a Southerner who loved his country, a states' righter dedicated to the Union, a slaveholder who regretted the institution and manumitted his slaves, and an aristocrat with a democratic political philosophy" (Newmyer 1968, 94). During his nearly three decades of judicial service, Taney wrote almost 300 judicial opinions, of which only a few were dissents. For the most part, he succeeded in uniting his primarily Democratic colleagues and in preserving an important role for the Supreme Court in the U.S. constitutional order.

The Old Guard

Joseph Story

Justice Joseph Story, of Massachusetts, was the chief justice's main rival on the bench during the early years of the Taney era. Among the greatest legal thinkers in the history of the Court and certainly one of the most eminent jurists of his day, Story served alongside Taney for eight years, during which time the two clashed on some of the most important issues to face the Court during this period. If Taney personified the new age in the history of the Court and of the Republic, Story came closest to representing an older era rapidly coming to a close by the time of Taney's appointment. Marshall's closest friend and associate, Story saw himself as the former chief justice's successor and attempted—often in vain—to carry on the work of his judicial hero.

Born in 1779 in the fishing village of Marblehead, Massachusetts, Story absorbed the values of his parents, Elisha and Mehitable Story, as well as those of New England culture. From his father—a member of the Sons of Liberty and an "Indian" in the Boston Tea Party—young Joseph received a fierce nationalism and a commitment to public service; from his mother—talkative and intelligent—he gained a boundless energy and tireless work ethic; from the place and time in which he grew up, he imbibed a Puritan sense of the social utility of religion and ethics. Educated at

Joseph Story (Mathew Brady, Collection of the Supreme Court of the United States)

Harvard, Story graduated in 1798 and returned to Marblehead to study law with Samuel Sewell, later the chief justice of Massachusetts. In 1801, Story was admitted to the bar and began practicing law in Essex County, Massachusetts. Although raised in Federalist-dominated New England, the young Story became a Jeffersonian Republican, in part because of his close association with the powerful and prominent Crowninshield family of Salem, leading Jeffersonians. This connection helped him win election to the Massachusetts House of Representatives, and Story later took Jacob Crowninshield's seat in Congress after his death. Despite this brief political experience, including a term in 1811 as speaker of the Massachusetts House of Representatives, Story's real love was the law.

As his biographer explains, law not only "suited [Story's] temperament and talents," it also took on for him great "moral and ideological" significance (Newmyer 1985, 38). As a practitioner of both law and politics in his early career, Story came to believe in the inefficiency and ineffectiveness, perhaps even the immorality, of political parties and the legislative branch of government. In contrast, law—scientifically conceived and properly applied by judges—served as a corrective to the ills of partisan politics. The judiciary, he came to believe, possessed a special obligation to study the law and apply it properly, so as to preserve the moral basis of the social order put at risk by the political branches of government. As he preached and practiced these principles, Story made a name for himself within the New England legal community. During the decade after his admission to the bar, he began publishing legal treatises that grew out of his own law practice. In these works, Story took leading English decisions and attempted to show how they applied to American legal development. He received high marks from his colleagues for his scholarship, as well as his advocacy, and when a vacancy arose on the U.S. Supreme Court with the death of Justice William Cushing, Story emerged as a potential nominee.

Story's name, however, was not among the first few on President James Madison's list. At the urging of former president Thomas Jefferson, Madison initially sought a more overtly partisan appointment, in order to help the Democratic-Republicans overtake the Federalist majority that still dominated the Court under Marshall. Madison's first choice, former U.S. attorney general Levi Lincoln, declined the appointment because of his age and poor health, despite being confirmed by the Senate. The president's second choice, former U.S. customs collector Alexander Wolcott, failed to win confirmation because of what Federalists perceived as his excessive partisanship. Madison then turned to his minister to Russia, John Quincy Adams, who, because of his publicly expressed distaste for the law and his privately held political ambitions, declined the post. Only then did the president nominate the young, Harvard-educated legal scholar. Democratic-Republicans greeted the appointment with little enthusiasm, particularly Jefferson, whom Story had angered years before as a U.S. representative when he opposed Jefferson's controversial Embargo

Act of 1807. Still, with the Senate and the nation tired of the parade of potential justices, confirmation came quickly. Within three days of his appointment, on November 18, 1811, Story won Senate approval. At thirty-two years of age, Story was the youngest person ever nominated or confirmed to serve on the Court.

Before Taney's arrival on the Court in 1837, Story made a name for himself as a staunch judicial nationalist and a prominent legal scholar. A supporter of all of Marshall's major decisions, Story took a particular interest in expanding the power and jurisdiction of the federal judiciary, especially in maritime and commercial law cases. His most famous opinion, though, had come in *Martin v. Hunter's Lessee* (1816), a case involving the power of a state court to challenge a decision of the U.S. Supreme Court. During the American Revolution, Virginia had enacted legislation confiscating land held by British subjects. Litigants challenged the law, and the Supreme Court initially ruled, in *Fairfax's Devisee v. Hunter's Lessee* (1813), that the Virginia confiscation law violated treaties between the United States and England. But the Virginia Court of Appeals, under the leadership of Judge Spencer Roane, refused to acknowledge the U.S. Supreme Court's jurisdiction in the case. When the issue came back to the Supreme Court a second time in *Martin v. Hunter's Lessee*, Story issued his most forceful statement of national supremacy. Denouncing the notion of states' sovereignty, Story argued that the Constitution had been created not by the states, but by the people—as stated in the Constitution's preamble. For this reason, he argued, Congress had the power to give the U.S. Supreme Court appellate review of state decisions, as it had done in the Judiciary Act of 1789. Popular sovereignty, in Story's hands, thus became the constitutional foundation for national supremacy. The state needed to yield to the Court's decision, Story argued, because the people themselves had authorized the powers given to the U.S. Supreme Court. Story furthered these ideas apart from his role as a Supreme Court justice, when he was appointed the first Dane Professor of Law at Harvard. During his sixteen years there, Story wrote nine legal treatises, including his *Commentaries on the Constitution* (1833), in which he explicated and systemized the Marshall Court's nationalistic view of the Constitution.

After Taney assumed the chief justiceship, Marshall's and Story's nationalism fell somewhat out of favor. In 1837, the new chief justice's first year on the bench, Story found himself dissenting in three of the Court's most important decisions. In *New York v. Miln*, the first major Commerce Clause case to come before the Taney Court, the majority upheld a New York statute that required the captains of foreign vessels arriving in the Port of New York to provide information on arriving passengers. The intent of the law was to regulate the inflow of indigents who might become wards of the city. Story insisted that the law violated what he viewed as the exclusive power of Congress to regulate commerce under the Constitution. In *Briscoe v. Kentucky*, Story again stood against the majority, this time on the issue of whether a state-chartered bank had the power to issue circulating notes. In contrast to his colleagues, who granted wide latitude to states to control banking and currency within their states, Story argued in his dissenting opinion that state-chartered notes violated the Constitution's ban on state-issued "bills of credit." Finally, in *Charles River Bridge v. Warren Bridge*, Story defended the Marshall Court's traditional position that corporate charters needed protection from state interference. Utilizing all of his intellectual and scholarly abilities, Story passionately argued that a 1785 Massachusetts charter granted a monopoly to the Charles River Bridge Company, thus contradicting the majority's decision that the state had a right to charter a new bridge to serve the public interest.

Despite these defeats, Story succeeded in convincing his colleagues on the Taney Court of the need for national uniformity in the area of commercial law. In *Swift v. Tyson* (1842), perhaps Story's most significant judicial opinion, a unanimous Court granted the authority of the federal courts to establish national principles of commercial law. The case dealt with a bill of exchange involving parties from two different states. In such diversity of citizenship cases, Section 34 of the Judiciary Act of 1789 required that federal courts abide by state laws that applied to the commercial transaction—in this case, the laws of New York. In the absence of state legislation regulating the type of transaction at issue in the case, the defendant, Tyson, argued that New York judicial decisions applied. Were they followed, these state precedents might have invalidated the bill as infected by the fraudulent nature of the original transaction. Seeking to protect the integrity of bills of exchange as a medium of commerce, particularly interstate commerce, Story held that state court decisions did not constitute "laws" that federal courts were bound to respect. Instead, according to Story, federal courts were free to apply general commercial law principles. By upholding the validity of the bill and rejecting the applicability of state precedents, Story thus sought to prevent commercial transactions from being upset by state and local rules. The fact that he convinced all of his colleagues in the case—especially given the Taney Court's overall tendency to uphold state economic regulations—attests to Story's powers of persuasion.

Story's commitment to establishing national legal rules collided with his personal convictions, however, with regard to the slavery issue. From the earliest days of his career, Story publicly denounced slavery as a moral and political evil, opposed the extension of the institution into new western territories, and condemned the international slave trade in his charges to grand juries while riding circuit. In the celebrated U.S. Supreme Court case of *United States v. Amistad* (1841), he succeeded in freeing a group of Africans who had entered U.S. jurisdiction after engaging in mutiny on a slave ship from Cuba, by narrowly construing the terms of a treaty. But in a much more doctrinally significant case the following year, *Prigg v. Pennsylvania*, Story's devotion to the Union and to national legal norms triumphed over his antislavery principles. Joined by seven of his colleagues, Story upheld the Fugitive

Slave Act of 1793, declared Pennsylvania's 1826 personal liberty law unconstitutional, and ruled that the Constitution's Fugitive Slave Clause established the right of slave owners to recapture their slaves. Perhaps in an effort to persuade the nation of the necessity of conciliation on the issue of slavery, Story claimed that the Fugitive Slave Clause had resulted from a critical compromise at the Constitutional Convention of 1787. The right of recapture, Story claimed, "was so vital to the preservation of [the South's] domestic interests and institutions, that it cannot be doubted that it constituted a fundamental article, without the adoption of which the Union could not have been formed" (41 U.S. 539, 611). There is no evidence, however, that the fugitive slave issue played a significant role in the Philadelphia convention, and Story's opinion in *Prigg* makes sense only in the context of his devotion to a national legal order. The power to enact legislation pertaining to the rendition of fugitive slaves, Story argued, lay exclusively with Congress. Abolitionist critics of the opinion insisted that it merely demonstrated "the moral bankruptcy of Story's legal science" (Powell 1994, 444). Regardless, that one of the U.S. Supreme Court's most proslavery opinions came from the pen of a lifelong opponent of the institution demonstrates the extraordinary tensions that at times marked the work of the Taney Court.

Although Story's influence on the Court lessened during Taney's chief justiceship, the New Englander maintained a reputation as the foremost American legal thinker of his day. His work at Harvard, both as a law teacher and a scholar, lent authority to his judicial opinions, even as Taney led the Court away from some of the Marshall Court's principles and precedents. Pessimistic about the future of the Court and the Republic, particularly in light of criticism he received for his *Prigg v. Pennsylvania* decision, in early 1845 Story announced he would retire from the bench later that year to focus on teaching and scholarship. After an especially grueling summer of circuit riding, he died on September 10, 1845.

Smith Thompson

Like Story, the moderate Justice Smith Thompson represented the older generation on the Court at the time of Taney's arrival. Born in 1768 in Dutchess County, New York, Thompson graduated from the College of New Jersey (later Princeton) and studied law under the well-known conservative jurist James Kent and his partner, Gilbert Livingston. Thompson married Livingston's daughter Sarah in 1794, and his father-in-law's political connections helped catapult Thompson to prominence within the state. A Democratic-Republican, he served briefly in the state assembly and as a member of New York's 1801 constitutional convention. In 1802, Thompson received an appointment to the New York Supreme Court, where he typically deferred to legislative enactments, and in 1814 he replaced Kent as chief justice. Politically ambitious, in 1818 Thompson left his seat on the bench to accept President James

Smith Thompson (Charles Bird King, Collection of the Supreme Court of the United States)

Monroe's nomination to be secretary of the navy. When Justice Henry Brockholst Livingston, a New Yorker, died in 1823, Monroe looked to the Empire State for a new justice. Passing over more prominent potential nominees such as Kent and U.S. Senator Martin Van Buren, Monroe appointed Thompson, whom he knew and trusted. Thompson served fourteen of his twenty years on Supreme Court before Taney arrived.

Thompson in many ways embodied the transition from the Marshall Court to the Taney era. During his years on the bench, Thompson consistently championed a considerable degree of state control over economic activity. In *Renner v. Bank of Columbia* (1824), he held that local custom, rather than uniform standards, ought to govern the execution of contracts, and in *Ogden v. Saunders* (1827) he joined the majority of his colleagues to hold that state bankruptcy legislation did not violate the Contract Clause. Thompson's willingness to grant power to states at times clashed with the Marshall Court's nationalist outlook. For example, he found himself in dissent in *Brown v. Maryland* (1827), in which he held that states could require sellers of imported goods to obtain licenses, as well as in *Craig v. Missouri* (1830), in which he attempted to uphold the issuance of state loan certificates.

During the Taney period, Thompson's belief in the idea of concurrent powers—the notion that states possessed power to regulate commerce in the absence of congressional action—became the view of the majority of the justices. In two of the major decisions of the 1837 term, *Briscoe v. Bank of Kentucky* and *New York v. Miln*, Thompson wrote concurring opinions, in which he sanctioned state authority over currency and over the registration of immigrants, respectively. Despite his general agreement with Taney on the constitutional contours of economic regulation, Thompson became a bitter political enemy of Andrew Jackson and Martin Van Buren, and as a justice he sometimes expressed fear of the decentralizing excesses of the new democratic order. He once confided to a friend his belief that the Jackson administration was attempting "to resolve the Government of the Union into the national imbecility of the old Confederation" (Swisher 1974, 45). In a brief opinion, Thompson concurred "entirely in all the principles and reasonings" in Justice Story's dissent in the *Charles River Bridge* case, a sure sign of at least some discomfort with the Taney's Court's new direction (36 U.S. 420, 650).

Thompson's most significant opinion came in a highly politicized constitutional case involving the separation of powers. When President Jackson's newly appointed postmaster general, Amos Kendall, refused to obey a federal court order that he honor a contract negotiated by his predecessor, Congress enacted legislation commanding him to do so. Kendall, who believed the contract was tainted by political favoritism, again refused to obey the order and charged that the act infringed on the powers of the executive branch under the Constitution. In a stinging rebuke of Kendall and the president who appointed him, the Court ruled against the postmaster general in *Kendall v. United States ex rel. Stokes* (1838). Writing for a six-justice majority, Thompson held that the federal court order—a writ of mandamus—had been properly issued and that Congress did have power over officials in the executive branch of government. "It would be an alarming doctrine that Congress cannot impose upon any Executive officer any duty they may think proper, which is not repugnant to any rights secured and protected by the Constitution," wrote Thompson, "and in such cases the duty and responsibility grow out of and are subject to the control of the law, and not to the direction of the President" (Warren 1928, 45).

Like his fellow northerner Justice Story, Thompson struggled with the constitutional issues surrounding slavery. In *Groves v. Slaughter* (1841), a case involving a provision in Mississippi's 1832 constitution that prohibited the introduction into the state of slaves for sale, Thompson avoided the major constitutional question at hand—whether state legislation regulating slavery encroached on national power to regulate commerce. When a slave trader challenged the constitutionality of the Mississippi rule, Thompson simply held that the state constitution's ban on importation of slaves was invalid because it had not been implemented by legislative action. The following year, Thompson concurred with his colleagues in *Prigg v. Pennsylvania* in upholding the Fugitive Slave Law of 1793. Still, he wrote a separate opinion so as to articulate again his belief in concurrent powers. In this instance, Thompson believed that states possessed the power to enact legislation pertaining to the rendition of fugitive slaves, so long as such enactments did not conflict with congressional legislation on the matter.

Thompson proved to be a moderate justice during the Taney period. Age, experience on the Marshall Court, and a contempt for President Jackson made Thompson at times an ally of Justice Story. Still, the New Yorker's belief in concurrent powers usually placed him on the side of Taney, states' rights, and slavery. He wrote eighty-five majority opinions, five concurrences, and eleven dissents during his two decades of judicial service. Collegial and well respected by his colleagues, Thompson initiated a new trend in the living arrangements of the justices when he appeared in Washington for the 1837 term with his bride and found a place to stay apart from the other justices, who had left their wives at home. The tradition of the justices lodging in a common boardinghouse thus came to end, as the other members of the Court eventually followed suit. As Thompson's decision on his living arrangements coincided with the arrival of the new chief justice, the 1837 term proved to be a break with the past in more ways than one. Thompson served on the Court until his death in 1843, just a few years before that of Story.

Jackson's Early Appointments

John McLean

When Taney assumed the chief justiceship, he joined three other justices who already owed their places on the Court to President Andrew Jackson. John McLean, the first of these, had arrived in 1829. Born in 1785 in Morris County, New Jersey, he moved during childhood to Morgantown, Virginia (now West Virginia), then to Kentucky, and later to Warren County, Ohio. There he received his only formal education—a few years of classical instruction—and in 1804 he began the study of law. Three years later, he was admitted to the bar, married Rebecca Edwards, and moved to Lebanon, Ohio, where he published a pro-Jeffersonian newspaper and practiced law. Elected to Congress in 1812, McLean served until the state legislature elected him to the Ohio Supreme Court, where he sat from 1816 to 1822.

President James Monroe's appointment of McLean as commissioner of the Public Land Office in 1822 and head of the Post Office Department a year later brought him back to Washington and fueled his political ambitions. McLean's success in administering the post office won him the favor of President John Quincy Adams, elected in 1824, who allowed him to retain his position in the new administration. Four years later, the politically savvy McLean cultivated ties to the Jacksonians while at the same time trying not to alienate the Adams administration. When Jackson won the election, the new president appointed McLean to the Supreme Court. Not only did Jackson want to reward McLean for refusing to work for Adams's reelection, the new president also hoped to eliminate a potential political rival. McLean, who was very popular in the West, had begun to be mentioned as a possible future presidential candidate.

Despite a promise not to pursue his political aspirations as a member of the Court, McLean proved to be one of the most political justices in U.S. history. Unrelenting in his quest for the presidency, he ran for the office four times while he was a member of the Court—each time with a different political party or faction. Over a period of thirty years, McLean flirted with the Jacksonians, the Anti-masons, the Free Soilers, the Know-Nothings, and the Republicans. Although his multiple political affiliations reflected to some degree the changing political landscape of the era, they also demonstrated the depth of his desire to attain the nation's highest office, by whatever means he thought expedient. Indeed, McLean's extensive political activities prompted his biographer to refer to him as "a politician on the United States Supreme Court." But McLean's political adroitness did not mean that he lacked convictions. A devout Methodist, a temperance advocate, and honorary president of the American Sunday School Union, McLean committed himself to the values represented by the antebellum North, particularly the antislavery cause. As the sectional conflict

John McLean (Collection of the Supreme Court of the United States)

unfolded, he supported the Wilmot Proviso and opposed the annexation of Texas and the Mexican-American War.

The evolution of McLean's political principles was evident in his Supreme Court opinions. In the early years of his judicial tenure, McLean gave every indication that he favored giving states wide latitude to regulate economic matters, a typically Jacksonian position. In *Craig v. Missouri* (1830), for example, the first major case in which he participated, McLean found himself on the opposite side of Chief Justice Marshall. In contrast to Marshall's majority opinion, McLean, along with Justices William Johnson and Smith Thompson, argued that a Missouri statute authorizing the issuance of state loan certificates did not violate the Constitution's ban on state-issued bills of credit. When the opinion of the dissenters became the majority view seven years later in *Briscoe v. Commonwealth Bank of Kentucky* (1837), McLean wrote the Court's opinion upholding the validity of notes issued by a state-chartered bank. Moreover, that same year, in *New York v. Miln*, he voted with the majority in upholding state registration of indigent immigrants

But even by 1837 McLean showed signs of drifting away from the Jacksonian states' rights position. His odd separate opinion in the *Charles River Bridge* case, although it denied that the Supreme Court had jurisdiction and thus had the practical effect of affirming Taney's majority opinion in favor of the state's chartering of the new Warren Bridge, agreed with the Charles River Bridge Company on the merits of the case. Indeed, the dissenting Justice Story praised McLean's opinion in the case and thereafter found himself allied with Jackson's first judicial appointee more than with any of his other colleagues. The two became good friends, and they roomed together during much of their time in Washington. McLean eventually sent his son to Harvard Law School to study with Story, and in later years the venerable New Englander lamented to McLean the passing of the old order and the inferiority of the Court's newer justices.

McLean became increasingly nationalistic over time, and he ultimately embraced the idea that Congress possessed the exclusive power to regulate interstate commerce. The Court struggled with the question of commercial regulation throughout the antebellum era, and the justices often found themselves deeply divided over whether state regulation infringed on congressional power. McLean asserted his belief in the exclusive power of Congress to regulate commerce in *Groves v. Slaughter* (1841), a case involving the interstate sale of slaves. "The necessity of a uniform commercial regulation, more than any other consideration, led to the adoption of the federal Constitution," he wrote. "And unless the power be not only paramount, but exclusive, the Constitution must fail to attain one of the principal objects of its formation" (40 U.S. 449, 504). Because the issue of commercial regulation had tremendous implications for the future of slavery, the debate over the exclusivity of congressional power led to deep divisions among the justices during the Taney Era. Both the *License Cases* (1847) and the *Passenger Cases* (1849), for example, produced multiple opinions but resulted in no conclusive doctrine on the issue. McLean upheld state taxation and regulation of alcoholic beverages imported into three New England states in the *License Cases*, which he justified as "police laws" rather than regulation of commerce. In the *Passenger Cases*, a pair of cases involving state attempts to tax ships' passengers coming into Massachusetts and New York, McLean reiterated his belief in the exclusivity of congressional power over commerce and joined the majority of his colleagues in striking down the state taxes. The Court reached some resolution of this question of the scope of congressional power under the Commerce Clause in *Cooley v. Board of Wardens* (1852). Here the majority adopted the notion of "selective exclusiveness," the idea that some subjects of commercial regulation were national, whereas others were local. True to his convictions, McLean joined his nationalist colleague Justice James Wayne in dissent. McLean's insistence on the exclusivity of congressional power prompted Whig Justice Benjamin Curtis, who wrote the majority opinion in *Cooley*, to label McLean and Wayne "the most high-toned Federalists on the bench" (Weisenburger 1937, 168).

Like Story, McLean had a difficult time reconciling his belief in national supremacy with his firm antislavery convictions. A longtime opponent of slavery, during his service in Washington as commissioner of public lands and postmaster general in the 1820s McLean had purchased a slave family, given them their freedom, brought them to Cincinnati, and helped them establish themselves. As a member of the Ohio Supreme Court, McLean argued that slavery could have no existence where it was not sanctioned by positive law, and he reiterated this view on the Supreme Court in *Groves v. Slaughter* (1841). Although it was in that case that he articulated his belief in the exclusivity of congressional power over commerce, McLean excluded slaves from the domain of national regulation. "The power over slavery belongs to the States respectively. It is local in its character and in its effects" (40 U.S. 449, 508). McLean believed that if states lacked the power to regulate slavery, northern free states in particular would be subject to the spread of this social evil. Each state, he thus held, had a right to protect itself against "the avarice and intrusion of the slave dealer" (40 U.S. 449, 508). The subject of who controlled slavery would not soon go away. The following year, McLean parted ways with Story and dissented alone in *Prigg v. Pennsylvania.* In *Prigg*, McLean continued to hold that states could exercise control over slaves—in this case fugitives—and he thus upheld Pennsylvania's personal liberty law. Despite his dissent in *Prigg*, McLean adhered to the Court's decision in a series of subsequent circuit cases involving fugitive slaves, where he usually ruled in favor of masters' rights to reclaim their slave property. Indeed, his failure to speak out against slavery from the bench during the late 1840s and early 1850s disappointed many of his antislavery friends.

But McLean did not disappoint antislavery forces in *Dred Scott v. Sandford*

(1857), in which he issued one of the case's two dissenting opinions. Contrary to the decision of Taney and the proslavery majority, McLean argued that Dred Scott could legally sue for his freedom in circuit court and that African Americans could in fact be citizens. Noting that various states—both free and slave—had conferred the right of suffrage on free blacks and that the nation had "made citizens of all grades, combinations, and colors" under the Treaty of Guadalupe Hidalgo, McLean argued that there was no legal basis for denying citizenship to African Americans. Moreover, as he had done in his previous slavery decisions, he argued that slavery had a right to exist only "by positive law of a municipal character" and was "without foundation in the law of nature, or the unwritten and common law" (60 U.S. 393, 533). Finally, he held, again contrary to the majority view, that Congress possessed the power to regulate slavery in the territories. His decision, although overshadowed by the lengthier and abler dissenting opinion of Justice Benjamin Curtis, renewed the talk of a presidential bid for the venerable Ohioan in 1860.

McLean's advanced age as well as other political factors, however, prevented him from again seeking the office he had so desired. He died just a month after the inauguration of Abraham Lincoln, in April 1861. By the end of his judicial career, John McLean had strayed about as far as possible from the values associated with Andrew Jackson, the president who had nominated him. A committed nationalist on questions of economic regulation and firm in his antislavery convictions, McLean rarely found himself allied with Chief Justice Taney.

Henry Baldwin

In contrast to McLean, President Jackson's second appointee to the Court, Henry Baldwin, had few productive years as a justice. Born in New Haven, Connecticut, in 1780, Baldwin graduated from Yale and studied law in Philadelphia with Alexander Dallas, the first reporter of the U.S. Supreme Court. In 1799 Baldwin settled in Pittsburgh, where he practiced law, served as part owner of a Democratic-Republican newspaper, and became involved in the iron industry. He owned three mills in western Pennsylvania, including the Union Rolling Mill, one of the largest in the region. In 1816 he won election to the U.S. House of Representatives, and during his three terms in Congress he advocated a protective tariff and supported General Andrew Jackson's prosecution of the Seminole wars. Illness forced Baldwin to resign his seat in Congress, but he maintained his political ties to Jackson. Baldwin played an important role in Jackson's presidential campaign in Pennsylvania in 1828, and the new president subsequently attempted to reward him with appointment as secretary of the treasury. Baldwin's support for a high tariff generated enough opposition to prevent his confirmation to the cabinet post, but Jackson succeeded in putting Baldwin on the Supreme Court in 1830.

Henry Baldwin (Vic Boswell, National Geographic, Collection of the Supreme Court of the United States)

Baldwin had an erratic, controversial, and undistinguished career as a justice. Early in his tenure, he expressed extreme dissatisfaction with what he deemed the Court's unwarranted expansion of its own powers, even to the point of threatening to resign. He dissented seven times during the 1831 term, including in *Ex parte Crane*, in which he strongly criticized Marshall and the majority for upholding the Court's power to issue a writ of mandamus to a circuit court. In 1832 he angered President Jackson and then Treasury Secretary Taney for issuing a circuit opinion in Pennsylvania that ran counter to the administration's policy regarding the national bank. Addicted to smoking Spanish cigars—which he was forbidden from doing while on duty—Baldwin often became impatient and irritable on the bench. He apparently suffered a breakdown in 1832, and his admission to the hospital caused him to miss much of the 1833 term. His absence probably proved a relief to his colleagues, who, regardless of their political persuasion, had a difficult time dealing with their irascible fellow justice.

Baldwin's penchant for occasionally issuing separate opinions, combined with his contentious relationship with Supreme Court reporter Richard Peters, led him to issue a group of his opinions in pamphlet form in 1837, the year of Chief Justice Taney's arrival. Published as *A General View of the Origin and Nature of the Constitution and Government of the United States . . .*, the pamphlet included opinions in four cases decided that year by the Court, along with a statement of Baldwin's theory on the proper relationship between the national government and the states. Baldwin took issue with the idea that the Constitution could be interpreted as "the grant of the people of the United States in the aggregate," an argument used by Marshall and Story in previous years to establish national supremacy. Baldwin contended, in contrast, that the Constitution was "the grant of the people of the several states" (Baldwin 1837, 1). The national and state governments thus emerged from a common source. Acceptance of this principle would allow the justices to ascertain the true meaning of the Constitution. Because Baldwin believed that recent decisions of the Court had not taken account of this interpretive perspective, he published his opinions separately and for public consumption. Baldwin, however, exaggerated the significance of his constitutional maxim, for in all of the controversial decisions of 1837 (*Charles River Bridge*, *Miln*, and *Briscoe*) he concurred with the majority. His insistence on publishing his opinions and theories in this way only alienated him further from his colleagues on the Court.

Despite his contentious relations with fellow justices, Baldwin gained southern allies over the next few years. South Carolina senator and constitutional theorist John C. Calhoun read Baldwin's exposition of his constitutional views "with very great satisfaction." Calhoun's only complaint was that Baldwin had not taken his analysis a step further to advocate the doctrine of "state interposition," which Calhoun believed followed "as a necessary consequence" from Baldwin's assertion of dual sovereignty (Meriwether 1959, 13: 644). Baldwin further captivated southerners with his vigorous support of state police powers. In *Holmes v. Jennison* (1840), he joined three of his colleagues (the justices split 4–4) in upholding a Vermont Supreme Court decision that allowed the state's governor to order the extradition of an indicted murderer to Canada. Baldwin made the most forceful statement of his career in favor of state sovereignty in the case, and he chastised his four opposing brethren for their eagerness to exercise judicial oversight of matters he deemed under state control. Finally, Baldwin took an overtly proslavery stance by the end of his career. In the *Amistad* case (1841), he dissented from the majority's decision to free a boatload of Africans who had resisted enslavement by mutinying on a slave ship, and in *Prigg v. Pennsylvania* (1842), he concurred with the Court's decision upholding the Fugitive Slave Law of 1793. His most proslavery opinion, though, came in *Groves v. Slaughter* (1841), in which the Court invalidated the Mississippi constitution's ban on the importation of slaves. In no uncertain terms, Baldwin proclaimed his belief that the U.S. Constitution protected the property rights of southern slaveholders: "I feel bound to consider slaves as property, by the law of the States before the adoption of the Constitution, and from the first settlement of the colonies: that this right of property exists independently of the Constitution, which does not create, but recognizes and protects it from violation, by any law or regulation of any State" (40 U.S. 449, 513). On the slavery issue, Baldwin proved an ally of the South and the Chief Justice.

In general, Baldwin's disagreeable personality, his recurrent illness, and his chronic financial problems made his years on the Court difficult ones—both for him and his colleagues. Although reportedly more competent and efficient when riding the circuit than when working with his fellow justices in Washington, Baldwin wrote relatively few opinions, and his personal and professional problems overshadowed his judicial accomplishments. He died in April 1844 after a long period of ill health.

James Wayne

James Moore Wayne, President Jackson's third appointee to the Supreme Court and the most recently appointed when Taney took his seat, ended up matching McLean in length of service. Born in Savannah, Georgia, in 1790, the son of a rice planter, Wayne was the twelfth of thirteen children. He received instruction from a private tutor during childhood, and at age fourteen he enrolled at the College of New Jersey (later Princeton), as the sons of many prominent southern families did at that time. After graduating in 1808, Wayne studied law in Savannah and in New Haven, Connecticut, before settling in his hometown. There he was admitted to the bar in 1811 and began his law practice. Although he served as an officer in the Georgia Hussars during the War of 1812, he saw no military action. In 1813, he married Mary Johnston Campbell, and the couple eventually had three children.

James Wayne (Collection of the Supreme Court of the United States)

The next several years saw Wayne establish a place among the state's political and legal leadership. He began a promising political career in 1815, when his opposition to a series of debtor relief laws enacted by the state propelled him into public life. He won a seat in the legislature and instantly became popular. After winning reelection handily in 1816, he was elected mayor of Savannah the following year at age twenty-seven. Although he resigned the mayorship in the summer of 1819, reportedly for personal reasons, Wayne remained prominent in Georgia affairs. His lucrative law practice kept him well connected to the state's business and political elite, and later that year the legislature elected him to serve on the newly created Savannah Court of Common Pleas, where he heard cases involving misdemeanors and small claims. Wayne added to his judicial experience in 1822, when the legislature selected him to serve as Judge of the Superior Courts of Georgia for the Eastern Circuit, and he held the post until his election to Congress in 1828. Wayne took his seat in the House of Representatives at the same time that Andrew Jackson moved into the White House, and during his three terms in Congress the young Georgia representative proved to be in lockstep with the president. Wayne supported Jackson on all of the major political issues of the day: the nullification question, Indian removal, and the war on the national bank. Wayne's political record, combined with geographical considerations—he replaced South Carolinian William Johnson after his death—made him a logical choice for the Supreme Court. Jackson appointed him to the Court in January 1835. Although largely unknown outside his home state, the political reaction to his nomination was generally favorable. Whigs praised Wayne as a gentlemanly and honorable man, and the Senate speedily and overwhelmingly confirmed him. Scarcely a week passed from the time of his appointment to his taking the oath of office.

Whig support for Wayne proved to be well founded, for it was not long before the new justice demonstrated that he, like McLean, would be independent of the president who had appointed him. Justice Wayne, for example, defended the opinion of his colleague Justice Thompson in *Kendall v. United States* (1838), a controversial case involving the separation of powers in which President Jackson had a great political stake. While Thompson was delivering the Court's decision and criticizing the position taken by the president in the case, the attorney general rose and charged that Thompson was misrepresenting one of his arguments. In open court, Wayne promptly rebuked the attorney general, a bold move by one who had only a few years before gained his seat because of his loyalty to Jackson.

Over the next several years, moreover, it became evident that Wayne's constitutional philosophy gave much more authority to the national government than states' rights Democrats typically favored. Wayne wrote opinions in a series of cases during the 1840s that both limited state efforts to interfere with national authority and expanded the jurisdiction of the federal courts. In *Dobbins v. Erie County* (1842),

Wayne spoke for a unanimous Court in striking down a Pennsylvania tax imposed on the income of federal revenue officers. Drawing on the Marshall Court's landmark ruling in *McCulloch v. Maryland*, Wayne concluded that the tax interfered with the constitutional means by which the national government collected its revenue. A few years later, Wayne expanded the power of corporations to sue in federal courts, this time by overturning a Marshall-era decision. Marshall had previously held that corporations could sue only if all stockholders claimed citizenship in states other than the defendant's, a rule that severely restricted the possibility of corporate lawsuits. In *Louisville Railroad Company v. Letson* (1844), Wayne held that "a corporation created by a state . . . seems to us to be a person, though an artificial one, inhabiting and belonging to that State, and therefore entitled, for the purpose of suing and being sued, to deemed a citizen of that State" (43 U.S. 497, 555). Wayne's decision meant that the citizenship or residency of stockholders ceased to be relevant and that corporations now had easy access to federal courts. Finally, Wayne expanded the admiralty jurisdiction of federal courts. In *Waring v. Clarke* (1847), a case involving a steamboat collision ninety-five miles upriver from New Orleans, he drew on rules established in British admiralty courts to argue that admiralty jurisdiction extended beyond the high seas and included "arms of the sea, waters flowing from it into ports and havens, and as high upon rivers as the tide ebbs and flows" (46 U.S. 441, 462). A few years later, in another decision, Wayne argued that federal admiralty jurisdiction extended even further up the Mississippi, in the areas beyond the influence of the tidal flow of the sea.

If Wayne envisioned an expanded jurisdiction for federal courts, he also broadly construed congressional power under the Commerce Clause and limited state powers under the Contract Clause. The Court confronted the question of how much power states possessed to regulate commerce in *New York v. Miln* (1837) and the *License Cases* (1847), but in both instances Wayne had not joined the debate. In the *Passenger Cases* (1849), however, a pair of cases involving attempts by New York and Massachusetts to tax immigrants into the state, Wayne made known his belief in Congress's exclusive power over commerce. Although he sided with the majority in invalidating the laws in question, the divisions within the Court on the question of commercial regulation became glaringly apparent. Wayne's belief in the exclusivity of congressional control over commerce allied him with McLean and set him against Chief Justice Taney. Much of Wayne's lengthy opinion in the case, in fact, took issue with Taney on what exactly the Court had decided in the *Miln* decision twelve years earlier. Wayne's nationalism became even more apparent in *Cooley v. Board of Wardens* (1852), in which the Court attempted to reach a compromise of sorts on the issue of commercial regulation. While the majority upheld a Pennsylvania law and argued that states possessed the power to regulate matters of local, rather than national significance, Wayne and McLean dissented. Both continued to argue in favor of Congress's exclusive power over commerce. At times Wayne's restrictive view of state powers overlapped explicitly with his conservative background and his positive view of business corporations. He wrote the majority's opinion, for example, in *Dodge v. Woolsey* (1856), in which a divided Court struck down Ohio's effort to impose a tax on corporations, in violation of the tax provisions of a previously enacted state bank incorporation statute. Arguing that the initial law constituted a contract, Wayne held that an Ohio constitutional amendment repealing the tax preferences granted to corporations in the state violated the U.S. Constitution's Contract Clause.

Unlike his southern colleagues on the bench, Wayne seemed to have little difficulty reconciling his generally nationalistic views with his strong commitment to slavery. Because he believed that the Constitution explicitly sanctioned slavery, he never thought that advocating the exclusive power of Congress over commerce posed a threat to the South's control over the "peculiar institution." On this point Wayne differed from Chief Justice Taney. Both men believed strongly that the Constitution protected the rights of slaveholders, but Wayne was less vigilant about and less attuned to the possible constitutional implications for slavery in any given case. Whereas Taney frequently spoke out for the rights of slaveholders, during the course of his judicial career Wayne remained relatively silent on the issue, although he himself owned slaves all his life. The Georgian concurred with Justice Thompson's opinion in *Groves v. Slaughter* (1841), which held invalid the Mississippi constitution's ban on the importation of slaves into the state. Moreover, he concurred with the majority in *Prigg v. Pennsylvania* (1842), in which the Court struck down a Pennsylvania personal liberty law and upheld the Fugitive Slave Act of 1793. In *Prigg*, Wayne issued his most complete judicial statement on slavery. He contended that the power to legislate on fugitive slaves under the Constitution's Fugitive Slave Clause rested exclusively with Congress and that states had surrendered their sovereignty on this issue for the sake of national unity. Wayne supported this position primarily by examining the history of the Constitutional Convention. Like Justice Story, Wayne argued that the framers had compromised on the issue of fugitive slaves, and that this compromise had proved essential to the convention's adoption of the Constitution. Wayne's matter-of-fact attitude about slavery's protected constitutional status was most evident in *Dred Scott v. Sandford* (1857), in which he issued a brief opinion wholly concurring with Chief Justice Taney. Wayne was the only justice to agree completely with Taney's lengthy and controversial opinion, which held that Scott was not a citizen and that Congress lacked authority to legislate on the issue of slavery in the territories.

Despite his extreme proslavery position, Wayne remained on the Court during the secession crisis and the Civil War. Like his fellow southerner and Jackson-appointee John Catron, Wayne had spent too many years of his life in service to the federal government to abandon the Union. During the war, Wayne fulfilled all the obligations of his office, including presiding as senior associate justice during Taney's frequent absences and calling on President Lincoln at the White House. Georgians, of course, vilified Wayne for his decision to cast his lot with the Union. In 1862, the Confederate District Court in Georgia confiscated his property and a grand jury declared him an "alien enemy." Wayne's judicial record during the war showed his strong support for federal military actions, for he sustained Lincoln's blockade of the South in the *Prize Cases* (1863) and upheld the federal military's arrest of a leading Confederate sympathizer in *Ex parte Vallandigham* (1864). After the war, Wayne constituted part of an important five-member majority of justices who invalidated the loyalty oaths enacted during wartime. These measures required persons practicing various occupations to swear that they had never offered aid or sympathy to the Confederacy. Despite his Unionist principles, Wayne opposed any policy that limited southerners' rights on account of their support for the Confederacy. In *Cummings v. Missouri* (1867) and *Ex parte Garland* (1867), the Court held that such legislation violated the Constitution's ban on bills of attainder and ex post facto laws.

Compared with his contemporaries, McLean and Catron, whose service on the Court overlapped almost exactly with Chief Justice Taney's, Wayne wrote a small number of opinions. In thirty-two years on the Court, he wrote separately only 180 times; he reportedly exerted much of his influence during conference with the other justices, where he often tried to manage procedures and decision making. Neither an original thinker nor a great legal theorist, Wayne served conscientiously and diligently as a justice until his death from typhoid in 1867. Convivial and genteel, Wayne and his wife played a prominent role in the capital's social life, and they had many friends and connections in both the North and the South. Wayne's old school manners and charm made him a respected public figure, though not an outstanding jurist.

Jackson's Later Appointments

Philip Pendleton Barbour

Philip Pendleton Barbour took his seat on the Court in 1836, at the same time as Chief Justice Taney. Born in 1783 in Orange County, Virginia, to a prominent planter family, Barbour received an informal education from a local Episcopal minister, primarily because of the economic hardships his family experienced as a result of the Revolutionary War. He gained admission to the Virginia bar in 1800 and briefly practiced law in Kentucky, but he soon returned to his home state to continue his legal studies under the distinguished Virginia jurist St. George Tucker at the College of William and Mary. After succeeding in the practice of law in Virginia, Barbour served briefly in the Virginia House of Delegates before winning election to Congress in 1814, where he served as Speaker of the House of Representatives from 1821 to 1823.

Philip Pendleton Barbour (Neagle, after portrait by George Healy, Collection of the Supreme Court of the United States)

A part of the "Old Republican" leadership in Virginia, which included Judge Spencer Roane, John Randolph, and *Richmond Enquirer* editor Thomas Ritchie, Barbour clung tenaciously to a states' rights, strict constructionist constitutional position. As a U.S. representative, he opposed funding of national internal improvements, fought the protective tariff, and served as counsel for the state of Virginia in the landmark U.S. Supreme Court case *Cohens v. Virginia* (1821), in which Chief Justice Marshall and his colleagues extended the jurisdiction of the Court. In 1825, after declining the first law professorship at the University of Virginia, Barbour left Congress for a seat on the Virginia General Court for the Eastern District. Two years later, he returned to Congress, where he became an outspoken opponent of the national bank. His stance on this issue in particular, along with his staunch political support of President Jackson, caught the president's eye. In 1830, Jackson appointed him to the U.S. District Court for Eastern Virginia, and six years later, when an opening appeared on the U.S. Supreme Court, Jackson appointed Barbour to the vacancy. Although Barbour's nomination outraged nationalists, Jackson's political opponents focused their efforts on defeating Taney, and Barbour won Senate confirmation by vote of 30–11. He took his seat, along with the new chief justice, at the beginning of the 1837 term.

Barbour wrote one major opinion during his brief tenure on the Court. *New York v. Miln* (1837) presented the Court with the question of whether a New York statute regarding immigrants constituted a state attempt to regulate interstate commerce, in violation of the Constitution's Commerce Clause. The law in question required captains of ships sailing into the Port of New York City to provide information—names, places of birth, ages, and occupations—on all ship passengers, so that the city could prevent the immigration of paupers for whom it could not provide. Barbour declared that the New York act did not constitute a regulation of commerce. Rather, he contended, the law was an exercise of the state's police power, designed to protect the health, safety, and welfare of the people of the state. Distinguishing the case from previous decisions regarding the Commerce Clause, Barbour argued that people—the subject of the regulation in question—could not be articles of commerce. "They are not the subject of commerce," Barbour wrote, "and, not being imported goods, cannot fall within a train of reasoning founded upon the construction of a power given to Congress to regulate commerce, and the prohibition of the States from imposing a duty on imported goods" (36 U.S. 102, 136–137). Barbour's narrow definition of the federal commerce power and broad view of state power to regulate fit with his states' rights constitutional vision and struck a blow at Marshall Court nationalism. In the other two significant decisions of the 1837 term, *Charles River Bridge v. Warren Bridge* and *Briscoe v. Bank of the Commonwealth of Kentucky*, Barbour voted with the majority in granting more power to states as well.

In the other major cases in which he wrote opinions, Barbour supported Jacksonian political goals and states' rights constitutional principles. In *Kendall v. United*

States ex rel. Stokes (1838), Barbour opposed the majority's decision upholding the power of a federal court to issue a writ of mandamus directed at the postmaster general. Barbour's dissenting opinion, in support of Postmaster General Amos Kendall, one of President Jackson's chief political lieutenants, argued that the court in question had no legal power to issue such a writ. As the case had aroused much controversy over the power of Andrew Jackson's White House, Barbour demonstrated a loyalty to the former president displayed only by Old Hickory's other closest friends on the Court, Chief Justice Taney and Justice John Catron of Tennessee. A few years later, in *Holmes v. Jennison* (1840), a case involving the extradition of a fugitive from the state of Vermont to Canada, Barbour made his most forceful argument in favor of state power. In contrast to Chief Justice Taney, who held that a state governor possessed absolutely no power to deal with foreign governments, Barbour argued exactly the opposite. Because the state's extradition conflicted with no explicit power of the national government, he claimed, the ability to take such action rested with state governments. The governor of Vermont was perfectly within his rights to order the extradition. Because the Court split 4–4 on the issue, the governor's actions were sustained.

Barbour died suddenly of a heart attack in February 1841. Although his tenure on the Court was brief, historians agree that had he lived, Barbour would have emerged as one of the Court's most significant and outspoken advocates of states' rights constitutionalism and the rights of slaveholders. The owner of a large Virginia plantation, Barbour sided with fellow southerners Chief Justice Taney and Justice Catron more than he did with his other colleagues, but he earned the respect and friendship of the most nationalistic members of the Court, Joseph Story and John McLean. Barbour's integrity, legal acumen, and work ethic made him an effective member of the Court.

John Catron

Jackson's last Supreme Court appointee, John Catron, came closer than any other to representing Jackson's own constitutional and political vision for the nation. Jackson and Catron were old friends from Tennessee. Born in Grayson County, Virginia, in 1786 to poor German immigrants, Catron grew up in Virginia and Kentucky, where he received a rudimentary education. In 1807, he married Matilda Childress, and in 1812 the couple moved to Sparta, Tennessee, where Catron drove cattle, groomed his father's racehorse, and began to study the law. Creek Indian raids on a white military outpost in central Alabama soon drew Catron into military service under the command of young Andrew Jackson. After brief involvement in expeditions against the Indians, Catron returned home, gained admission to the bar, and won election as attorney general for Tennessee's Third Circuit. In 1818, after serving two years, Catron moved to Nashville on the recommendation of Jackson and began to establish

John Catron (Handy Studios, Collection of the Supreme Court of the United States)

himself in the community. Although hindered by his lack of education and indelicate manners, Catron made his way in the legal profession and Nashville society, and after six years of successful practice there, in 1824 the legislature elected him judge of the state supreme court. There he served with distinction until 1835, the last four years as the state's chief justice.

Throughout his state judicial career, Catron supported Jackson and his agenda. In 1828, during Old Hickory's second run for the White House, when Jackson's opponents charged his wife, Rachel, with being an adulterous woman (she had married him after believing incorrectly that she had obtained a legal divorce from her first husband), Catron and a group of prominent Nashville citizens united to refute the charges. The following year, Judge Catron became an outspoken critic of the national bank, well before Jackson himself attempted to veto the rechartering of the bank. In a series of essays in a Knoxville newspaper, Catron characterized the national bank as a monopoly run by wealthy eastern investors who cared nothing about average men and women in places like Catron's home state. His arguments foreshadowed Jackson's own complaints about the bank's aristocratic nature and unconstitutionality. Catron also did his part to support Jackson's policy of Indian removal. In a state supreme court opinion regarding the status of the Cherokee in Tennessee, Catron issued a lengthy rebuttal to the Marshall Court's ruling that upheld Cherokee sovereignty. In *State v. Foreman* (1835), Catron's Tennessee Supreme Court opinion argued that white Europeans had the right as Christian "discoverers" to conquer and seize the lands of Native Americans.

Catron's commitment to Jackson, in the end, both cost him his state judicial post and won him his Supreme Court appointment. Not surprisingly, in 1836 Catron supported Jackson's chosen successor, Martin Van Buren, for the presidency. Most Tennesseans, however, opposed Jackson's efforts to elect his vice president, favoring instead the candidacy of Hugh Lawson White, a former state supreme court judge and U.S. senator from Tennessee. By the end of 1835, Catron made known his support for Van Buren, and his unpopular public pronouncements coincided with the election of state supreme court judges in accordance with Tennessee's newly drafted constitution. Primarily because of his political stance, the legislature voted Catron off the bench and chose a less experienced jurist to take his seat on the court. Forced from the judicial post he had held for twelve years, Catron devoted his energies to running Van Buren's presidential campaign in the state. Van Buren lost Tennessee, but he won the White House. Soon thereafter, in early 1837, Congress passed a judiciary act that created two new federal court circuits and added two seats to the U.S. Supreme Court. The need for a westerner to ride the new circuit encompassing Tennessee, Kentucky, and Missouri made Catron a logical candidate. As a reward for his political loyalty, the departing Jackson made Catron's appointment to the Supreme Court one of the final acts of his presidency. On March 3, 1837, Jackson nominated his fellow Tennessean, and five days later the Senate confirmed him with little controversy.

Catron's judicial record, particularly with regard to corporations, clearly reflected Jacksonian values. Although early in his career he concurred without opinion in cases such as *Bank of Augusta v. Earle* (1839) and *Louisville Railroad Company v. Letson* (1844), both of which expanded the ability of corporations to conduct business nationwide, Catron eventually came to believe that corporate power posed a threat to many Americans. In a series of cases in the 1850s, Catron expressed his unwillingness to expand the rights of corporations by conferring on them status as "citizens." Justice Wayne had first described corporations in this way in *Letson* for the purposes of expanding the right to sue corporations in federal courts. Although Catron favored giving federal courts jurisdiction in suits involving corporations, he clearly opposed the idea that all stockholders could be regarded collectively as a citizen. Rather, he argued in *Rundle v. Delaware and Raritan Canal Company* (1853), the president and members of the board were the responsible parties in any case involving the corporation, and, in Catron's view, they should have access to federal courts in cases involving citizens of other states. Catron met any attempt to expand the rights of corporations as citizens with suspicion.

During the 1850s, Catron expressed his opposition to growing corporate power in a series of dissents. *Piqua Branch of the State Bank of Ohio v. Knoop* (1854) raised the issue of whether a corporate charter constituted a contract between a state and a bank. The bank's original charter had granted it exemption from state taxation, but a subsequent legislature sought to repeal that provision and impose a tax. Along with Justices John Archibald Campbell and Peter V. Daniel, Catron dissented from the majority's ruling that the charter was a contract that could not be repealed under the Constitution's Contract Clause. "The sovereign political power is not the subject of contract so as to be vested in an irrepealable charter of incorporation, and taken away from, and placed beyond the reach of, future legislatures," Catron argued (14 U.S. 369, 404). When an Ohio constitutional convention subsequently passed an amendment repealing the tax exemption for banks, the Court struck it down as a violation of the Contract Clause in *Dodge v. Woolsey* (1855). Catron again joined fellow southerners Campbell and Daniel in dissent. Both cases raised questions about the proper role of corporations in American society, particularly whether corporations had come to wield more power than the states that had chartered them. In another case involving corporations, Catron expressed typically Jacksonian sentiments when noting his concern about "the vast amount of property, power, and exclusive benefits, prejudicial to other classes of society that are vested in and held by these numerous bodies of associated wealth" (*Ohio Life Insurance and Trust Co. v. DeBolt*, 57 U.S. 416, 442–443.)

On questions of state regulation of commercial activity, Catron held the middle ground and voted with the majority in every leading case. Unlike his colleagues Justices McLean and Wayne, who consistently argued that the power to regulate commerce rested exclusively with Congress, Catron claimed that in the absence of congressional action states were free to exercise their police powers. In the *License Cases* (1847), which involved a series of state laws taxing and otherwise regulating spirituous liquors, Catron wrote one of six separate opinions upholding the regulations. Examining the original intentions of the framers, as well as a line of Commerce Clause cases decided by the Marshall Court, Catron concluded that the Court had never held congressional authority over commerce to be exclusive. Moreover, the unprecedented growth of the American economy made it extraordinarily difficult—if not impossible—in a practical sense to enact national commercial regulations. If the states went too far in attempting to regulate, Catron contended, the Congress and the Court would be there to stop them. Such a position, Catron believed, was "moderate" and "prudent" (12 U.S. 504, 608). A few years later, in the *Passenger Cases* (1849), Catron constituted part of a five-person majority, this time in invalidating state taxes on incoming ship passengers, including immigrants. When the justices reached somewhat of a compromise on the issue of commercial regulation in *Cooley v. Board of Wardens* (1852), where the Court ruled that some subjects of commerce required national uniform regulation while others were best left to state authorities, Catron concurred without opinion.

Like his fellow southerners on the Court, Catron took a proslavery position. He remained silent in the vast majority of the Court's cases involving slavery, and his only notable opinion on the subject came in *Dred Scott v. Sandford* (1857), in which he concurred with the majority decision but took a slightly less extreme proslavery position than Chief Justice Taney. In that case, Catron avoided entirely the question of whether Scott was a citizen with standing to sue in a federal court, and he privately dismissed Taney's lengthy discussion of that issue as mere obiter dictum. Instead, Catron focused his opinion on the question of whether Scott remained a slave after his sojourns in Illinois and Minnesota Territory and the issue of congressional power over slavery in the territories. On the first of these, Catron, in the words of one historian, "reaffirm[ed] the principles of the old tacit agreement between the sections" (Fehrenbacher 1978, 396): He held that domiciling a slave in a free state brought about his emancipation, whereas temporary residence there did not. Thus, Catron held, Scott remained a slave. On the matter of congressional power, Catron took a decidedly different tack from the chief justice's. Whereas Taney contended that the Fifth Amendment's Due Process Clause protected slave property and invalidated any congressional attempts to regulate that "peculiar institution," Catron emphasized the restrictions imposed on Congress by the terms of the Louisiana Purchase. The treaty with France had guaranteed the property rights of the inhabitants of the territory, and Congress could not repeal the provision. Moreover, Catron contended, American citizens enjoyed the rights of "common property" in the territories, and if Congress could prohibit slave property, it could just as easily prohibit other types of property—cattle, horses, or farm implements, for example. Because the Constitution secured

Table 2.1 Justices of the U.S. Supreme Court during the Taney Era, 1836–1864

Roger B. Taney, Chief Justice 1836–1864 (Maryland)			
Joseph Story 1811–1845 (Massachusetts)	Levi Woodbury 1845–1851 (New Hampshire)	Benjamin Curtis 1851–1857 (Maine)	Nathan Clifford 1858–1881 (Maine)
Smith Thompson 1823–1843 (New York)	Samuel Nelson 1845–1872 (New York)		
John McLean 1830–1861 (Ohio)			Noah H. Swayne 1862–1881 (Ohio)
Henry Baldwin 1830–1844 (Pennsylvania)	Robert C. Grier 1846–1870 (Pennsylvania)		
James M. Wayne 1835–1867 (Georgia)			
Philip P. Barbour 1836–1841 (Virginia)	Peter V. Daniel 1841–1860 (Virginia)		Samuel Miller 1862–1890 (Iowa)
John Catron 1837–1865 (Tennessee) Seat created by Judiciary Act of 1837			
John McKinley 1837–1852 (Alabama) Seat created by Judiciary Act of 1837		John A. Campbell 1853–1861 (Alabama)	David Davis 1862–1877 (Illinois)
Stephen J. Field 1863–1897 (California) Seat created by act of 1863			

"to the respective states and their citizens an entire equality of rights, privileges, and immunities," Congress could not prohibit the introduction of slaves in the territories (60 U.S. 393, 529). A lifelong slaveholder, Catron took a firm stand in support of the South's "peculiar institution."

Despite his support of slavery, Catron—like Jackson—proved to be a staunch friend of the federal Union. As the storm clouds of war gathered in the spring of 1861, Catron continued with his judicial duties in hopes of preserving federal authority throughout his southwestern circuit, where Union and Confederate sympathizers battled for control. After holding court in Kentucky, he returned to his home state of Tennessee, where he supported the Unionist cause. In June 1861, Tennesseans voted in favor of secession, and Catron found himself behind enemy lines. Meanwhile, his circuit duties required his presence in St. Louis, where he and his circuit court colleagues issued a forceful charge to a grand jury proclaiming that support for the rebellion constituted treason. The charge, published in newspapers throughout the country, also proclaimed that obstructing the operation of a federal court was included among treasonous activities. After completing his work in St. Louis, Catron attempted to return to Nashville, but a group of citizens met him outside the city, where they ordered him either to resign his seat on the Court or leave the city within twenty-four hours. Although he fled in despair, later, when Union forces occupied much of the state within the next year, he returned to open the federal court in Nashville under the protection of federal troops. His support for the Union, though, did not always translate into advocacy of President Lincoln's war policies. Catron dissented in the *Prize Cases* (1863), for example, in which the majority upheld Lincoln's naval blockade of the South. Nevertheless, Catron cast his lot wholly with the Union. While on circuit, he ordered the arrest of the governor of Kentucky and upheld the confiscation of a pro-Confederate newspaper. As the war continued, Catron's health deteriorated, and he missed the 1864–1865 Supreme Court term because of illness. He died at home in Nashville on May 30, 1865, a little more than a month after the downfall of the Confederacy.

The Democratic Justices

John McKinley

Despite a decade and a half of service on the Court, Justice John McKinley wrote the fewest opinions (24) and had the lowest average number of opinions per term (0.85) of any member of the Taney Court. Only three of these opinions were dissents. In the overwhelming majority of cases in which he participated, McKinley silently voted with the majority of the justices; thus, his written contribution to the constitutional debates of the day was minimal. Born in 1780 in Culpepper County, Virginia, the son of a physician, McKinley grew up in Kentucky. At age twenty, he was admitted to the bar and practiced first in Frankfurt, Kentucky, and later in Louisville. In 1819, after McKinley had married and had children, he and his family settled in Huntsville, Alabama.

For almost the next two decades, McKinley figured prominently in Alabama politics, during which time his political leanings evolved from Federalist to Jacksonian-Democratic. Although defeated for a circuit judge position in 1819, McKinley won

John McKinley (Albert Rosenthal, Collection of the Supreme Court of the United States)

election to the legislature the following year. In 1822, he unsuccessfully sought a seat in the U.S. Senate as a Federalist, but four years later he won election to Alabama's other U.S. Senate seat after the death of the incumbent. In his second Senate race, McKinley ran as a committed Jacksonian, although probably more out of political expediency than principle. As a senator, he championed internal improvements in Alabama, as well as lower prices on the sale of public lands. His support for internal improvements put him at odds with President Jackson, as McKinley voted to override the president's veto of the Maysville Road Bill in 1830. After a term in the Senate, McKinley lost a bid for reelection, and he came home to serve in the Alabama legislature. In 1833, he returned to Washington to serve in the U.S. House of Representatives, where he strongly supported Jackson's removal of the deposits from the national bank. He decided against running for a second term in Congress. Instead, he returned to Alabama, where he worked for the election of Martin Van Buren and sought a seat in the state legislature, which he hoped would serve as springboard to reclaiming his old Senate seat. McKinley's political plans succeeded on both counts. He regained his place in the Senate, and before he took his seat Van Buren tapped him for service on the U.S. Supreme Court.

McKinley joined the Court in January 1838, and a few months later rendered the most significant decision of his career. In the midst of a nationwide financial panic, Alabama citizens defaulted on debts owed to banking corporations from out of state. When the banks brought suit in the U.S. Circuit Court in Mobile, McKinley ruled that out-of-state corporations had no right to do business in Alabama under the state's laws. The circuit opinion shocked the nation's commercial community, and an appeal quickly made its way to the Supreme Court in the case of *Bank of Augusta v. Earle* (1839). An eight-justice majority overturned McKinley's ruling, and the newly appointed justice from Alabama filed a dissent. "Alabama, as an independent foreign state, owing no duty, nor being under any obligation to either of the states by whose corporations she was invaded," McKinley wrote, "was the sole and exclusive judge of what was proper or improper to be done, and consequently had a right to examine and determine whether she could grant a favor to either of those states without injury to herself" (38 U.S. 519, 606). Denying that any constitutional principle prevented Alabama from prohibiting out-of-state corporations from operating within its borders, McKinley relied on the Tenth Amendment to the Constitution to argue that such powers rested with the state of Alabama. McKinley's passionate articulation of an agrarian, states' rights position hostile to business corporations in this case showed how far the justice had apparently drifted from his early political ideology.

McKinley's other opinions followed a states' rights trajectory but, curiously, avoided overt discussions of the major constitutional questions of the day. In *Groves v. Slaughter* (1841), for example, McKinley dissented from the majority and argued that the Mississippi constitution's ban on slaves imported from other states ought to be upheld, but he shied away from any discussion of the scope of the federal commerce power. And in the *Passenger Cases* (1849), McKinley constituted part of a five-justice majority that invalidated New York and Massachusetts laws levying taxes on ship passengers coming into those states. Again, however, rather than arguing over the validity of the state regulations in light of the Constitution's Commerce Clause, McKinley interpreted a clause of the Constitution commonly understood as referring to imported slaves—what most referred to as the Slave Trade Clause—as applicable in this instance. He argued that since Congress had the exclusive power to regulate "the migration or importation of such persons as any of the States now existing shall think proper to admit," the states in question lacked power to dictate the terms on which persons migrated into the state. None of the seven other justices who wrote opinions in the case addressed McKinley's unorthodox interpretation of this clause. McKinley never did make clear his position on the federal commerce power. Because he was near death when the Court decided *Cooley v. Board of Wardens* (1852), he did not participate in that most famous of antebellum Commerce Clause cases.

McKinley's virtual silence from the bench stemmed in part from his frequent absences, owing both to his onerous circuit riding duties and his recurring health problems. The ninth circuit, for which he was responsible, at the time encompassed Alabama, Mississippi, Louisiana, and Arkansas. To be sure, McKinley's circuit required more extensive and difficult travel than any other. Largely in response to his complaints, in 1839 the secretary of state compiled a report on the circuit riding duties of the justices, in which McKinley estimated that he traveled 10,000 miles a year. Although the figure was probably exaggerated, his sparsely populated southwestern circuit lacked sufficient roads, and he often found it best to stick to water routes that required him to travel well out of his way. McKinley's greatest accomplishment as a justice may indeed have been his ability to convince Congress to consider reordering the circuits, which it finally did in 1842. Thereafter, McKinley handled cases only from Alabama and Louisiana. (This fact greatly pleased McKinley, as he had been physically assaulted in Jackson, Mississippi, by a deputy marshal, and in 1841 the justice had refused to hold court in the state.) Still, health problems made the remainder of his tenure on the Court difficult. He missed the entire 1840 term because of illness, and in 1842 he suffered a paralytic attack. He died in 1852. The least impressive and least significant member of the Taney Court, McKinley's contributions as a justice were minimal.

Peter V. Daniel

A staunch proponent of the values of traditional agrarianism and strict constructionism, Peter V. Daniel was the most conservative justice of the era. By far the most frequent dissenter of the Taney period, Daniel often stood alone in defending his

Peter V. Daniel (J. Daniel, Collection of the Supreme Court of the United States)

traditional "Old Republican" principles. Born in Stafford County, Virginia, in 1784, Daniel grew up in a prominent gentry family. He received his early education from private tutors, briefly attended the College of New Jersey (later Princeton), and studied law in Richmond with former Virginia governor and leading Federalist Edmund Randolph. As a member of the Virginia aristocracy, Daniel lived by the code of honor, and when a dispute arose between Daniel and another man in 1808—probably over some political issue—Daniel mortally wounded his opponent in a duel. Despite rumors initially alleging some impropriety in the proceedings, Daniel's reputation remained intact. A few years after the incident, he married Randolph's daughter, Lucy, a move that brought him Spring Farm plantation and immediately made him part of Virginia's ruling elite.

From the start, Daniel proved more successful in politics than in the practice of law. Despite his close association with the Federalist Randolph, Daniel became an ardent "Old Republican," a champion of the principles of agrarianism, states' rights, and strict constructionism associated with the Virginia and Kentucky Resolutions of 1798. After gaining admission to the bar in 1808, he served two terms in the legislature before winning election to the council of the state, an executive advisory body. In 1818, he became presiding officer of the council, thus serving as de facto lieutenant governor of Virginia. He also played a significant role in national politics, as a supporter of William H. Crawford in 1824 and Andrew Jackson in 1828 and 1832. Daniel shared Jackson's opposition to nullification, and he opposed banks with even more passion than Old Hickory did. As a believer in traditional agrarian ideals, Daniel viewed banks and corporations in general as the greatest threats to a free society. His political work on behalf of Jackson, particularly his loyalty on the bank issue, proved important to the advancement of his career. After Daniel made an unsuccessful bid for the governorship in 1830 and subsequently lost his position on the state council, Jackson offered him the post of attorney general when Taney moved to the Treasury Department. Daniel declined, but the following year, he accepted Jackson's offer to serve as U.S. District Judge for the Eastern District of Virginia when Judge Philip P. Barbour vacated that position to take one on the U.S. Supreme Court. Daniel served as a federal judge for four years before Barbour's sudden death in February 1841. With but a few days remaining in office, President Van Buren quickly nominated Daniel to fill the vacancy on the Court, and Democratic outmaneuvering of the nomination's Whig opponents led to Daniel's confirmation. The Virginian took his seat on the Court the following January.

Daniel ascended to the bench with a confident assurance that he would bring true constitutional principles to the Supreme Court, which in his view had long ago permitted the unjustified encroachment of national power on state authority. Daniel's extreme version of strict constructionism and states' rights soon became apparent in *Searight v. Stokes* (1845), a case involving a toll levied by Pennsylvania on carriages that transported U.S. mail over the Cumberland Road. Whereas his colleagues debated the constitutionality of the toll, Daniel took the opportunity to question the federal government's authority to build the road at all. Narrowly interpreting the Constitution's grant of power to Congress to "establish Post Offices and Post Roads," Daniel claimed that the clause only gave Congress power to choose postal routes and not to build the actual roads. The national government had no power, he believed, "to construct roads, nor any other description of what have been called internal improvements, within the limits of the states" (44 U.S. 151, 180).

Daniel took a similarly restrictive view of the Commerce Clause. He sharply dissented in the *Passenger Cases* (1849), where the majority invalidated state efforts to regulate and tax immigrants as violative of the Commerce Clause. "I am unable to suppress my alarm at the approach of power claimed to be uncontrollable and unlimited," he stated in the opening of his opinion (48 U.S. 283, 494). Fearing the majority's interpretation of the clause as well as his colleagues' strict adherence to treaties guaranteeing the rights of British subjects in American ports, Daniel bluntly warned of the implications of the ruling for the South: "If it should suit the commercial speculations of British subjects to land within the territory of any of the States cargoes of Negroes from Jamaica, Hayti, or Africa, it would be difficult . . . to designate any legitimate power in the states to prevent this invasion of their domestic security" (48 U.S. 283, 508). Such concerns echoed those of Chief Justice Taney, who also viewed the majority's ruling through the lens of the slavery conflict, and demonstrated the way in which Daniel closely identified southern agrarian interests with state and local autonomy. Even when most of his judicial colleagues agreed on a compromise involving the scope of the federal commerce power, Daniel would have none of it. Although he concurred with the Court's ruling upholding a Pennsylvania pilot regulation in *Cooley v. Board of Wardens* (1852), he took issue with the majority's reasoning that the law was constitutional because pilotage was of local rather than national importance. Instead, he claimed, the power to enact pilot laws had "been exercised by the States from the very origin of their existence" and represented the most basic expression of state sovereignty (53 U.S. 299, 325).

If congressional power posed a threat to the sovereignty of states, in Daniel's view, so did the expansion of the jurisdiction of the federal courts. Daniel consistently fought attempts to enlarge federal judicial power. In *Pennsylvania v. Wheeling and Belmont Bridge Company* (1852), he argued in dissent along with Chief Justice Taney that the Court lacked jurisdiction in a dispute involving a railway bridge over the Ohio River that interfered with steamboat transportation. Although the majority deemed Pennsylvania a party to the case because of financial losses incurred by state-owned internal improvements, Daniel denied that the state possessed a right to sue because it lacked any "property in or title to the River Ohio within the limits of Virginia, and no property in or title to the steamboats which ply upon that river" (54

U.S. 518, 595). Moreover, in *Genesee Chief v. Fitzhugh* (1852), in which the rest of the justices expanded federal admiralty jurisdiction to include inland waterways, Daniel issued a stinging dissent in which he held to the traditional common law rule that jurisdiction was confined to tidal waters. "My opinions may be deemed to be contracted and antiquated, unsuited to the day in which we live," Daniel wrote, "but they are founded upon deliberate conviction as to the nature and objects of limited government." Ironically, on this particular issue the strict constructionist Daniel found himself on the same side as those who done the most to expand federal judicial power over the years. "I have at least the consolation—no small one it must be admitted—of the support of Marshall, Kent, and Story in any error I may have committed," he concluded (53 U.S. 443, 465). Finally, in a series of cases Daniel expressed his belief, again in dissent, that corporations lacked the right to sue or be sued in federal courts. Daniel, who displayed a strong disdain for corporations and frequently referred to them in disparaging language, did all within his power halt the advance of corporate influence. Denying that corporations were citizens, Daniel maintained that corporations could claim no access to federal courts under the doctrine of diversity of citizenship.

Although often out of step with his colleagues, Daniel did speak for the majority of the Court in one major constitutional case. *West River Bridge v. Dix* (1848) involved the extent to which states could exercise the power of eminent domain. A 1795 Vermont charter had authorized a bridge company to maintain a toll bridge for a hundred years, but when the state later decided to turn it into a free public highway, it took the bridge and provided compensation to its owners. The bridge owners contended that this violated the Constitution's Contract Clause. Writing for an eight-justice majority, Daniel sustained the state's actions and held that no difference existed between incorporated and unincorporated property when it came to the exercise of eminent domain. "This power, denominated 'eminent domain' of the State, is, as its name imports," Daniel wrote, "paramount to all private rights vested under the government, and these last are by necessary implication, held in subordination to this power, and must yield in every instance to its proper exercise" (47 U.S. 507, 532). Daniel's hostility to corporations and his belief in state sovereignty lay behind his opinion, and although the majority did not share Daniel's extreme views on these subjects, they agreed on the need for states to have extensive power of eminent domain in order to promote the public interest.

Not surprisingly, Daniel also agreed with the majority of his colleagues in supporting the rights of slaveholders. A lifelong slave owner, he viewed the "peculiar institution" as the foundation on which the South's civilized society rested, and he saw state control over slavery as the only way to preserve the southern way of life. Daniel concurred in upholding the Fugitive Slave Law of 1793 and invalidating Pennsylvania's personal liberty law in *Prigg v. Pennsylvania* (1842), although he wrote a separate opinion to express his views on the fugitive question. Vigorously denying that the national government possessed exclusive power over fugitives, Daniel contended that individual slave owners as well as states played a critical role in the rendition process. The small number of federal officials in the states meant that too many slaves could successfully escape without state involvement. Over time, Daniel became more strident in his support of slavery and more sectional in his constitutional outlook. His first visit to New England while riding circuit in 1847 only confirmed his worst impressions of the region, for he detested its bustling mercantilism and uncouth incivility. His separate opinion in the *Dred Scott* case paralleled that of Chief Justice Taney. Like Taney, Daniel explicitly denied the citizenship of blacks. "The African . . . was regarded and owned in every State in the Union as property merely," Daniel wrote, "and as such was not and could not be a party or an actor, much less a peer in any compact or form of government established by the States of the United States" (60 U.S. 393, 481). Having long argued that the Missouri Compromise violated the Constitution and that Congress lacked power to legislate on slavery in the territories, moreover, Daniel accepted this portion of Taney's opinion as given. Daniel even explicitly claimed that the Northwest Ordinance of 1787, which had banned slavery in the Old Northwest Territory north of the Ohio River, was unconstitutional as well. This contention made Daniel's opinion more extreme than that of any of his fellow justices.

Daniel died in May 1860, nearly a year before the start of the Civil War. Bitter and lonely after the death of his second wife in 1857 (she died horribly when her clothes caught afire), the last few years of his life took a great toll on Daniel, who had never exhibited a very cheery disposition in the first place. Known for his dry wit and acerbic tongue, Daniel clung tenaciously to his old style agrarianism, however outmoded it may have been. Nearly a third of his written opinions were dissents, and he averaged nearly two and a half dissents per term on the Court, a much higher rate of dissent than any of his colleagues. Although a close friend of Roger Taney, with whom he shared a boardinghouse, Daniel never acquired the diplomacy and moderation that came to characterize the work of the Chief Justice.

Samuel Nelson

Samuel Nelson was among the most prolific opinion writers of the Taney era, although few of his decisions concerned the most important constitutional questions of the day. Born in 1792 in Hebron, New York, the son of Scotch-Irish immigrants, Nelson obtained his early education in common schools and private academies before attending Middlebury College in Vermont. Although his parents had planned for him to enter the ministry, on graduation Nelson read law with two judges in Salem, New York, gained admission to the bar in 1817, and opened a law office in Cortland. Spe-

Samuel Nelson (Mathew Brady, Collection of the Supreme Court of the United States)

cializing in real estate and commercial law, Nelson developed a successful practice, while also serving briefly as the local postmaster. In 1820, he entered political life for the first time when he became a presidential elector for James Monroe, and the following year he attended New York's constitutional convention as a delegate from Cortland County. A member of Martin Van Buren's faction in New York politics, Nelson advocated the expansion of suffrage and the restructuring of the state judiciary while he was a member of the convention.

Nelson's work at the convention led to a judicial career. In 1823, he received an appointment as circuit judge under the terms of the new constitution, and he held this position until 1831, when he began service on the New York Supreme Court. He served as an associate justice of the court until 1836, when he was elevated to the position of chief justice. During his years on the state supreme court, Nelson earned a reputation for fairness and directness as well as for possessing a reservoir of common sense. Nelson's sound judgment and nonpartisan nature made him an ideal nominee to the U.S. Supreme Court for President John Tyler. The embattled president, who had gained his office after the death of William Henry Harrison and never really received the backing of his own party, had unsuccessfully attempted to fill two vacancies on the Court in 1843 and 1844. Not until Tyler's last few weeks in office in 1845 did he submit Nelson's name to the Senate, which quickly approved the nomination.

Nelson's first few years on the Court proved the justice's unwillingness to enter the partisan fray. At a time when the Court was beginning to come to terms with the conflict over the commerce power and the slavery question, Nelson maintained a low profile. He voted to uphold state regulations of liquor and of ships' passengers in the *License Cases* (1847) and the *Passenger Cases* (1849), respectively, but in neither case did he write an opinion. He silently joined Justice Benjamin Curtis's majority opinion, moreover, in *Cooley v. Board of Wardens* (1852), which upheld a Pennsylvania pilot law. His only written opinion of any importance in a Commerce Clause case came in *Pennsylvania v. Wheeling and Belmont Bridge Company* (1852), the conclusion of a dispute that came before the Court three times. In 1852, a majority of the justices had held that a bridge chartered by Virginia constituted a public nuisance because it obstructed the passage of large steamboats. When Congress subsequently passed legislation designating the bridge lawful at its existing height, Nelson deferred to the legislative branch. He wrote the majority opinion declaring that the bridge was not an obstruction of interstate commerce, thus overruling the Court's previous decision and bringing an end to six years of litigation on the subject.

Much of Nelson's work on the Court dealt with relatively uncontroversial matters, such as admiralty and patent law. His most significant admiralty opinion came in *New Jersey Steam Navigation Co. v. Merchants Bank* (1848), a case involving a steamboat disaster that occurred in Long Island Sound in 1840. A fire consumed nearly all who were aboard as well as a crate of gold and silver shipped by the Merchants Bank of Boston. At issue was whether the steamboat company's negligence made them liable to the bank for the loss of the money as well as whether the case came under federal admiralty jurisdiction. Nelson sided with the bank and upheld federal jurisdiction over the matter.

Because he served the Second Circuit, a hotbed of enterprise and innovation that included New York, Nelson heard a number of patent cases while on circuit and wrote the opinion in many such cases that made it to the Supreme Court. In *Hotchkiss v. Greenwood* (1851), a dispute involving a patent on clay and porcelain doorknobs, Nelson held that an improvement of a product based solely on the use of better materials did not warrant the grant of a patent. "The improvement consists in the superiority of the material, and which is not new, over that previously employed in making the knob," he stated. "But this, of itself, can never be the subject of a patent" (52 U.S. 248, 266). Nelson also played an important part in the ongoing litigation over the patent on Cyrus McCormick's reaper, a machine that revolutionized grain production during the early nineteenth century. Nelson decided *Seymour v. McCormick* (1857) in McCormick's favor, a ruling that eventually drove Seymour and other inventors out of the reaper business.

Even on the most controversial of issue of his tenure—slavery—Nelson attempted to steer clear of partisan conflict. When the *Dred Scott* case was initially argued, Nelson believed that the question of black citizenship was not before the Court, and he attempted to forge a majority among the justices that would decide the case on the narrow grounds of whether Scott became free because of his temporary residence in free territory. The eagerness of some of the more proslavery and antislavery justices to write extensive opinions addressing the broader questions of black citizenship, as well as the extent of congressional power over slavery in the territories, however, pushed Nelson's compromise opinion to the side. He still issued it as a concurrence, and close scrutiny of the opinion shows that Nelson offhandedly supported Chief Justice Taney's argument that Congress lacked power to legislate on slavery. Although Nelson's opinion in *Dred Scott* never aroused the ire of the northern press in the way Taney's opinion did, the New Yorker nevertheless came under fire for his tacit support of the position advocated by the southern proslavery wing of the Court.

As America approached civil war, Nelson fretted about the country's future and urged political compromise. During the winter of 1861, he joined with Justice John A. Campbell, of Alabama, and served as an intermediary between representatives of the South and the incoming Lincoln administration, but Nelson became brooding and pessimistic when talks broke down and hostilities began. Although loyal to the Union, he opposed the war and at times criticized Lincoln's policies. Nelson wrote for the four dissenters in the *Prize Cases* (1863), a series of cases involving Lincoln's blockade of southern ports, arguing that Lincoln had no authority, prior to a declaration of war by Congress, to act as though a state of war existed between the United States and the Confederacy and impose the blockade. Near the end of the war, Nelson dissented alone in another prize case, *The Circassian* (1865), which involved the capture of a British merchant steamer bound for New Orleans in 1862. He argued that since New Orleans was at that point occupied by federal troops, no blockade of the city existed at the time of the ship's capture.

Nelson's impact on the nation's constitutional development, considering the number of opinions he wrote, was limited. Although respected for his integrity and diligence, his desire to avoid the most contested issues of his time blunted his effectiveness among his colleagues and adversely affected his reputation among historians. Ill health forced him to retire in 1872, and he died the following year.

Levi Woodbury

For someone who served so briefly—only five years—Levi Woodbury wrote opinions in some of the most important cases to reach the Court during his tenure. Born in 1789 in Portsmouth, New Hampshire, Woodbury graduated from Dartmouth College in 1809 and subsequently went to Tapping Reeve's Litchfield Law School in Connecticut. The first member of the Supreme Court to have attended law school, Woodbury also studied in Boston with Judge Jeremiah Smith. He was admitted to the bar in 1812, and he initially practiced in Francestown, New Hampshire, before moving to Portsmouth in 1819. Woodbury became active in politics in 1812, when he made speeches in support of the war with England, and he soon emerged as a leader of the local Democratic-Republican Party. His loyalty to the party won him the position of clerk of the state senate in 1816, and the following year his political connections paid off, when his friend Governor William Plumer appointed the young and inexperienced Woodbury to the state supreme court.

Woodbury performed respectably on the state bench, and over the next several years he played a leading role in New Hampshire political and legal circles. He served a term as governor of the state (1823–1824) and as U.S. Senator (1825–1831) before receiving an appointment from President Jackson to become secretary of the navy. Although he did not share Jackson and Taney's virulent opposition to the national bank, in 1833 Woodbury accepted the position of treasury secretary after the Senate rejected Taney for the job. He held the cabinet post through the controversial years after the bank war as well as during the panic-plagued Van Buren presidency, and he returned to the Senate in 1841. Woodbury believed in states' rights and strict constructionism, although he was not regarded as an ideologue. He was politically ambitious and was mentioned as a potential vice presidential candidate in 1844, although his nomination to the Court forestalled whatever future political plans he may have entertained. In 1845, after Justice Joseph Story died, President James K. Polk nominated

Levi Woodbury (Mathew Brady, Collection of the Supreme Court of the United States)

Woodbury for the New England seat on the Court. Woodbury easily won Senate confirmation, despite having limited judicial experience more than twenty years earlier.

Only a few years into his tenure on the Court, Woodbury wrote an important majority opinion for the Court in one of the era's major slavery cases. *Jones v. Van Zandt* (1847) involved the Fugitive Slave Act of 1793, under which a Kentucky slave owner sued an Ohio farmer who had assisted in the escape of the Kentuckian's slaves. The case presented the issue of the constitutionality of the act, and Woodbury wrote for a unanimous majority in upholding the law. Citing Justice Story's opinion in *Prigg v. Pennsylvania* (1842), in which the Court had previously upheld the Fugitive Slave Act, Woodbury contended that "the Constitution itself . . . flung its shield, for security, over such property as is in controversy in the present case, and the right to pursue and reclaim it within the limits of another State" (46 U.S. 215, 229). Woodbury's opinion, moreover, dismissed the argument that the provision of the Northwest Ordinance of 1787 banning slavery north of the Ohio River made the Fugitive Slave Law illegal. Slavery, he argued, was "a political question, settled by each State for itself" (46 U.S. 215, 231). Thus, Congress had no power over the institution. Although personally opposed to slavery throughout his New Hampshire political career, Woodbury's opinion in Van Zandt earned him a reputation as a "doughface," a northern supporter of the South.

Woodbury's other major constitutional opinions also advanced states' rights principles. He wrote a lengthy dissent in *Waring v. Clarke* (1847), in which the majority extended the admiralty jurisdiction of the federal courts to include inland waters influenced by the ebb and flow of the tide. Woodbury argued in favor of limited jurisdiction under traditional English rules, and he warned against allowing federal courts to extend their reach too far. He took a similar position in Commerce Clause cases, where he sought to protect states' sovereign powers and urged judicial restraint. In the *License Cases* (1847), for example, Woodbury voted with the majority to uphold state liquor licensing laws, arguing that "the States stand properly on their reserved rights, within their own powers and sovereignty, to judge of the expediency and wisdom of their own laws" (46 U.S. 504, 631). Moreover, he joined the states' rights wing of the Court in dissent in the *Passenger Cases* (1849), arguing in favor of state power to regulate immigrants. Like southerners Taney and Daniel, Woodbury noted the implications of the Court's ruling for slavery. If Congress possessed exclusive power over the admission of aliens into the several states, as the majority concluded, did the national government also have control over the admission of slaves and free blacks? Wanting to keep such matters within the purview of the states, Woodbury defended the state laws at issue in the case. As the sectional crisis heightened and the Court debated the constitutional questions associated with states' rights and slavery, Woodbury seemed to ally himself with the Court's pro-South wing.

Woodbury's Contract Clause opinions took the middle ground that typified the work of the Taney Court in this area. Here Woodbury had to balance his belief in the inherent powers of states to legislate for the public good with the need to protect contractual relationships. He concurred in *Cook v. Moffat* (1847), in which the Court ruled that a state bankruptcy statute did not affect one's debts incurred out of state. Further, in *Planters' Bank of Mississippi v. Sharp* (1848), although he argued for a presumption of constitutionality when state legislation was at issue, Woodbury nonetheless struck down a state statute that interfered with a bank's ability to transfer bills and notes, powers that the bank had been granted in the state's original charter. In *West River Bridge v. Dix* (1848), though, Woodbury concurred in upholding Vermont legislation that eliminated the exclusive franchise of a toll bridge. The state possessed the power of eminent domain to promote the public good, Woodbury argued, and the taking did not constitute a violation of the Contract Clause.

Woodbury worked hard as a justice, writing on average more than eleven opinions per term, but the lengthy and convoluted nature of his judicial writings hampered his effectiveness on the Court. Second only to Justice McLean in terms of political ambition among the justices, moreover, Woodbury sometimes seemed more interested in the presidency than in his judicial post. Some historians speculate that his pro-South judicial record represented an effort on his part to position himself for the White House and that, had he lived longer, he—rather than Franklin Pierce, New Hampshire's other leading Democrat—would have been nominated to run for president in 1852. Woodbury died in 1851.

Robert Cooper Grier

A key member of the Democratic bloc that dominated the Court during the 1850s, Robert Cooper Grier figured prominently in the major questions that faced the nation during the Taney period and afterward. Grier was born in Cumberland County, Pennsylvania, in 1794, the oldest of eleven children and the son of a Presbyterian minister. Soon after Robert's birth, the Grier family moved to Lycoming County, where the Rev. Grier farmed, preached, and taught school. Young Grier received a classical education under his father's direction, and later he enrolled in Dickinson College and graduated in 1812. After teaching at Dickinson for a year, he returned home to assist his father in running the private Northumberland Academy. On his father's death in 1815, Grier assumed command of the school and studied law on the side. Admitted to the bar in 1817, he practiced first in Bloomsburg, Pennsylvania, and soon in nearby Danville, where he worked for the next fifteen years.

Grier's success at the bar, his loyal service as a Jackson Democrat, and his 1829 marriage to Isabella Rose—the daughter of a wealthy Scotsman—improved his prospects. In 1833, he received an appointment as judge of the District Court of Allegheny County, on the opposite end of the state, where Grier soon ingratiated himself with the Pittsburgh bar. After thirteen years of steady but unspectacular service,

Robert Cooper Grier (Mathew Brady, Collection of the Supreme Court of the United States)

peculiar political circumstances led to the appointment of the relatively obscure judge to the U.S. Supreme Court. The death of Pennsylvanian Henry Baldwin in 1844 and President Tyler's subsequent inability to fill the seat on the Court left the appointment to his successor, President James K. Polk. After failing to secure the nomination of either of his first two choices—both were also Pennsylvanians—Polk nominated Grier for the position. He won unanimous Senate confirmation in August 1846.

As a justice Grier exhibited pragmatism and moderation. Author of only a dozen dissenting opinions during his twenty-four years of service on the Supreme Court, Grier staked out the ideological center among his colleagues and almost always constituted part of the majority. His thinking about contracts, for example, fit with the Taney Court's overall emphasis on the public interest, as Grier generally struck a balance between protecting property rights and promoting the welfare of the community. In *Cook v. Moffat* (1847), he wrote one of his first major opinions of the Court. Here he held that a Maryland bankruptcy law had no effect on a contract made by a Maryland citizen with a New Yorker, where the contract was to be performed in New York. Upholding a precedent lain down by the Marshall Court, Grier ruled that state insolvency laws only discharged debts made between citizens of that particular state. In other contract cases, Grier proved more responsive to changing social and economic circumstances. In *Richmond, Fredericksburg, and Potomac Railroad Company v. Louisa Railroad Company* (1852), Grier spoke for the majority in narrowly defining a railroad's charter so as to allow the construction of another railroad along a similar route. Citing Taney Court precedents regarding corporate charters and eminent domain, Grier championed the public interest. "The grant of a franchise is of no higher order, and confers no more sacred title, than a grant of land to an individual," he wrote, "and, when the public necessities require it, the one, as well as the other, may be taken for public purposes on making suitable compensation" (54 U.S. 71, 83).

Grier's opinions in Commerce Clause cases also represented the predominant view among the justices. In the *License Cases* (1847), he concurred in a brief opinion with the majority decision upholding state liquor regulations. Grier went as far as any of his brethren in asserting the state's power over such matters. "The police power, which is exclusively in the States, is alone competent to the correction of these great evils, and all measure of restraint or prohibition necessary to effect the purpose are within the scope of that authority," he argued (46 U.S. 504, 632). Although he believed the question of whether or not Congress possessed exclusive power over commerce to be irrelevant in the case, a few years later Grier jumped into the thick of the debate over the extent of the federal commerce power. Joining nationalists McLean and Wayne as well as Justices Catron and McKinley, Grier voted to strike down state regulations and taxation of immigrant passengers in the *Passenger Cases* (1849). Quoting the Marshall Court's decision in *Gibbons v. Ogden* (1824), Grier argued that treaties negotiated by the U.S. government and laws enacted by Congress precluded any state from interfering with commerce. In 1852, Grier again was in the majority when the Court reached a middle ground on the Commerce Clause issue in *Cooley v. Board of Wardens.*

Like the other northern Democrats on the Court during the decade before the Civil War, Grier's record on the slavery issue placed him squarely in the "doughface" camp. Because he often held circuit court in Pennsylvania, an important state for slaves attempting to escape to freedom, Grier heard an unusually large number of fugitive slave cases. Soon after joining the Court, he invoked the ire of Pittsburgh's antislavery activists when he charged the jury strongly in favor of a Virginia slave owner who sought an indemnity against a Pennsylvania man for harboring the Virginian's runaway slave. The jury in *Van Metre v. Mitchell* (1847) heeded Grier's charge and returned a judgment in favor of the slaveholder. It would not be the only time Grier brought the wrath of the antislavery movement upon himself. After the passage of the Fugitive Slave Law of 1850, part of the famous Compromise of 1850, tensions over the fugitive issue in Pennsylvania only increased. In 1851, armed free blacks and abolitionists in Christiana, Pennsylvania, skirmished with a party of slave catchers from Maryland. The riot resulted in the death of a Maryland slave owner who had gone to Christiana to reclaim his escaped slave. Federal authorities indicted the suspects for treason, and the trial proceeded before a jury and Justice Grier. His charge to the jury in *United States v. Hanway* (1851) made clear that federal officials had gone too far in charging the defendants with treason; the jury agreed and acquitted the men. Still, Grier was remembered not for his temperate interpretation of the law, but for his bitter criticisms of the abolitionists, whom he described as "infuriated fanatics and unprincipled demagogues" who "promulgate doctrines subversive of all morality and all government" (Swisher 1974, 580).

Such rhetoric on the circuit won Grier no friends among abolitionists, and his opinions in Supreme Court cases involving slavery proved equally offensive to them. In *Moore v. Illinois* (1852), Grier wrote the opinion for an eight-justice majority upholding an Illinois statute that made it a crime to harbor runaway slaves. Grier concluded that the power to aid in the rendition of fugitives was a concurrent power, possessed by both the state and the federal governments. By so ruling, Grier effectively ignored Justice Story's majority opinion in *Prigg v. Pennsylvania* (1842), which had placed the issue under federal control, and instead enshrined Taney's concurrence in that case as the established rule regarding fugitive slaves. Grier issued a brief opinion in *Dred Scott v. Sandford* (1857), in which he supported Justice Nelson's view that the Missouri courts ought to decide Scott's status, while agreeing with Taney that the Missouri Compromise was unconstitutional. The only northerner on the Court to agree with Taney on this question, Grier again came under attack from northern abolitionists for his southern sympathies.

Despite his strong support of the rights of slaveholders, Grier firmly supported the Union cause during the Civil War. He vehemently denied that any state or portion of the Union possessed a right to secede, and, in an 1861 circuit case, he even referred to "the total insanity of the people in the South altogether" (Swisher 1974, 873). When the *Prize Cases* (1863) came before the Court, the only time the Court ruled on the constitutionality of President Lincoln's wartime policies, Grier spoke for a 5–4 majority in upholding the Union blockade of the southern states. Deftly handling the constitutional questions raised in the case, Grier held that the president, as commander in chief, had the power to impose the blockade in the absence of congressional authorization. Because the seceding states were engaging in an insurrection against the United States, Grier contended, a state of war existed, even though not formally declared. Grier's opinion gave the Lincoln administration everything it wanted. By ruling that a state of war existed, the Court sanctioned the president's actions without ever acknowledging the sovereign existence of the Confederacy. Although he opposed other elements of the administration's prosecution of the war—the issuing of greenbacks as well as the government's seizure of a Democratic newspaper—Grier's opinion in the *Prize Cases* (1863) displayed his loyalty to the Union cause and proved to be one of the most significant statements on presidential war powers in U.S. history.

Grier served another six years on the Court beyond the Taney era. Ill health severely limited his capacity to perform his job as early as 1862, when he gave up his circuit duties. By 1869, his Supreme Court colleagues were urging him to retire, which he did in early 1870. He died later that year. A large, corpulent man who enjoyed trout fishing, Grier possessed an occasionally rough manner. During nearly two and a half decades of service on the Court, he made important contributions to U.S. constitutional development, although his devotion to upholding the legal rights of slaveholders undoubtedly damaged his reputation among historians.

John Archibald Campbell

The last of the Democratic justices who served during the decade before the Civil War was John A. Campbell. Although he spent only eight years as a justice of the Supreme Court, Campbell played an important part in the Court's handling of cases involving states' rights and slavery. Born in Washington, Georgia, in 1811, Campbell was the son of a well-educated lawyer and planter of Scotch-Irish ancestry. After demonstrating extraordinary intellectual abilities as a child and briefly attending a local academy, Campbell enrolled at the University of Georgia at age eleven and graduated in 1825 with honors. With hopes for a military career, Campbell earned admission to West Point Military Academy, but the deaths of two of his siblings and his father during his attendance there prompted him to resign and return to the South. He taught in Florida Territory for a year to help pay the family's debts before returning home and earning admittance to the Georgia bar in 1829. The following year he moved to Alabama, a

John Archibald Campbell (Mathew Brady, Collection of the Supreme Court of the United States)

relatively new state where opportunities abounded for ambitious, young lawyers. Campbell settled in Montgomery, where he met and married Anne Goldthwaite, who came from one of the community's most prominent families. Campbell practiced law in Montgomery until 1835. He fought in the Creek Indian War and won election to the state legislature as a Democrat in 1836, and he moved to Mobile in 1837. Campbell was disillusioned by state politics, and his political career was brief. He served a year in the legislature from Montgomery in 1836 and a year from Mobile in 1842.

Campbell spent the vast majority of his public life as a lawyer. In the course of twenty-three years of practicing law in Alabama, he earned a first-class reputation. A specialist in land titles, especially those based on complicated Spanish grants, Campbell argued a number of high-profile cases before the state supreme court and federal courts, including the famous case of Myra Clark Gaines, who fought for two decades to gain title to extensive lands in Mississippi and Louisiana. Campbell also argued many cases before the Supreme Court, during which time he impressed many of the justices with his skills as an advocate as well as with his legal learning. Campbell reportedly possessed one of the largest personal law libraries in America, and his knowledge of Anglo-American and continental law, some claimed, rivaled that of Joseph Story. Although twice asked to serve on the state supreme court, Campbell rejected the offer both times, choosing instead to continue practicing.

By the late 1840s Campbell took a more active role in politics. He wrote a series of essays on the sectional conflict and slavery, in which he predicted the ultimate extinction of slavery and advocated the moral and educational advancement of blacks. These seemed more like philosophical ruminations, however, than genuine expressions of his views. (He regularly bought and sold slaves during his lifetime; the maximum number of slaves he owned at any one time was fourteen, in 1846.) Campbell jumped headlong into the political fray in 1850, when the legislature chose him as one of Alabama's delegates to the Nashville Convention, where representatives from most of the southern states gathered to condemn the Wilmot Proviso and discuss ways to protect the rights of slaveholders—either in or out of the Union. Campbell introduced a series of resolutions at the convention arguing that Congress had no power to prohibit slavery from any territory and that states possessed sole power over slave property. In the summer of 1852, when Justice John McKinley died, fellow Alabaman Campbell emerged as the likely nominee to replace him. Incoming President Franklin Pierce consulted Justices Catron and Benjamin Curtis, who both wholeheartedly endorsed Campbell's appointment. Soon after his inauguration, Pierce, as expected, nominated Campbell for a position on the Court. Within days, the Senate unanimously confirmed the appointment, and Campbell took his seat on the bench in April 1853.

The most important cases during Campbell's early years on the Court involved corporations, and on such matters he asserted states' rights principles. As a Jacksonian Democrat, Campbell looked on corporate power with suspicion and favored local control of corporate development. As a member of the Supreme Court, he opposed the gains that had been made by corporations in U.S. constitutional law up to that point—the right to sue under diversity of citizenship as well as the protection corporations enjoyed under the Court's interpretation of the Contract Clause. His views on the first question became known early in his tenure, when he issued a vigorous dissent in *Marshall v. Baltimore and Ohio Railroad Company* (1854). Although the majority in the case affirmed the right of a corporation to sue a citizen of another state in federal court and struck down a state statute forbidding such suits, Campbell issued a thorough dissent, in which he outlined the history of the Court's decisions on this question. Citing Justice Marshall's earliest ruling on the issue, in which the chief justice had denied the notion that a corporation could be a citizen, Campbell described the Court's more recent opinions as diverging from the true spirit of the Constitution and the framers. "A corporation is not a citizen," Campbell declared simply. "It may be an artificial person, a moral person, a juridical person, a legal entity, a faculty, an intangible, invisible being, but," he argued, quoting Marshall, "'it certainly is not a citizen'" (57 U.S. 314, 351).

Campbell's later opinions involving corporations pertained to state regulation rather than the citizenship issue. In *Piqua Branch of the State Bank of Ohio v. Knoop* (1854), the Court faced the question of whether a charter exempting a corporation from taxation in Ohio constituted a contract between a state and a bank. When the Court held that it did and thus struck down a state tax, Campbell dissented. Later, when an Ohio constitutional convention passed an amendment repealing the tax exemption and the Court, in *Dodge v. Woolsey* (1855), declared it a violation of the Contract Clause, Campbell again found himself in the minority. Viewing the Court's decision as a dangerous expansion of judicial power and a serious threat to state sovereignty, Campbell saw the ruling as a stark example of the ever-increasing power of a privileged few, who obviously had an ally in the Supreme Court. The decision, Campbell warned, "will establish on the soil of every State a caste made up of combinations of men for the most part under the most favorable conditions in society, who will habitually look beyond the institutions and authorities of the State to the central government for the strength and support necessary to maintain them in the enjoyment of their special privileges and exemptions" (59 U.S. 331, 373). The welfare of society, in Campbell's view, required that states maintain control over the development of corporations. Campbell succeeded in persuading his colleagues of the correctness of this approach in at least one instance, the case of *Christ's Church Hospital v. County of Philadelphia* (1861), where he spoke for a unanimous Court in upholding Pennsylvania's repeal of a hospital's tax-exempt status.

As sectional antagonisms grew more pronounced during the late 1850s, Campbell continued to assert his states' rights views in other areas of the law. On more than one occasion, he spoke out against the expansion of federal admiralty jurisdiction. He dissented, for example, in *Jackson v. Steamboat Magnolia* (1858), a case involving a steamboat collision in his home state. "The Alabama River flows entirely within the State, and discharges itself into the Mobile River, and through that and the Mobile Bay connects with the Gulf of Mexico," he wrote, arguing that the cause was a state matter. "The collision occurred two hundred miles above the ebb and flow of the tide, and on a river upon which no port of entry or delivery before that time had been established" (58 U.S. 296, 322). As in his decisions in cases involving corporations, Campbell discussed at length the history of admiralty law and came to the conclusion that the Court's recent decisions violated precedent as well as the spirit of the Constitution. The "revolution in the admiralty administration of the courts of the United States," he predicted, would "produce heart-burning and discontent, and involve collisions with State legislatures and State jurisdictions" (58 U.S. 296, 343). On the slavery issue as well, Campbell sought to limit the power of the national government. In *Dred Scott v. Sandford* (1857), the only major slavery case in which he wrote an opinion, Campbell concurred with most of Chief Justice Taney's majority opinion. In particular, Campbell held that Scott was still a slave, that Congress had no power over slavery in the territories, and that the Missouri Compromise violated the Constitution. He outlined a narrow view of the Constitution's Territories Clause by claiming that it did not grant Congress the power "to determine the internal polity, or to adjust the domestic relations, or the persons who may lawfully inhabit the territory." Instead, Campbell argued for territorial self-government. This fit with his overall view of the national government's relationship to slavery. He believed that Congress could exercise "no power over the subject of slavery within the States, nor control the intermigration of slaves, other than fugitives, among the States" (60 U.S. 393, 500).

Although he adhered to southern orthodoxy in his commitment to states' rights and slavery, Campbell at times displayed moderation in the midst of sectional hysteria. He incurred the wrath of southern expansionists during the 1850s, for example, when he twice used all the powers of his judicial office while on circuit to halt filibustering expeditions in Central America. Campbell came down hard on John A. Quitman and William Walker—who hoped to lead invasions of Cuba and Nicaragua, respectively—for violating U.S. neutrality laws. Despite the popularity of these leaders' extralegal efforts to acquire new lands for the United States, Campbell used at times high-handed tactics to halt their efforts. When secession fever hit the South in 1861, moreover, Campbell argued against separating from the Union. Because of his deep belief in states' rights and the constitutional protections afforded to slaveholders, he thought the South had little to fear with the election of Lincoln. Campbell served as an intermediary between Union and Confederate officials during the weeks before the outbreak of the Civil War, but when the war began he resigned his seat on the Court and returned to the South. He was the only southern member of the Court

Table 2.2 Numbers of Opinions by the Ten Most Significant Members of the Taney Court

	Years Served	Majority Opinions	Concurring Opinions	Dissenting Opinions	Average Number of Opinions per Term*	Average Number of Dissents per Term
Taney 1836–1864	28	260	7	14	10.32	.46
Story 1811–1844	33	270	1	13	8.7	.39
McLean 1829–1861	32	245	5	33	9.31	1.03
Wayne 1835–1867	32	144	6	5	4.97	.16
Catron 1837–1865	28	157	12	26	7.5	.93
Daniel 1841–1860	19	87	9	47	7.68	2.42
Nelson 1845–1872	27	290	6	22	11.85	.78
Grier 1846–1870	23	194	7	12	9.17	.48
Curtis 1851–1857	6	48	3	8	10.5	1.17
Campbell 1853–1861	8	92	5	18	14.5	2.25

*Includes majority opinions, concurrences, dissents, and other opinions.

to do so. Although he agreed to serve in the War Department of the Confederacy, he did so reluctantly and tried in vain during the war to negotiate peace between the sections. After the war, Campbell spent four months in prison for his service to the Confederate government before receiving a pardon from President Andrew Johnson.

Campbell's brief but significant Supreme Court career coincided with one of the most difficult periods in the history of the Court and the nation. His strongly held views regarding states' rights and slavery meant that he dissented relatively frequently—on average more than any of his contemporaries except for Justice Daniel. Despite his significant contributions to the constitutional debates of the day, some historians argue that Campbell's most important work came after the war, when he returned to the practice of law. He argued many more cases before his former colleagues, including the landmark *Slaughterhouse Cases* (1873), in which he represented a group of disgruntled New Orleans butchers who challenged the constitutionality of a state slaughterhouse regulation. He died in 1889.

The Lone Whig

Benjamin Robbins Curtis

Only one Whig justice graced the bench of the Supreme Court during the Taney era. Justice Benjamin Robbins Curtis, of Massachusetts, served from 1851 to 1857, during which time he sat on a Court composed entirely of Democrats (except for Justice McLean, who associated himself with a variety of political parties over the course of his career). Most of the justices, moreover, hailed from the South at a time when the sectional conflict dominated the nation's political consciousness, and Curtis wrote one of two dissents in the famous case of *Dred Scott v. Sandford* (1857). Still, Curtis fit in among his fellow justices more easily than might have been expected. "My brethren here have received me very kindly," he wrote during his first term on the Court, "and there are some pleasant gentlemen among them" (Warren 1928, 233). He dissented only once that year, and he did so infrequently over the course of the next six years. Despite an acrimonious exchange of letters between Curtis and Chief Justice Taney in the midst of the *Dred Scott* case, after which Curtis resigned, the Massachusetts native harbored no resentment toward the chief justice. Unlike some northerners who came to despise Taney as the head of the southern slaveocracy, Curtis heaped praise on his former colleague at Taney's death in 1864. The aristocratic Curtis admired the chief justice's "dignity, his love of order, his gentleness, his caution, his accuracy, his discrimination" during conferences (Swisher 1974, 968). He respected Taney's qualities of judicial leadership, and—despite their obvious differences in the *Dred Scott* case—the two men agreed on most matters of constitutional interpretation.

Born in Watertown, Massachusetts, in 1809, Curtis came from one of the state's oldest and most respected families, which traced its roots back to Puritan settlers in the 1630s. Although Curtis's father, a member of the merchant marine, died at sea when Curtis was still a child, his mother managed to send him to nearby Harvard College, from which he graduated in 1829. He subsequently enrolled in Harvard Law School just in time to study with Justice Joseph Story, who had recently arrived there. In intense moot court sessions run by Story, students gained valuable experience before one of the nation's foremost judges. After graduating and being admitted to the bar in 1832, Curtis built up a respectable law practice in Northfield, Massachusetts, in the western part of the state. He soon discovered that he disliked the small town atmosphere, and his family connections (his uncle taught at Harvard Law School) afforded him the opportunity to return to Boston in 1834 and join a prominent firm run by a distant cousin, Charles Pelham Curtis.

For the next several years, Benjamin Curtis practiced law in Boston, specializing in admiralty and commercial law. He argued his first fugitive slave case, *Common-*

Benjamin Robbins Curtis (Collection of the Supreme Court of the United States)

wealth v. Aves, in 1836, which involved a black child who had been emancipated when accompanying her owner into Massachusetts. A conservative who disdained both the excesses of abolitionism in the North and the extreme advocates of slavery in the South, Curtis argued that the principle of comity demanded that Massachusetts law recognize the right of property in slaves. Although he lost the case, Curtis caught the eyes of those who would later favor his appointment to the Supreme Court. During a brief stint in the Massachusetts legislature, from 1849 to 1851, Curtis emerged as an important figure in the state in the midst of the national debate over the fugitive slave law and the Compromise of 1850. Senator Daniel Webster recruited Curtis, in fact, to argue fugitive slave cases in Massachusetts. Viewing enforcement of the new fugitive slave law as essential to maintaining sectional harmony, Curtis consistently argued that federal law needed to be upheld and that runaways be returned to their owners. On the death of Justice Woodbury in 1851, Webster recommended Curtis's appointment to President Millard Fillmore, who specifically wanted to nominate a young Whig from New England. Curtis fit the bill and had little trouble winning confirmation.

The new justice's impact on the Court was immediate. Just a few months after the Senate confirmed his nomination, Curtis wrote the majority opinion in one of the most important Commerce Clause cases in U.S. history. *Cooley v. Board of Wardens* (1852) raised the issue of whether or when states could regulate commercial activity—a question that had bedeviled the justices for decades. In upholding a Pennsylvania law regulating ships' pilots, Curtis wrote for five of eight justices (McKinley was not present) in declaring that the power to regulate commerce did not rest exclusively with Congress. Instead, he formulated the doctrine of "selective exclusiveness," the idea that some areas required national uniform regulations set by Congress, whereas other matters were essentially local in character and best left to states. "Either absolutely to affirm, or deny, that the nature of this power requires exclusive legislation by Congress, is to lose sight of the nature of the subjects of this power," he wrote (53 U.S. 299, 319). Thus, Curtis stressed that pilotage statutes in particular had long been enacted by states and that Congress had even recognized state authority over "pilots in the bays, inlets, rivers, harbors, and ports of the United States" (53 U.S. 299, 317). By placing an emphasis on the subject of commercial regulation—and whether it was national or local in nature—Curtis moved the debate away from the question of whether Congress possessed exclusive power over commerce and implied that in the future the Court would decide such questions on a case-by-case basis. Given his reputation as a nationalist, Curtis correctly predicted that his opinion "would excite surprise, because it is adverse to the exclusive authority of Congress" (Curtis 1879, 168). Moderates such as Taney and Catron praised the decision, but Justice McLean—who dissented in *Cooley*—later the same year ignored the new doctrine and continued to assert that Congress's power of commerce was exclusive. Still, Curtis's opinion helped the Court resolve a seemingly intractable problem by establishing a new, pragmatic standard of interpretation.

In spite of a history of support for federal fugitive slave laws and a reputation among abolitionists as a "slave-catching judge," Curtis became the judicial icon of the antislavery cause with his powerful dissent in *Dred Scott v. Sandford* (1857). Curtis's lengthy opinion took aim at both of Chief Justice Taney's major conclusions—that blacks lacked any claims to citizenship and that Congress had no power over slavery in the territories. First, Curtis claimed, before 1789 U.S. citizenship was synonymous with state citizenship; the Articles of Confederation prohibited Congress from making any citizenship rules, and the Constitution itself referred to "citizens at the time of the adoption of the Constitution." Because five states recognized free blacks as citizens at the time of the Constitution's adoption and because the Constitution did not provide in any way for altering their status, Curtis argued, no valid claim existed against black citizenship. Dred Scott, therefore, had the right as a citizen to bring his case into federal court. Second, Curtis interpreted the Territories Clause of the Constitution broadly, so as to grant Congress power to organize and govern territories in whatever way it wished. This included the power to pass legislation pertaining to slavery, as Congress had done with the Northwest Ordinance of 1787. On the most basic question involved in the case—the status of the slave, Scott—Curtis argued that he became emancipated upon his residence in free territory. Echoing the contention of antislavery advocates that slavery had no existence where not given positive legal protection, Curtis contended that Congress had absolutely forbidden slavery in the territories subject to the Missouri Compromise. This act of Congress changed the status of slaves brought within its jurisdiction. Thus, when Scott traveled with his master in free territory, he ceased being a slave.

At the time of Curtis's appointment, Whigs held high hopes that he would advance their agenda of nationalism and economic development and that he would fill the intellectual void left by Story's death in 1844. In many ways, Curtis did not disappoint. He favored expanded admiralty jurisdiction for the federal courts, voting with the majority in the landmark case *Genesee Chief v. Fitzhugh* (1852), and he wrote for the Court in *Steamboat New World v. King* (1854), in which he held that the navigability of a river—rather than whether it was subject to the ebb and flow of the tide—determined whether it fell under federal admiralty jurisdiction. He also believed in expanding corporations' rights to sue in federal courts by holding, in *Lafayette Insurance v. French* (1856), that corporations were citizens of the states in which they were formed. Curtis was the first member of the Court to graduate from law school, and his opinions were learned, crisp, and well reasoned. In his *Dred Scott* dissent, some historians have argued, Curtis showed signs of judicial greatness, as he thoroughly outmatched the chief justice in a way that only Story had been able to do.

Still, Curtis never felt comfortable as a justice of the Supreme Court. He hated traveling the circuit, living in a Washington boardinghouse, and spending time apart from his family. He constantly complained about the low salary, and he surely missed his lucrative Boston law practice. And there were other problems. According to one scholar, "Curtis's natural conservatism in politics turned into pessimism of the deepest kind, and the gap between his political outlook and that of the coming group of leaders in national affairs became steadily wider" (Leach 1952, 518). He had a distaste of politics and a distrust of politicians. The increasingly harsh tenor of political debate over slavery fed Curtis's worst fears that the future of the Union was in peril. A disagreement with Taney over Curtis's release of his *Dred Scott* dissent to a Boston newspaper before the Court had issued its opinion in the case prompted Curtis to resign. The chief justice came down hard on Curtis for his inappropriate behavior, although Curtis maintained that he mistakenly thought the majority decision in the case had already been filed. Curtis left the bench after six years but continued to play an important role in the nation's legal community. He returned to the practice of law in Massachusetts, argued a number of cases before the Supreme Court, and successfully defended President Andrew Johnson in his 1868 impeachment trial. Curtis died in 1874.

The Civil War Justices

Nathan Clifford

During the last six years of the Taney era, from 1858 until the chief justice's death in 1864, five new justices came to the Supreme Court. These men served the vast majority of their years on the Court well after the Civil War and thus played a minor role during the Taney period. The first of these, Nathan Clifford, was the last Democratic appointment to the Court under Taney—and the last for many years to come. In fact, with Union victory in the Civil War and the triumph of the Republican Party, not until 1887 would another Democratic president appoint a member of the Court.

Born in 1803 in Rumney, New Hampshire, Nathan Clifford gained admission to the bar in 1827 and eventually established a law practice in Newfield, Maine. Over the course of his political career, Clifford served in the Maine legislature, held the position of state attorney general, and spent two terms in the U.S. House of Representatives. In 1846, President Polk appointed him U.S. attorney general, and a few years later Clifford helped negotiate peace terms at the end of the war with Mexico. At the conclusion of the Polk administration, Clifford returned to practice law in Maine. A Democrat and a close associate of James Buchanan, who had served as secretary of war under Polk, Clifford's political connections figured prominently in his eventual appointment to the Court. With Justice Curtis's resignation in 1857, President Buchanan wanted to appoint a New Englander and a loyal party man to the Court.

Nathan Clifford (Mathew Brady, Collection of the Supreme Court of the United States)

Buchanan appointed Clifford to the post, but antislavery forces nearly succeeded in blocking the nomination. In the wake of Curtis's *Dred Scott* dissent and subsequent resignation, the appointment of yet another "doughface" infuriated some northerners. Clifford barely won Senate confirmation, by a vote of 26–23.

Taking his seat on the eve of the Civil War, Clifford resembled the Court's other northern Democrats in his sympathy for the South and the rights of slaveholders. A little more than a year after his appointment, Clifford wrote to Buchanan about the impending crisis: "My views are fully expressed in the opinion of the Supreme Court in the case of Dred Scott, and I most fully approve the principles of your Administration" (Swisher 1974, 733). As a justice, Clifford was part of the Court's unanimous decision in *Ableman v. Booth* (1859), a case involving a fugitive slave in which Chief Justice Taney wrote a proslavery opinion. Clifford opposed secession, and he urged his colleague Justice Campbell not to resign from the Court to return to Alabama when the war began. Still, Clifford was part of a trio of justices—which included Taney and Nelson—who seemed determined to frustrate the Union war effort. In the *Prize Cases* (1863), Clifford sided with the dissenters led by Nelson, who argued that Lincoln lacked the power, in the absence of congressional authorization, to impose a blockade against the Confederacy.

Most of Clifford's tenure stretched well beyond the Taney era. His most important opinions came during the Reconstruction period, as he took the side of the majority in banning the use of loyalty oaths for voters and public officials, narrowly interpreting civil rights and voting rights guarantees for former slaves, and declaring the issuing of federal paper money unconstitutional. Undistinguished as a justice, his claim to fame was the fact that he served as president of the Electoral Commission, which Congress created to resolve the disputed presidential election of 1876. His frustration with the election of Republican President Rutherford B. Hayes, along with an occasionally contentious relationship with his Republican colleagues on the Court, made Clifford stubborn and irascible during his last years on the bench. Despite poor health and a deteriorating mind, he refused to resign while a Republican was in the White House. He died in 1881, thus giving Republican President Chester A. Arthur the chance to appoint his successor.

Noah H. Swayne

President Abraham Lincoln's first Supreme Court appointee and the first Republican member of Court, Noah Haynes Swayne served during the last few years of the Taney era. Born in Frederick County, Virginia, in 1804, Swayne was educated at a Quaker Academy in Waterford, Virginia, and later started to study medicine with a local physician. He abandoned this pursuit on the death of his teacher and turned to the study of law in Warrenton, Virginia. He was admitted to the bar in 1823. That same

Noah H. Swayne (Mathew Brady, Collection of the Supreme Court of the United States)

year Swayne moved to Ohio, probably because of his strong opposition to slavery. His successful practice there quickly led to his appointment as prosecuting attorney for Coshocton County, and in 1829 he won election to the state legislature as a Jacksonian Democrat. In 1830, President Jackson appointed him U.S. attorney for the District of Ohio, a position in which served until 1841.

Swayne's renown as a trial lawyer, particularly his role in prominent fugitive slave cases during the 1850s, catapulted him to the top of the Ohio bar. As the slavery issue became increasingly divisive, Swayne embraced the newly formed Republican Party and worked for the 1856 presidential campaign of John C. Fremont and, four years later, for Lincoln's campaign. On the death of Justice McLean, who had been a good friend of Swayne's, Lincoln looked for another antislavery, pro-Union Ohioan to fill his seat on the Court. Swayne, eager to land the position, mobilized the entire Ohio congressional delegation to push for his appointment. Although Swayne lacked judicial experience, Lincoln saw political advantage in nominating a native southerner to the Court during wartime, and Swayne won Senate confirmation with only one dissenting vote.

Swayne's lengthy though undistinguished tenure on the Court included almost three years of service during Taney's chief justiceship. A staunch Republican and a firm nationalist, Swayne usually supported Lincoln's wartime policies. He voted with the majority in the *Prize Cases* (1863), in which the Court upheld Lincoln's blockade of southern ports. In cases that involved wartime issues but were decided after the war had ended, Swayne upheld the federal government's issuing of paper money, supported the use of military trials of civilians, and wrote the majority opinion in a case upholding the 1862 income tax implemented to pay for the war. His only break with administration policy came in an 1862 circuit ruling in a treason case, in which he held that domestic rebels could not be "enemies" within the meaning of the Constitution or federal law. Arguing that wartime circumstances ought to have no effect on the administration of the law, Swayne defended his narrow interpretation of treason. "Causeless and wicked as is this rebellion, and fearful as has been its cost already in blood and treasure, it is not the less our duty to hold the scales of justice, in all cases, with a firm and steady hand" (Swisher 1974, 953). His most significant opinion during the Taney era came in *Gelpke v. Dubuque* (1864), a case involving the validity of railroad bonds that also had implications for the scope of federal and state judicial power. Swayne held that because state court precedents were inconsistent in determining the validity of the bonds in question, federal courts possessed the power to interpret the state constitution and decide the issue. Swayne upheld the validity of the bonds, thereby pleasing investors and expanding federal judicial authority.

The ambitious Swayne twice lobbied to be appointed to the position of chief justice, first on Taney's death in 1864, and again after the death of Taney's successor,

Salmon P. Chase, in 1873. Known for his charm and his political scheming, Swayne was undoubtedly Lincoln's least effective appointment to the Court. He remained on the bench until 1881, and he died three years later.

Samuel F. Miller

Lincoln's second appointee to the Court, who served only two and a half years in the Taney Court, far outshined his first. Samuel F. Miller was born in 1816 in Richmond, Kentucky, and educated intermittently at a local academy. He worked in a drugstore as a boy and eventually studied medicine. After receiving his medical degree from Transylvania University in 1838, Miller practiced for a decade before pursuing his interest in the law. Admitted to the bar in 1847, Miller served as a justice of the peace and a member of the county court. He also took an active part in local politics. Advocating the gradual emancipation of slaves, in 1849 he announced his desire to run for delegate to the Kentucky constitutional convention, although he withdrew from the race to prevent a split in the antislavery vote when a friend of his announced his intention to run for the same position.

The following year, after the Kentucky constitutional convention solidified rather than weakened slavery in the state, Miller moved to Iowa, where his views on the subject fit more within the mainstream. There he became a prominent attorney, joined the Republican Party, and in 1856 ran unsuccessfully for the state senate. Miller's legal reputation and Republican connections, as well as geographical considerations, played a part in his appointment to the Supreme Court. Lincoln hoped to nominate someone from the West to cover the newly created Ninth Judicial Circuit, and he submitted Miller's nomination for the Court in July 1862. Despite a lack of political experience and his relative anonymity (some newspapers mistakenly referred to the nominee as "David Miller"), Miller won unanimous support in the Senate. He thus became the first Supreme Court justice born west of the Appalachian Mountains and the first to live west of the Mississippi River.

That summer Justice Miller began what would be a twenty-eight year Supreme Court career. Like Swayne, Miller proved to be an ally of the president in matters related to the prosecution of the war. He voted with the majority to uphold the blockade in the *Prize Cases* (1863), and in later cases he favored a federal loyalty oath for members of the bar and supported the constitutionality of issuing federal paper money during wartime. The sole dissenter in *Gelpke v. Dubuque* (1864), Miller argued that federal courts had no business interfering with existing state court precedents regarding railroad bonds. Himself an Iowan, Miller took offense at Swayne's dismissive attitude toward the Iowa Supreme Court's ruling on this matter. Miller, moreover, correctly predicted that the majority opinion would only stiffen the resolve of the Iowa Supreme Court, which subsequently tried to reassert its position on the issue.

Samuel F. Miller (Handy Studios, Collection of the Supreme Court of the United States)

The verbal jousting between Swayne and Miller in *Gelpke* revealed the first tensions among Lincoln's appointees. Despite the significance of the case, Miller wrote his most important opinions during the 1870s and 1880s, in disputes involving civil rights and voting rights. The most notable of these came in the *Slaughterhouses Cases* (1873), in which he narrowly defined the rights of national citizenship that could be protected by the federal government. Ranked by many scholars as a "near great" justice of the Court, Miller made significant contributions to American constitutional development. He served until his death in 1890.

David Davis

Although Lincoln did not really know Miller at the time of his selection, the president had long been acquainted with David Davis, his third nominee. Born in 1815 on a plantation on the Eastern Shore of Maryland, Davis graduated from Kenyon College at age seventeen, studied law and clerked in a Massachusetts law office, and in 1835 entered the New Haven Law School in Connecticut. After studying there for less than a year, Davis headed to Illinois, where he settled in Bloomington and established a law practice. Introduced to Abraham Lincoln at this time, Davis initiated a lifelong friendship with the future president that eventually led to his appointment to the Supreme Court.

Davis took an active role in Illinois politics soon after his arrival in the state. A Whig, he won election to the state legislature in 1845 and two years later served as a delegate to state's constitutional convention. In 1848 he became a state circuit judge, a position in which he served for the next fourteen years. During the next decade, Davis joined the Republican Party and supported Lincoln's unsuccessful campaign against Stephen Douglas for the U.S. Senate. Davis, who understood the electoral politics of the day better than most, managed Lincoln's 1860 presidential campaign and afterward worked closely with the president-elect on cabinet appointments and other matters pertaining to Lincoln's impending inauguration. When Congress rearranged the circuits in the federal court system, Lincoln chose his old friend to take the vacant seat on the Court that had been occupied by Justice Campbell.

Although Davis repeatedly expressed doubts about his fitness for the Court (he wrote to his wife that opinion writing would not come easily, for example), he performed respectably as a justice. Like all of Lincoln's appointees, he supported the administration's blockade policy in the *Prize Cases* (1863). But despite his long association with Lincoln, Davis opposed the Emancipation Proclamation, which he thought demonstrated the president's eagerness to please the radical wing of the Republican Party, and he took direct issue with the trying of civilians in military courts. Indeed, his only major constitutional opinion came in *Ex parte Milligan* (1866), a landmark case in which Davis held that neither the president nor Congress could authorize trials of civilians by military courts where regular civil courts were

David Davis (Collection of the Supreme Court of the United States)

still in operation. Because of his love of politics, Davis grew restless on the Court. He sought unsuccessfully to be nominated for president in 1872 and resigned from the bench to serve in the U.S. Senate in 1877. Davis died in 1886.

Stephen J. Field

The greatest of Lincoln's appointments, Stephen J. Field served thirty-four years on the Court, only one of which overlapped with Chief Justice Taney's tenure. Born in Haddam, Connecticut, in 1816, the son of a Congregational minister, Field spent his childhood in western Massachusetts. At age thirteen he went to live in Turkey with his sister, whose husband worked as a missionary, and the young Field gained invaluable experience living and traveling throughout the Mediterranean. He returned to Massachusetts at age seventeen and graduated from Williams College in 1837. He then moved to New York to study law with his brother, the famous legal reformer David Dudley Field Jr., and gained admission to the New York bar in 1841. Stephen Field practiced law with his brother for seven years, spent another year in Europe, and in 1849 moved to California in the midst of the Gold Rush. He settled in Marysville, where he was soon elected to the position of alcalde, a traditional Mexican office that combined the duties of a judge and a mayor. Field served a term in the state legislature in 1851 and thereafter became active in Democratic Party politics. After an unsuccessful campaign for the U.S. Senate, he became a judge on the California Supreme Court in 1857. In that position he confronted the unenviable task of sorting out conflicting land grants among miners and homesteaders in a state where Mexican and Anglo-American legal systems still coexisted.

In 1863, when Congress created the new Tenth Circuit that encompassed the new states of California and Oregon, Lincoln appointed Field to the U.S. Supreme Court. Field's expertise in California land law, combined with his Democratic yet Unionist politics, made him an ideal choice. Sworn in as a justice in May 1863, the most significant cases that Field heard during the war years were on circuit. In *United States v. Greathouse* (1863), for example, the Tenth Circuit took up the case of a privateer vessel seized in San Francisco that was making preparations for a trip to aid the Confederacy. Although attorneys in the case argued that the crew could not be guilty of treason because they had not yet begun their voyage, Field issued a stern charge to the jury, in which he all but stated the defendants' outright guilt. Technically agreeing with the definition of treason that Justice Swayne had previously articulated—that only foreign, and not domestic, enemies could be guilty—Field nevertheless argued that the privateers had aided the rebellion and thus levied war against the United States in violation of federal law. Appointed after the controversial *Prize Cases* (1863), Field later participated in *Ex parte Milligan* (1866), in which he joined

Stephen J. Field (Handy Studios, Collection of the Supreme Court of the United States)

the majority in prohibiting the use of military tribunals outside the theater of war, and in the *Test Oath Cases* (1867), in which he wrote the majority opinion invalidating oaths of loyalty to the Union as a precondition of employment.

Field's first few years on the Court constituted but a minor part of his thirty-four year judicial record. He later became best known for his interpretation of the Fourteenth Amendment, particularly his advocacy of substantive due process, the idea that the Constitution protected certain natural rights, such as property ownership and the freedom to practice one's trade. Always a loyal Democrat despite having been appointed by Lincoln, Field kept a hand in party politics, especially in California. After becoming ill and less productive as a member of the Court, he resigned his position in 1897, and he died in 1899.

Conclusion

As in any other period of the Court's history, the justices of the Supreme Court during the Taney era were uneven in judicial ability and accomplishment. Chief Justice Roger B. Taney and Justice Joseph Story routinely rank among the "great" justices in U.S. history, and Justice Benjamin Curtis's name usually appears in the "near great" category. Scholars regard almost all of the other members of the Taney Court as "average," with only Justice Philip P. Barbour falling in the "below average" category. (Justices Samuel Miller and Stephen Field are included in the "near great" category, but it is hardly justifiable to view them as members of the Taney Court, given how briefly their tenures overlapped with Taney's.) The fact that historians and legal scholars regard so many of the Court's members from 1836 to 1864 as "average" probably has more to do with scholars' lack of familiarity with many of the justices than with their actual abilities or accomplishments. The justices of the mid–nineteenth century are, after all, some of the least studied of all the members of the Supreme Court. Justices McKinley and Baldwin are perhaps just as—if not more—deserving of the "below average" label than Barbour. McKinley ranks among the least productive members in the Court's history, and Baldwin certainly takes the honors as the most cantankerous and disagreeable of the Taney period.

More important than obscurity in determining the justices' reputations has been the coincidence of their service with the great national conflict over slavery that culminated in the Civil War. Undoubtedly, the individual members of the Court have generally fared dismally in historians' assessments because of the Taney Court's many decisions upholding and expanding the institution of slavery. In this regard, quite simply, most justices of the Taney era were on the wrong side of history.

References and Further Reading

Abraham, Henry J. *Justices, Presidents, and Senators: A History of the U.S. Supreme Court Appointments from Washington to Clinton.* 4th ed. Lanham, MD: Rowman and Littlefield, 1999.

Baldwin, Henry. "A General View of the Origin and Nature of the Constitution and Government of the United States, Deduced from the Political History and Condition of the Colonies and States, from 1774 until 1788, and the Decisions of the Supreme Court of the United States, Together with Opinions in the Cases Decided at January Term 1837, Arising on the Restraints on the Powers of the States." Philadelphia: n.p., 1837.

Baxter, Maurice. *Daniel Webster and the Supreme Court.* Amherst: University of Massachusetts Press, 1966.

Burnette, Lawrence, Jr. "Peter V. Daniel: Agrarian Justice." *Virginia Magazine of History and Biography* 62 (1954): 289–305.

Chandler, Walter. "The Centenary of Associate Justice John Catron of the United States Supreme Court." *Tennessee Law Review* 15 (1937): 32–51.

Curtis, Benjamin R. *A Memoir of Benjamin Robbins Curtis*, vol. 1. Boston: Little, Brown, 1879.

Dictionary of American Biography. New York: Charles Scribner's Sons, 1928–1995.

Dunne, Gerald T. *Justice Joseph Story and the Rise of the Supreme Court.* New York: Simon and Schuster, 1970.

Fehrenbacher, Don E. *The Dred Scott Case: Its Significance in American Law and Politics.* New York: Oxford University Press, 1978.

Finkelman, Paul. "'Hooted Down the Page of History': Reconsidering the Greatness of Chief Justice Taney." *Journal of Supreme Court History* (1994): 83–102.

Frank, John P. *Justice Daniel Dissenting: A Biography of Peter V. Daniel, 1784–1860.* New York: Augustus M. Kelley, 1970.

Friedman, Leon, and Fred L. Israel. *The Justices of the United States Supreme Court, 1789–1969: Their Lives and Major Opinions*, vols. 1–2. New York: Chelsea House, 1969.

Garraty, John A., and Mark C. Carnes, eds. *American National Biography.* 24 vols. New York: Oxford University Press, 1999.

Gass, Edmund C. "The Constitutional Opinions of Justice John Catron." *East Tennessee Historical Society Publications* (1936): 54–73.

Hall, Kermit L., ed. *The Oxford Companion to the Supreme Court of the United States.* New York: Oxford University Press, 1992.

———. *The Oxford Guide to United States Supreme Court Decisions.* New York: Oxford University Press, 1999.

Hicks, Jimmie. "Associate Justice John McKinley: A Sketch." *Alabama Review* 18 (1965): 227–233.

Huebner, Timothy S. *The Southern Judicial Tradition: State Judges and Sectional Distinctiveness, 1790–1890.* Athens: University of Georgia Press, 1999.

Jordan, Christine. "Justice John Campbell: Last of the Jacksonians." *Supreme Court Historical Society Yearbook* (1980): 78–88.

Lawrence, Alexander A. *James Moore Wayne: Southern Unionist.* Chapel Hill: University of North Carolina Press, 1943.

Leach, Richard H. "Benjamin Robbins Curtis: Judicial Misfit." *New England Quarterly* 25 (1952): 507–524.

Meriwether, Robert L., ed. *Papers of John C. Calhoun.* Columbia: University of South Carolina Press, 1959.

Newmyer, R. Kent. *The Supreme Court Under Marshall and Taney.* Arlington Heights, IL: Harlan Davidson, 1968.

———. *Supreme Court Justice Joseph Story: Statesman of the Old Republic.* Chapel Hill: University of North Carolina Press, 1985.

Powell, H. Jefferson. "Joseph Story." In Melvin I. Urofksy, ed., *The Supreme Court Justices: A Biographical Dictionary.* New York: Garland, 1994.

Roper, Donald Malcolm. *Mr. Justice Thompson and the Constitution.* New York: Garland, 1987.

Saunders, Robert, Jr. *John Archibald Campbell: Southern Moderate, 1811–1889.* Tuscaloosa: University of Alabama Press, 1997.

Schmidhauser, John R. "Judicial Behavior and the Sectional Crisis of 1837–1860." *Journal of Politics* 23 (1961): 615–640.

Silver, David M. *Lincoln's Supreme Court.* Urbana: University of Illinois Press, 1957.

Strickland, W. P. *The Life of Jacob Gruber.* New York: Carlton and Porter, 1860.

Swisher, Carl Brent. *History of the Supreme Court of the United States*, vol. 5, *The Taney Period, 1836–1864.* New York: Macmillan, 1974.

———. *Roger B. Taney.* New York: Macmillan, 1936.

Taylor, M. Flavia. "The Political and Civic Career of Henry Baldwin, 1799–1830." *Western Pennsylvania Historical Magazine* 24 (1941): 37–50.

Tyler, Samuel, ed. *Memoir of Roger Brooke Taney, LL.D., Chief Justice of the Supreme Court of the United States.* Baltimore: John Murphy, 1872.

Warren, Charles. *The Supreme Court in United States History*, vol. 2. Boston: Little, Brown, 1928.

Weisenburger, F. P. *The Life of John McLean: A Politician on the United States Supreme Court.* Columbus: Ohio State University Press, 1937.

3

Major Decisions

The Supreme Court's major decisions during Chief Justice Roger B. Taney's tenure reflected the themes of change and continuity that mark the history of U.S. constitutional development. In some respects, particularly its general willingness to grant more authority to state governments than to the federal government to regulate in the public interest, the Taney Court's record represented a departure from the Marshall era. In other ways, however, the Taney Court built on the Marshall legacy, especially in preserving the significant role of the Supreme Court and the federal courts generally in the American constitutional system. Moreover, even if Marshall and Taney often differed in what they believed was the better method of promoting economic growth and development, the two chief justices shared a forward-looking belief in American entrepreneurship and the capitalistic marketplace. In short, although it is easy to characterize Marshall and Taney as situated on opposite ends of the ideological spectrum—as many contemporary partisans, particularly Taney's opponents, were apt to do—such a description fails to do justice to the many ways in which the Taney Court's record flowed out of the experience of the Court under Marshall. Only on the slavery issue—where the Marshall Court had no record to speak of—did the Taney Court stand apart from its predecessor.

Contracts, Finance, and Economic Development

During the mid–nineteenth century, the justices heard myriad cases involving the Contract Clause. Article I, Section 10 of the Constitution imposes a number of restrictions on the states, including a ban on the passage of any "law impairing the obligation of contracts." The Court's interpretation of these words proved to have significant consequences for the scope of state regulatory authority as well as for the future of economic enterprise. On the one hand, if the definition of contractual rights were to be drawn broadly and in support of property holders and commercial interests, states would have little power to restrict the activities of entrepreneurs. On the other hand, such limitations on state power might also hinder the state's ability to facilitate internal improvements and promote development in the public interest. During the Taney era, the Court thus attempted to strike a balance between the fundamental rights of property under the Contract Clause and the power of states to regulate and promote economic activity for the public good.

The *Charles River Bridge* case, decided during the new chief justice's first term, was the most important Contract Clause case of the era and one of the two most significant opinions of Taney's career. *Charles River Bridge v. Warren Bridge* (1837) contained all the ingredients of a great drama: a controversial new chief justice; a pair of famous lawyers in Daniel Webster and Simon Greenleaf; a dispute involving huge profits and supposed promises in Boston, one of America's largest and most prosperous cities; and a ringing dissent issued by Joseph Story, the Court's most respected scholar and best friend of the late Chief Justice Marshall. Although Taney's more famous *Dred Scott* decision contributed to the outbreak of the Civil War, that ruling became obsolete as a matter of law soon afterward, when slavery ceased to exist. In contrast, the *Charles River Bridge* decision stands as the Taney Court's most enduring legacy.

This celebrated case arose over the fate of two bridges spanning the Charles River and connecting Boston to the neighboring community of Charlestown. In 1785, the Massachusetts legislature had authorized a group of businessmen to build the Charles River Bridge and had granted a charter that guaranteed them revenue from tolls for a forty-year period. The charter required that the bridge company pay an annual sum to Harvard College, which had operated a ferry at the site for more than a century, to make up for the loss of income from the ferry, which was to be discontinued. Six years later, in 1791, the legislature extended the charter for another thirty years. During the ensuing three and a half decades, the bridge proved both popular and profitable. Local citizens, especially businessmen, preferred the bridge to the ferry, for the bridge made the movement of goods between the two communities more efficient and less expensive. As the populations of both Boston and Charlestown exploded during the early part of the nineteenth century, the bridge reaped impressive profits: by 1814 stock in the bridge corporation had increased more than 600 percent from its original value.

Dramatic population growth had made the Charles River Bridge proprietors very rich men; it also made necessary the construction of a new bridge. In 1828, the Massachusetts legislature chartered the Warren Bridge Company, which constructed a bridge nearly adjacent to the original span. When completed at the end of that year, the new bridge lay just 260 feet away from one end of the old bridge and 915 feet from the other. Not only was the Warren Bridge right next to the Charles River Bridge, but also the terms of the charter of the new bridge posed a serious threat to the old bridge's financial future. Tolls would be the same as those for the Charles River Bridge, but after six years the new bridge would revert to the state and become toll free. Faced with economic competition as well as a potential violation of its original charter, in 1828 the Charles River Bridge brought suit to halt completion of the new bridge. When the state supreme court refused to stop construction of the Warren Bridge or to offer any relief to the plaintiffs, the Charles River Bridge appealed its case to the U.S. Supreme Court.

The Supreme Court first heard arguments in the case in 1831, while Chief Justice Marshall was still presiding, but divisions among the justices and a series of vacancies on the bench kept the Court from deciding the case during Marshall's lifetime. Not until 1837, during Taney's first term as chief justice, did the justices hear the reargument, and by that time the Court's membership had changed considerably from six years before. The constitutional question at stake, both in the state court and again when argued before the U.S. Supreme Court, was whether the Constitution's prohibition of state laws "impairing the obligation of contracts" (Article I, Section 10) protected the interests of the Charles River Bridge and prohibited the construction of the Warren Bridge. (At the state level, attorneys for the Charles River Bridge had also claimed that the new bridge violated the Massachusetts constitution.) Although attorneys for the Charles River Bridge originally sought an injunction prohibiting construction of the Warren Bridge, by the time of reargument in 1837, the Warren Bridge had been a vital part of the Boston community for nearly a decade. A year before, the bridge had reverted to the state and become toll free.

Attorneys Daniel Webster and Simon Greenleaf engaged in some of the greatest intellectual jousting to take place before the Court during the entire nineteenth century. Representing the Charles River Bridge, Webster argued that his clients possessed an exclusive right to the operation of a bridge between the two cities. This right derived from the ferry franchise that had been transferred to the Charles River Bridge, as well as from the charter's implied prohibition against destructive competition. By authorizing the erection of a second bridge, Webster contended, the state of Massachusetts had voided the terms of the original charter, thus violating the constitutional protection against the impairment of contracts. Although recognized as one of the great lawyers and orators of the age, Webster seemed "uneasy and moody" during the course of argument, perhaps because he knew that the justices were leaning toward his opponents (Kutler 1971, 79). Greenleaf, lead counsel for the Warren Bridge Company and a colleague of Justice Story on the Harvard law faculty, argued for a strict interpretation of the Charles River Bridge charter. Neither Harvard College nor the Charles River Bridge Company ever possessed exclusive rights, he claimed, because none of the charters at issue in the case ever granted such rights. Nor could these rights be implied. If monopoly rights were implicit in every charter, he contended, all public improvements would be called into question. Attorneys for the Warren Bridge Company also emphasized the state's power of eminent domain—the power to take private property for public use, provided that an owner is fairly compensated. Greenleaf argued that accepting the

Charles River Bridge's interpretation of the charter would seriously compromise this essential attribute of a state's sovereign character. If all charters or contracts implied the right of monopoly, after all, states could never take property for public use.

Less than three weeks after oral arguments concluded, the Court issued its decision in the case. Chief Justice Taney, writing for four of the seven justices, ruled in favor of the Warren Bridge Company. His opinion incisively dealt with the arguments Webster had advanced. Taney denied, first of all, that any connection existed between the ferry franchise and the charter of the Charles River Bridge. "It does not, by any means, follow that because the legislative power in Massachusetts in 1650 may have granted to a justly favored seminar of learning, the exclusive right of ferry between Boston and Charlestown, they would in 1785 give the same extensive privilege to another corporation, who were about to erect a bridge in the same place" (36 U.S. 420, 543). The bridge's charter, he argued, ought to be understood on its own terms, and nowhere did it state that exclusive rights had passed to the bridge. Indeed, Taney contended, the building of the bridge extinguished the exclusive rights of the ferry franchise. Relying on an English precedent, Taney concluded that any ambiguity in the terms of the bridge charter ought to be interpreted in favor of the public. He then turned to a recent decision of the Marshall Court, *Providence Bank v. Billings* (1830), in which the former chief justice had held that a state could tax a bank despite the bank's claim that its charter implicitly exempted it from taxation. Taney viewed the case as analogous to the bridge dispute, because Marshall had ruled that the taxing power constituted a vital part of a state's sovereign powers. "The object and end of all government," Taney argued, "is to promote the happiness and prosperity of the community by which it is established, and it can never be assumed that the government intended to diminish its power of accomplishing the end for which it was created" (36 U.S. 420, 547). If all such charters carried with them exclusive rights, government would significantly curtail its powers to govern—to promote the public interest.

After devoting the first half of his opinion to a discussion of legal precedent, Taney turned to the practical implications of the issue. He noted that the rapid expansion of internal improvements throughout the country stood opposed to the principles advocated by the Charles River Bridge. For the forty or fifty years preceding the Charles River Bridge case, states had chartered and expanded turnpike lines, often over the same line of travel, and, more recently, states had chartered railroads that at times rendered existing turnpikes useless or obsolete. The fact that the dispute over the Charles River Bridge was the first such case to come to the Supreme Court proved, in Taney's mind, that no one understood state-issued charters to imply a grant of exclusive rights. Should such a doctrine become law, moreover, all of the nation's progress and advancement would suddenly be subject to litigation. "Let it once be understood that such charters carry with them these implied contracts, and give this unknown and undefined property in a line of traveling, and you will soon find the old turnpike corporations awakening from their sleep," Taney wrote, "and calling upon this court to put down the improvement which have taken their place" (36 U.S. 420, 552–553). A sudden explosion of such cases would jeopardize the nation's steady progress with regard to public works. "We shall be thrown back to the improvements of the last century, and obliged to stand still until the claims of the old turnpike corporations shall be satisfied," Taney warned (36 U.S. 420, 553). Sounding the theme of judicial restraint, the chief justice implied that the Court had neither the right nor the power to resolve disputes about matters such as the width of lines of travel supposedly granted by corporate charters. State legislatures, rather than judges, ought to make policies on the basis of the best interests of their communities. By ruling in this way, Taney placed the Court on the side of economic development and technological advancement at the same time that he affirmed Jacksonian principles of popular government and the public good.

In a lengthy dissent joined by Justice Smith Thompson, Justice Joseph Story sharply disagreed with Taney. Story claimed that the charter creating the Warren Bridge violated a contract between the state and the proprietors of the Charles River Bridge. Marshaling an array of precedents in support of his position, Story portrayed himself as the protector of ancient common law principles. "I stand upon the old law," Story proclaimed, "upon law established more than three centuries ago, . . . in resisting any such encroachments upon the rights and liberties of the citizens, secured by public grants. I will not consent to shake their title deeds by any speculative niceties or novelties." Story dismissed Taney's emphasis on the societal benefits of the new bridge. These were mere "niceties or novelties," unrelated to the fundamental legal issues at stake. Story directly challenged Taney's interpretation of the Charles River Bridge's charter by arguing that the 1785 charter ought to be viewed as analogous to a private contract. The state granted to the Charles River Bridge Company an exclusive right to operate a bridge in exchange for the benefits that such a bridge would generate for the public. Story thus portrayed the dispute as involving the vested rights of the Charles River Bridge Company—rights that needed protection, if contracts were to be enforced and capitalism to be preserved.

In the same way that Taney included in his opinion a dire prediction about the consequences of siding with the Charles River Bridge, Story proved equally compelling in his explanation of the economic implications of the majority's opinion. "[I]f at the moment of granting the charter the Legislature had said to the proprietors—you shall build the bridge; you shall bear the burdens; you shall be bound by the charges; and your sole reimbursement shall be from the tolls of forty years; and yet we will not ever guaranty you any certainty of receiving any tolls. On the contrary," Story continued, "we reserve to ourselves the full power and authority to erect other bridges, toll or free bridges, according to our own free will and pleasure, contiguous to yours, and having the same termini with yours; and if you are successful we may thus supplant you, divide, destroy your profits, and annihilate your tolls, without annihilating your burdens." If such had been the nature of the grant, Story asked, "is there a man living of ordinary discretion or prudence, who would have accepted such a charter upon such terms?" (36 U.S. 420, 615). Although Story's reasoning laid bare the main weakness in the majority's opinion, his argument also showed that on some level the two justices agreed on the need for promoting economic development. Taney thought that economic progress came through giving state legislatures a free hand to promote the public good, whereas Story believed that only with adequate protection of private investments would capitalists feel confident in investing in public enterprises. Both opinions rested on the assumption that economic development created a better society.

Still, the disagreement between Taney and Story was a significant one. In the simplest terms, Story's position represented the past, for he articulated the same views that the Marshall Court had championed during the previous three decades. The most significant Contract Clause decision rendered by the Marshall Court had come in *Dartmouth College v. Woodward* (1819), in which the justices had thwarted New Hampshire's attempts to alter the charter of Dartmouth College by bringing it under state control. Like Marshall in *Dartmouth College*, Story viewed state-issued charters as private contracts, the sanctity of which was essential to protecting investments and creating a stable economy. Taney's perspective, in contrast, represented the tenor of the times. Most Americans during the Jacksonian era favored a competitive economic order in which the public interest, rather than private rights, took precedence. Taney's opinion departed from the *Dartmouth College* interpretation of the Contract Clause and fashioned a new legal doctrine. The idea of "creative destruction," defined by one legal scholar as "a continuous process whereby new inventions and enterprises create new goods and services and . . . destroy existing ones," later grew out of Taney's opinion and became an important principle in American constitutional development (Kutler 1971, 160). Apart from the doctrinal differences evident in the contrasting opinions, Story's passionate dissent illustrated his pessimism about the future of the Court and its interpretation of the Constitution. "[T]he old constitutional doctrines are fast fading away," he wrote to a colleague "and a change has come over the public mind from which I augur little good" (Warren 1928, 28). The willingness of the Court's senior justice to break with the majority also showed the fissures on the Court that marked the Taney era. Whereas Marshall had succeeded remarkably in crafting unanimous majority opinions, Taney would prove less successful in this regard. The relative harmony and unanimity of an earlier time had come to an end.

Within weeks of the *Charles River Bridge* decision, the Taney Court handed down its ruling in *Briscoe v. Commonwealth Bank of Kentucky* (1837), another case with important ramifications for business activity in which the justices were divided. *Briscoe* involved Article I, Section 10's prohibition of states from "coin[ing] money" and "emit[ing] Bills of Credit." Under this provision, states were forbidden to "make any Thing but gold and silver Coin a Tender in Payment of Debts." Hoping to protect creditors from state policies that promoted inflation and assisted debtors, the framers essentially sought to prohibit states from issuing paper money. As the republic expanded, financial policies evolved and the exact definition of state-issued "bills of credit" became subject to debate. In 1830, the Marshall Court dealt with this question in *Craig v. Missouri*, in which a four-justice majority deemed state-issued paper money unconstitutional. That case involved the refusal of debtors to repay sums borrowed from the state in the form of loan certificates, on the grounds that these certificates constituted "bills of credit." *Briscoe* was similar. At issue was an attempt to avoid repayment of a debt incurred in borrowing state bank notes issued by the Bank of the Commonwealth of Kentucky. The bank—which was owned by the state and whose officers were chosen by the state—was intimately connected to the state; however, it acted officially in its own name, rather than that of Kentucky. Henry Clay, who argued the case for the bank, went to great lengths to distinguish the bank from the state. Because the bank and the state were distinct, he claimed, the bank's issuance of notes did not constitute a state emission of "bills of credit."

Although the facts in the case were similar to those in *Craig*, the Taney Court diverged from the recent precedent and upheld the constitutionality of the bank notes. Justice John McLean, writing for a six-justice majority, defined a bill of credit more narrowly than the Court had in *Craig*, in which it had basically held that all state-issued paper currency violated the Constitution. McLean instead argued that a bill of credit was "a paper issued by the sovereign power, containing a pledge of its faith, and designed to circulate as money" (36 U.S. 257, 314). This definition allowed him to pick up on Clay's distinction between the bank and the state. McLean, moreover, included a heavy dose of pragmatism in his opinion, given that a ruling that banned all paper money issued by state banks would prove disastrous for the nation's financial system. Such a doctrine "strikes a fatal blow against the State banks," he argued, "which have a capital of near four hundred millions of dollars and which supply almost the entire circulating medium of the country" (36 U.S. 257, 317). By 1837, President Jackson's dismantling of the national bank had made state banks the center of the nation's financial system, and the opinion in *Briscoe* reaffirmed the increased role of these institutions in the U.S. economy.

Justice Story, this time alone, again issued a powerful dissent. Story stood squarely on the Court's opinion in *Craig* and throughout invoked the name of the recently deceased Marshall in support of his position. Wondering why the Court was attempting again to define a bill of credit, since the Court had already done so in *Craig*, Story reiterated Marshall's broad definition—that a bill of credit constituted paper "intended to circulate through the community for its ordinary purposes as money" (36 U.S. 257, 329). Story made no distinction between money issued by a bank or by a state and argued that the only test to determine whether these notes violated the Constitution was whether they were "designed to circulate as currency." "All other tests which have hitherto been applied, and all other tests which can be applied," Story bluntly asserted, "will be illusory, and mere exercise of human ingenuity, to vary the prohibition and evade its force" (36 U.S. 257, 331). Believing this case to be of profound significance, Story concluded by defending his right to dissent, declaring the public's right to know the views of the Court's individual members, and again referring to the late Chief Justice Marshall. "Mr. Chief Justice Marshall is not here to speak for himself," Story observed, "and knowing full well the grounds of his opinion, in which I concurred, that this act is unconstitutional, I have felt an earnest desire to vindicate his memory from the imputation of rashness, or want of deep reflection. Had he been living, he would have spoken in the joint names of both of us" (36 U.S. 257, 350). As the Taney Court began to undo some of the work of the Marshall Court, Story thus clung tenaciously to the past.

If the decisions in *Charles River Bridge* and *Briscoe* seemed to confirm the worst fears about the Taney Court held by conservative champions of the old order, two subsequent cases involving contracts offered the Court's critics some reassurance. *Bank of Augusta v. Earle* (1839), which was argued along with *Bank of the United States v. Primrose* and *New Orleans and Carrollton Railroad v. Earle*, concerned the power of a corporation to make a contract outside the state in which it had been chartered. Alabama's constitution forbade the legislature from establishing any bank except one in which the state held part of the stock. This not only created a monopoly for the state in the banking industry, it also prompted Alabama businessmen—in the midst of the Panic of 1837—to claim that they need not pay debts owed to out-of-state banks. These banks, the debtors argued, had no right to conduct business in Alabama. In a circuit court opinion, Justice John McKinley, a states' rights Democrat, sided with the debtors and held that Alabama had prohibited foreign banking corporations from acting within the state. The economic implications of his decision were profound. As corporations throughout the country expanded their operations during this era, they increasingly conducted business across state lines. McKinley's circuit ruling, according to Justice Story, "frightened half the lawyers and all the corporations of the country out of their properties" (Warren 1928, 50). The decision potentially endangered the right of banks, insurance companies, or any corporation to contract or engage in interstate business.

McKinley's controversial opinion sparked much debate over the issue of corporate rights, and the U.S. Supreme Court agreed to hear an appeal. Daniel Webster argued the case for the banks and emphasized the notion of comity—the common law principle that binds each state to protect the rights and privileges of citizens of every other state. Webster claimed that the constitutional basis for comity lay in Article IV: "the citizens of each State shall be entitled to all privileges and immunities of citizens in the several States." Essential to Webster's argument was the idea that corporations could claim the rights of citizens, a controversial and somewhat novel claim. Leading lawyer Charles J. Ingersoll argued the case for the defendants. A staunch opponent of corporate power, Ingersoll rejected the notion of comity and contended that for a corporation to do business outside the state that chartered it, other states needed explicitly to allow such activity. The Constitution, rather than the idea of comity, he argued, defined the relationship of the states to each other, and he rejected Webster's claim that Article IV established the principle of comity in the United States and prevented states from enacting legislation restricting the activity of out-of-state corporations.

Writing for eight of the nine justices, Chief Justice Taney took a moderate stance on the issues presented. He agreed with Webster that a corporation could be understood as a "person," "for certain purposes in contemplation of law," and that the principles of comity applied to the states (38 U.S. 519, 588). "The intimate union of these States, as members of the same great political family; the deep and vital interests which bind them so closely together; should lead us, in the absence of proof to the contrary, to presume a greater degree of comity, and friendship, and kindness towards one another, than we should be authorized to presume between foreign nations," Taney wrote (38 U.S. 519, 590). The chief justice also took note of the fact that banks chartered in the several states frequently contracted and dealt with each other, and that the economic implications of the Court's decision could not be ignored. "These usages of commerce and trade have been so general and public, and have been practiced for so long a period of time, and so generally acquiesced in by the States," Taney argued, "that the court cannot overlook them when a question like the one before us is under consideration" (38 U.S. 519, 590–591). Still, Taney did not agree wholly with Webster's argument. The Court held that a state could exercise the power to regulate a corporation's activities within its borders, but that those regulations needed to be expressly stated in specific legislation. According to the Court, the state had done nothing to prevent out-of-state banks from operating in Alabama. As expected, Justice McKinley dissented from the ruling and argued that Alabama's law had restricted the activities of out-of-state banks. The majority decision put the nation's commercial community at ease and showed that the Taney Court did not have the strongly agrarian, states' rights orientation that many Whigs had feared. Justice Story praised Taney's opinion, declaring that "it does great honor to yourself as well as to the Court" (Schwartz 1993, 90).

Further adulation from commercial interests came with the Court's decision in *Bronson v. Kinzie* (1843). Like *Bank of Augusta*, this case involved state regulation of business transactions. In 1841, as a result of the financial panic that gripped the nation, a number of states enacted debtor relief laws. For its part, Illinois passed legislation limiting mortgage foreclosure sales. These regulations provided that a mortgagor's equity could not be lost for twelve months after a foreclosure sale and that no sale could occur unless two-thirds of the appraised value was bid for the property. The laws applied retrospectively—to mortgages made before the legislation was enacted. The state thus sought to assist debtors by restricting the ability of creditors to claim debtors' property. The constitutional question presented in the case was whether these laws "impaired the obligation of contracts" in violation of Article I, Section 10.

The Court held that the Illinois regulations were unconstitutional. In his majority opinion, Chief Justice Taney explained the extent to which a state could regulate contractual relationships. He noted that a state could legislate the manner in which the courts handled suits involving debts by, for example, exempting certain articles from the grasp of creditors. Even if such regulations made "the recovery of debts more tardy and difficult," they did not impair the obligation of the contract (42 U.S. 311, 316). "Whatever belongs merely to the remedy may be altered according to the will of the State," he summarized, "provided the alteration does not impair the obligation of the contract. But if that effect is produced, it is immaterial whether it is done by acting on the remedy or directly on the contract itself. In either case, it is prohibited by the Constitution" (42 U.S. 311, 316). Taney invoked the memory of the framers in praise of the Contract Clause. "[I]t would be unjust to the memory of the distinguished men who framed it, to suppose that it was designed to protect a mere barren and abstract right, without any practical operation upon the business of life," he argued. "It was undoubtedly adopted as a part of the Constitution for a great and useful purpose. It was to maintain the integrity of contracts, and to secure their faithful execution throughout the Union" (42 U.S. 311, 318). Taney's opinion, which made no reference to the nationwide financial panic and the plight of debtors, soothed the commercial community and again won the support of Justice Story, although he did not participate in the case.

The Court once more took the side of business interests in *Planters' Bank of Mississippi v. Sharp* (1848), a case involving state regulation of banking. In 1840, Mississippi enacted legislation banning the transfer of any bill or bank note. The state passed this law in order to enforce another state statute that required banks to accept their own notes for payment of debts. During the panic, many banks transferred notes that had depreciated in value to a third party. In this way, they could refuse to accept the less valuable notes as a form of payment. Public outcry against such banking practices spurred legislators to enact these regulations, and, when the Planters' Bank brought suit challenging the ban on transferring bank notes, the Mississippi Supreme Court upheld the law. When the Planter's Bank appealed, the U.S. Supreme Court had to decide whether the legislation impaired the obligation of contracts.

In the majority opinion, Justice Levi Woodbury held that the Mississippi bank regulation violated the Contract Clause. Arguing that the transfer of notes constituted part of the legitimate business of a bank, Woodbury proved unsympathetic to the state's attempts to interfere with such transactions. Banks, he wrote, "must be able to assign or sell those notes when necessary and proper, as, for instance, to procure more specie in an emergency, or return an unusual amount of deposits withdrawn, or pay large debts for a banking-house, and for any 'goods and effects' connected with banking which it may properly own" (47 U.S. 301, 323). The state law, he argued, not only violated the bank's original charter—which the Court considered a contract—it also interfered with the contractual relationship between the maker of the note and the bank. "[H]ere the duty imposed by the State to adhere to its own deliberate grant, and the duty imposed on the signer of the note to make payment to an assignee, as well as to the bank itself, are both interfered with and altered," the majority held (47 U.S. 301, 328). In dissent, Justice Peter V. Daniel argued vigorously in support of the state's power to impose such regulations on banks. Criticizing banks and corporations for abuses of power, Daniel deemed the majority opinion as "subversive of justice" (47 U.S. 301, 341).

Despite a decade of decisions protective of propertied and commercial interests, the Court issued a landmark decision that placed clear limits on the protection offered by the Contract Clause. In *West River Bridge v. Dix* (1848), the justices examined the question of a state's power of eminent domain and its implications for the obligation of contracts. Although the attorneys in the *Charles River Bridge* case had spent considerable time on this question, the Court had formulated no rule on the issue in that instance. The case of the West River Bridge thus provided an opportunity for the justices to revisit the issue nearly a decade later. In 1795, Vermont had incorporated a bridge company with exclusive rights to erect a bridge and collect tolls on traffic across the West River for 100 years. In 1839, well before the charter had expired, the state passed a law allowing county courts to take property for public use, provided that it offered just compensation to owners. Under the provisions of this law, proceedings soon began in the county in which the bridge lay to establish a free public road, of which the bridge would be a part. The county court assessed the value of the bridge franchise, took over the bridge, and awarded compensation to its owners. The bridge company then sued, and the Vermont Supreme Court affirmed the actions of the county court.

On appeal to the U.S. Supreme Court, the case attracted national attention. Despite defeat in defending the proprietors of the Charles River Bridge, Daniel Webster took up the cause of the West River Bridge. He argued that in the event of a conflict between the Contract Clause and a state's power of eminent domain, the Contract Clause occupied a superior position. In no way, he claimed, could a state impair the obligation of contracts through an exercise of its power to take property in the public interest. Webster pleaded with the Court to limit the state's power of eminent domain and expressed particular concern over how popularly elected state legislatures might choose to exercise such authority. "[A]s to the exercise of this power of eminent domain, the Legislature, or their agents, are to be the sole judges of what is to be taken, and to what public use it is to be appropriated, the most leveling ultraisms of Antirentism or Agrarianism or Abolitionism may be successfully advanced," he noted (47 U.S. 507, 521). Such statements no doubt reflected Webster's own conservative fears about democratic threats to rights of established property owners. In contrast, lawyers and partisans in support of Vermont's exercise of eminent domain grounded their arguments in the state's constitution, which provided that "private property ought to be subservient to public uses when necessity requires it" (47 U.S. 507, 522). But they also included a heavy dose of practical arguments in support of Vermont's actions. Lawyers cited the building of roads, canals, and railroads as all resulting from state exercises of eminent domain.

Justice Peter V. Daniel's majority opinion focused on the ideas of state sovereignty and the rights of the community. The power of eminent domain, he argued, was an inherent attribute of sovereignty that allowed states to legislate in the interest of the public. "[I]t cannot be justly disputed," he stated, "that in every political sovereign community there inheres necessarily the right and the duty of guarding its own existence, and of protecting and promoting the interests and welfare of the community at large" (47 U.S. 507, 531). In contrast to Webster's claim that the protection of private contracts held a superior constitutional position to eminent domain, Daniel took the opposite stance. The power of eminent domain, he argued, was "paramount to all private rights vested under the government, and these last are, by necessary implication, held in subordination to this power, and must yield in every instance to its proper exercise" (47 U.S. 507, 532). Daniel even thought it "somewhat strange" that any opposition would be raised against state construction of internal improvements, as "the whole policy of the country relative to roads, mills, bridges, and canals rests upon this single power" (47 U.S. 507, 533). Concluding the opinion, Daniel wrote that the Court found no reason to inquire into whether the compensation provided by the state in this instance was just and reasonable. Such matters rested with the states, not with the U.S. Supreme Court.

In a concurring opinion, Justice Woodbury agreed with the Court's decision in the case, based on the facts in this particular dispute. Still, he was unwilling to go along with the majority's sweeping statements about the superiority of the power of eminent domain. "If any property of any kind is not so situated as to be either in the direct path for a public highway, or be really needed to build it," Woodbury wrote, "the inclination of my mind is, that it cannot be taken against the consent of the owner. Because, though the right of eminent domain exists in some cases, it does not exist in all, nor as to all property, but probably, as to such property only as from its locality and fitness is necessary to the public use" (47 U.S. 507, 545). By rejecting Woodbury's standard, the Court gave broad powers to states under the principle of eminent domain. The decision won support from southern advocates of state sovereignty, as well as from Jacksonians who opposed corporate privilege, and it contributed to ongoing state efforts to expand internal improvements.

Later, in *Richmond, Fredericksburg, and Potomac Railroad Company v. Louisa Railroad Company* (1852), the Court built on the principles established in both *West River Bridge* and *Charles River Bridge.* Here the Court interpreted an 1834 Virginia charter granting the Richmond, Fredericksburg, and Potomac Railroad Company an exclusive right to carry passengers between Richmond and Fredericksburg for a period of thirty years. In 1848, well within the thirty-year duration of the charter, the state legislature provided for the establishment of the Louisa Railroad, which traversed a similar route while transporting coal and other freight. In a 4–3 decision, the Court held that the charter of the Louisa Railroad did not "impair the obligation of contracts." Taking his cue from *Charles River Bridge,* Justice Robert C. Grier took a narrow view of the Richmond, Fredericksburg, and Potomac Railroad Company's charter and quoted Chief Justice Taney's opinion to the effect that "the corporation can claim nothing but what is clearly given by the act" (54 U.S. 71, 81). Since the railroad company's charter pertained only to "transporting passengers," which the new railroad was not permitted to do between the two cities, the Court saw no reason to interfere with the state's effort to promote the public good. Citing *West River Bridge* with approval, Justice Grier noted that "the grant of a franchise is of no higher order, and confers no more sacred title, than a grant of land to an individual" (54 U.S. 71, 83). Under eminent domain, therefore, the state possessed the power to take a franchise, just as it could take any other form of property for the benefit of the public. The three dissenters noted that the Louisa Railroad would carry passengers along portions of the route between Richmond and Fredericksburg, a violation of the Richmond, Fredericksburg, and Potomac Railroad Company's original charter. Still, the majority ruling's interpretation of the Contract Clause made it clear that states retained extensive powers to regulate economic matters and to promote the public good.

In cases involving contracts and finance, the Taney Court produced a moderate and pragmatic record. Attempting to balance the often competing ideals of preserving state sovereignty, promoting the public good, and protecting contractual rights, the justices exhibited a flexibility that served well both the Court and the nation. Taney and his colleagues gave extensive powers to states when it came to fostering internal improvements and exercising the power of eminent domain. Yet, at the same time, the Court gave numerous assurances to investors that democratically elected legislatures could not overstep their bounds in their zeal to regulate and reform banking practices or creditor-debtor relations. Because the first years of Taney's chief justiceship coincided with a nationwide financial panic, the Court's disciplined decision making proved significant both in assisting the republic on a path toward economic prosperity and in helping the Court retain the respect of the American people.

The Legal Status of Corporations

By offering legal sanction to corporations to conduct business across state lines, the Court's decision in *Bank of Augusta v. Earle* (1839) led to a huge expansion in the number of corporations in the United States. As the number of such entities dramatically expanded during the 1840s and 1850s, the Court increasingly took up cases that involved the place of corporations in the nation's legal order. Although many of these disputes arose under the Contract Clause, others involved the issue of the rights of corporations—particularly whether they had the status of "citizens" to sue in federal courts. According to Article III, Section 2 of the Constitution, the jurisdiction of the federal courts includes disputes "between citizens of different states." This came to be known as the idea of "diversity of citizenship." Ever since 1809, when the Marshall Court issued its opinion in *Bank of the United States v. Deveaux*, the Court had upheld the notion that the citizenship status of a corporation constituted that of its shareholders. In other words, in order for a corporation to sue or be sued in federal court on the basis of diversity jurisdiction, all of its shareholders had to reside in a state other than that of the other party involved in the suit.

The Taney Court first confronted the question of whether corporations could have access to federal courts in *Commercial and Railroad Bank of Vicksburg v. Slocumb* (1840). A year earlier, Congress had expanded federal court jurisdiction to include cases involving multiple parties from different states, even though some of the parties might be from the same state. Many lawyers believed that this act had opened the federal courts to corporations whose members resided in different states, even if some members of the corporation resided in the same state as the plaintiffs. Despite this new legislation, in *Slocumb* the justices relied on the authority of *Bank of the United States v. Deveaux* and upheld the existing strict standard regarding jurisdiction. The Court unanimously concluded in *Slocumb* that only complete diversity of citizenship—when all members of a corporation resided in states other than that of the plaintiff—would permit suits involving corporations in federal courts.

Just four years later, the Court revisited this issue in the case of *Louisville v. Letson.* This complicated dispute involved Thomas Letson, a citizen of New York, and the Louisville, Cincinnati, and Charleston Railroad Company, a South Carolina corporation. Of course, had all the stockholders in the corporation been South Carolinians, the jurisdiction of the federal court in which the case was originally heard would have been unquestioned. However, since two of the corporation's stockholders resided in North Carolina and because the Bank of Charleston—some of whose stockholders were New York residents—held stock in the company, the question of federal jurisdiction was a convoluted one. The suit demonstrated the need for a clear statement on this important jurisdictional issue.

With three justices not participating and one justice having died, five members of the Court voted unanimously to eliminate the residency restrictions that had limited corporate access to federal tribunals. Where the stockholders of the corporation resided, the Court concluded in *Letson*, was irrelevant. "The corporators as individuals are not defendants in the suit," Justice James Wayne reasoned, "but they are parties having an interest in the result. . . . It may be said that the suit is against the corporation, and that nothing must be looked at but the legal entity, and then that we cannot view the members except as an artificial aggregate" (43 U.S. 497, 554). Forced to confront precedents to the contrary, Wayne simply stated that previous cases had been wrongly decided and that the justices had regretted making those rulings. He singled out *Bank of the United States v. Deveaux* in particular as a case "not . . . entirely satisfactory to the Court" and announced that the late Chief Justice Marshall had "repeatedly expressed regret" about the Court's decisions on this matter (43 U.S. 497, 555). In addition to overturning the Court's recent ruling in *Slocumb*—which, Wayne stated, the justices had decided solely on the basis on precedent and with great reluctance—the decision in *Letson* settled the matter of the residency and citizenship status of corporations and thus provided them access to federal courts. "When the corporation exercises its powers in the State which chartered it," Wayne summarized, "that is its residence, and such an averment is sufficient to give the circuit courts jurisdiction" (43 U.S. 497, 559). The *Letson* decision, by allowing federal lawsuits by corporations, augmented the place of the federal courts in American life, led to the development of a body of corporate law, and facilitated the growth of business corporations.

But *Letson* was not the last case in which the Court would address the issue. Less than a decade later, the rule established in *Letson* came under fire from the Court's southern agrarian members. In *Rundle v. Delaware and Raritan Canal Company* (1853), Justice Peter V. Daniel of Virginia, who had been absent when the Court issued its opinion in *Letson*, charged in a dissent that only a natural person could claim the rights of citizenship under the Constitution. "When distributing the judicial power, that article [III] extends it to controversies between citizens of different States. This must mean the natural physical beings composing those separate communities, and can, by no violence of interpretation, be made to signify artificial, incorporeal, theoretical, and invisible creations," Daniel asserted. "A corporation, therefore, being not a natural person, but a mere creature of the mind, invisible and tangible, cannot be a citizen of a State, or of the United States . . . and can therefore neither plead nor be impleaded in the courts of the United States" (55 U.S. 80, 98). Although he had constituted part of the majority in the *Letson* decision, Justice John

Catron of Tennessee joined Daniel in criticizing the Court's conferring of citizenship status on corporations. In arguing that the residency of a corporation's president and director ought to determine the question of jurisdiction, Catron seemed to reiterate the standard that had existed prior to the *Letson* decision.

These dissenting opinions in *Rundle* foreshadowed continued debate among the justices on the issue. Later that same term, in fact, the Court again confronted the matter in *Marshall v. Baltimore and Ohio Railroad Company* (1854). Here the justices engaged in spirited debate over whether a corporation could claim the right of a citizen to sue and be sued in federal courts. The majority opinion, written by Justice Grier, attempted to settle the issue once and for all. Grier's decision contained an extensive review of the Court's previous ruling on federal court jurisdiction with regard to corporations. Noting that none of the justices had dissented in *Letson*, Grier described that ruling as having been "received by the bar as a final settlement of the questions which have so frequently arisen under this clause of the Constitution" (57 U.S. 314, 325). He then proceeded to describe the nature of a corporation and its economic and legal relationship with others. Although Grier acknowledged a corporation as merely an "artificial person" in the abstract sense, he noted that when individual engaged in contracts with corporations, they dealt with real human beings. "[A] citizen who has made a contract, and has a controversy with a corporation . . . did not deal with a mere metaphysical abstraction, but with natural persons. . . . [H]is contract was made with them as the legal representatives of numerous unknown associates, or secret and dormant partners" (57 U.S. 314, 327). The modern market economy required that the numerous stockholders of a corporation be represented in this way. The fact that these individuals collectively organized into a corporation was no reason to deny their basic rights, nor those of any who might choose to sue them. "It is not reasonable that those who deal with such persons [as corporations]," Grier argued, "should be deprived of a valuable privilege by a syllogism, or rather sophism, which deals subtly with words and names, without regard to the things or persons they are used to represent." Opening the federal courts to suits involving corporations, Grier concluded, protected the rights of corporations as well as plaintiffs.

The three dissenters in the cases—Daniel, Catron, and the recently arrived Justice John A. Campbell—took issue with the majority's reasoning. Relying on precedents before *Letson*—especially *Bank of the United States v. Deveaux*—that denied corporations the right to sue in federal courts, the dissenters maintained that corporations could never be given the legal standing of citizens. Daniel's dissent was particularly caustic. After repeating many of the arguments he had made in *Rundle*, Daniel attacked the majority for their faulty reasoning as well as for their indifference to the meaning of the Constitution and the intent of its framers. "It is indeed a sad symptom of the downward progress of political morals, when any appeal to the Constitution shall fail to 'give us pause,' and to suggest the necessity of solemn reflection," Daniel lamented. "Still more fearful is the prevalence of the disposition, either in or out of office, to meet the honest or scrupulous devotion to its commands with a sneer, as folly unsuited to the times, and condemned by that new-born wisdom which measures the Constitution by its superior and infallible standard of policy and convenience" (57 U.S. 314, 345–346). Knowing that his attempts to halt the expansion of corporations went against the tenor of the times, Daniel thus made an appeal to the spirit of the framers and to a literal reading of the text of the Constitution. The dissents in *Marshall v. Baltimore and Ohio Railroad Company* showed the deep divisions among the justices in their attitudes toward corporations.

A case decided the following year demonstrated the justices' continued disagreement on questions of corporate power. *Piqua Branch of the State Bank of Ohio v. Knoop* (1854) presented the issue of whether a legislature could change the extent to which and the way in which taxes were levied on corporations. In 1845, the state of Ohio passed a statute making banks subject to a 6 percent tax on their profits; under the law, banks would be exempt from all other state taxes. Six years later, the legislature enacted new legislation that subjected banks to the same tax on property to which all individuals in the state were subject. After the Ohio Supreme Court upheld the 1851 tax, the U.S. Supreme Court heard the case. The dispute posed the question of whether the original banking law constituted a contract that could not be altered by future legislatures.

By a 6–3 vote, the Court held that the 1845 banking legislation did constitute a contract and that the subsequent tax on banks violated the Contract Clause of the Constitution. In the majority opinion, Justice John McLean distinguished between municipal (public) corporations and private corporations. "A municipal corporation, in which is vested some portion of the administration of government, may be changed at the will of the legislature." McLean explained. "But a bank, where the stock is owned by individuals, is a private corporation" (57 U.S. 369, 380). The private nature of the investments in the bank meant that lawmakers' attempts to establish rules for such institutions took on the status of a contract. McLean, moreover, rejected the claim that a state's taxing power was an essential attribute of state sovereignty, as the Court had held with regard to eminent domain in *West River Bridge v. Dix* (1848). Rather, he contended, "the exemption of property from taxation is a question of policy and not of power" (57 U.S. 369, 384). Because every government hoped to establish a "sound currency," bankers and investors needed guarantees from the state that taxing policies with regard to banks would not change at the whim of the legislature. "To establish such institutions as shall meet the public wants and secure the public confidence, inducements must be held out to capitalists to invest their funds," he wrote. "They must know the rate of interest to be charged by the Bank, the time the charter shall run, the liabilities of the company, the rate of taxation, and other privileges necessary to a successful banking operation" (57 U.S. 369, 384). When a state established the terms and conditions under which banking was to be conducted, a legislature made a contract with investors—a contract that could not be violated by a future legislative body.

Once more, the southern dissenters took issue with the majority's view of state regulation of corporations. Justice Daniel expressed his belief that the Court lacked jurisdiction in the case, and Justices Catron and Campbell both wrote extensive dissents. Citing the *West River Bridge* decision, Catron discussed the state's taxing power as analogous to eminent domain—as an essential element of state sovereignty. "The sovereign political power," he concluded, "is not the subject of contract so as to be vested in an irrepealable charter of incorporation, and taken away from, and placed beyond the reach of, future Legislatures" (57 U.S. 369, 404). Campbell's opinion, which relied on a host of federal and state court precedents, addressed the interpretation of charters, the taxing power, and the attributes of sovereignty. He reached the same conclusion as Catron. The power of a state to regulate or tax banks "is not properly a matter for bargain or barter, but the enactment is in the exercise of sovereign power, comprehending within its scope every individual interest in the state" (57 U.S. 369, 415). The southern dissenters thus viewed the case as a dispute between a state's power to legislate in the public interest versus the protection of private corporate interests.

During the same term as *Knoop*, the Court adjudicated another Ohio dispute involving the same 1851 tax on banks. In this case, *Ohio Life Insurance and Trust Company v. DeBolt* (1854), banks chartered before the 1845 law that had exempted banks from most state taxes brought suit against the 1851 banking legislation. These older institutions as well claimed that their contractual rights had been violated by the tax. This time the majority of the justices held that the tax did not violate the Contract Clause—nothing in their charters, according to Taney, granted them specific exemptions from taxation—but the justices remained as divided as ever on the issues. The six justices in the majority took a variety of positions, and the significance of the case lies more in the reasoning and rhetoric they employed than in the actual holding. The language of Justice Catron, for example, who had originally voted with the majority in *Letson* in 1844 in favor of granting corporations the legal status of citizens, showed the extent to which he had come to adopt a negative view of corporate power. Catron warned of the "unparalleled increase of corporations throughout the Union within the last few years; the ease with which charters, containing exclusive privileges and exemptions are obtained; the vast amount of property, power and exclusive benefits, that are vested in and held by these numerous bodies of associated wealth." Such boldly stated sentiments showed that Jacksonian political ideals influenced constitutional debates through the middle of the nineteenth century. Before the slavery issue transformed the political landscape, opposition to special privileges constituted an important part of American political and constitutional thought.

The culmination of the Court's pre–Civil War rulings regarding corporations came in *Dodge v. Woolsey* (1855), a third case dealing with the taxation of banks in Ohio. After the filing of the original Piqua Branch suit, which questioned the constitutional validity of the 1851 legislation repealing the tax exemption for banks, the state of Ohio amended its constitution by inserting a repeal clause. In other words, legislators hoped to blunt any legal opposition to the repeal of the tax exemption by sanctioning such a measure in the Ohio constitution. After passage of the amendment, the legislature enacted new legislation in 1852 imposing a tax on the property of banks. After deciding the *Piqua Branch* case, the Supreme Court heard a challenge to the validity of this legislation, again on the grounds that the exemption repeal violated the Contract Clause of the U.S. Constitution.

Justice Wayne's majority opinion, which represented the views of six of the justices, addressed a number of broad constitutional questions, including the scope of judicial power and the sovereignty of states. As the defense counsel had wanted to know how much sovereignty a state could possibly retain were the Court to sustain its jurisdiction in the case, Wayne devoted much of the opinion to a discussion of this foundational question of American constitutionalism. To Wayne and the other justices in the majority, the formation of the Union required that states surrender a portion of their sovereignty for the sake of the republic. "In such a union," Wayne wrote, "the States are bound by all of those principles of justice which bind individuals to their contracts. They are bound by their mutual acquiescence in the powers of the Constitution, that neither of them should be the judge, or should be allowed to be the final judge of the powers of the Constitution, or of the interpretation of the laws of Congress" (59 U.S. 331, 351). Any claim on behalf of the state, in other words, that its constitutional repeal of the tax exemption removed the dispute from the purview of the U.S. Supreme Court was contrary to basic constitutional principles. Wayne argued forcefully for the supremacy of the U.S. Supreme Court in matters of constitutional interpretation. Without the Court, he claimed, "neither the Constitution nor the laws of Congress passed in pursuance of it, nor treaties, would be in practice or in fact the supreme law of the land" (59 U.S. 331, 355). Only the Supreme Court, Wayne contended, could settle differences that existed between the governments of the states and that of the United States.

Having gone to great lengths to establish the authority of the nation's highest judicial tribunal, Wayne's majority opinion decisively stated the Court's ruling. Even though the people of Ohio had amended their constitution to end the tax exemption for banks, the 1852 tax legislation—enacted after the amending of the state constitution—violated the Contract Clause of the U.S. Constitution. "A change of constitution cannot release a State from contracts made under a constitution which permits them to be made," Wayne wrote. "The moral obligations never die. If broken by states and nations, though the terms of reproach are not the same with which we are accustomed to designate the faithlessness of individuals, the violation of justice is not the less" (59 U.S. 331, 360). Thus, the Court held that the Contract Clause sheltered the state's banks from Ohio's attempt to impose taxes, and for the first time in history, the justices ruled that a state constitutional provision violated the Constitution of the United States.

Not surprisingly, Campbell, Catron, and Daniel again took issue with the majority. Campbell penned an elaborate dissent, with which Daniel agreed entirely and Catron with its "conclusions." Reiterating earlier debates over the rights of corporations, Campbell again maintained that corporations had no rights as citizens to sue in federal courts. He blasted the majority's ruling by comparing its ideas about property and contracts to the traditional status of landholding in the Turkish Empire. But Campbell reserved his harshest rhetoric for the Court's arrogant assertion of its own power. "The inquiry recurs, have the people of Ohio deposited with this tribunal the authority to overrule their own judgment upon the extent of their own powers over institutions created by their own government . . . ?" (59 U.S. 331, 374). Denying that the Supreme Court even had jurisdiction over the matter, Campbell announced that he felt "no anxiety nor apprehension in leaving to the people of Ohio a 'complete power' over their government, and all the institutions and establishments it has called into existence" (59 U.S. 331, 380). The dissenters favored permitting the state to impose the bank tax.

If many of the Court's early decisions in the area of contracts and finance exhibited moderation and pragmatism, the justices' later rulings on the rights and status of corporations—many of which also involved the Contract Clause—demonstrated a bias in favor of this new and important form of business organization. In part because of these mid–nineteenth-century precedents, corporations came to wield enormous power in U.S. life during the three decades after the Civil War. The Court's willingness to grant access to the federal courts on the basis of diversity of citizenship allowed corporations to achieve a national reach, and the Ohio bank decisions proved to be the earliest examples of the Supreme Court's willingness to confer rights on business interests on the basis of the constitutional protection of contracts.

Separation of Powers

The constitutional allocation of powers among the three branches of the national government—the executive, legislative, and judicial—lay at the heart of some of the most significant decisions of the Taney era. Other than the many Marshall Court rulings that had established the jurisdiction and power of the federal judiciary, the Supreme Court had few occasions to address such matters during the years before Taney's arrival. In general, the nation's first six presidents—with the exception of Thomas Jefferson—had treaded cautiously in carrying out the constitutional powers of their office. But during Andrew Jackson's two tumultuous terms, the place of the presidency in U.S. public life expanded to an unprecedented degree. Hailed by his supporters as a bold leader and derided by his detractors as a dangerous despot, Jackson used the presidential veto, the power of appointment, and the force of his personality as no president before him ever had. In contrast to the Marshall Court's claim of judicial review, Jackson espoused the departmental theory of government, which held that all three branches of the government possessed the right to determine the constitutionality of legislation. As president, Jackson asserted, he had as much authority to decide whether an act was constitutional as the Court had. The Age of Jackson thus ushered in new controversies over presidential authority as well as the larger question of the relationship among the three branches of government. By the end of the Taney era, the Civil War augmented these questions as the president, Congress, and the Court worked in an uneasy alliance against the Confederate States of America.

The first case of the Taney period that pertained to the separation of powers, *Kendall v. United States ex rel. Stokes* (1838), arose from Postmaster General Amos Kendall's refusal to obey a federal circuit court order. Charging that it was tainted by political favoritism, Kendall declined to honor a contract that had been negotiated by the previous postmaster with the firm Stockton and Stokes. Congress subsequently ordered the solicitor of the treasury to adjust the claims, and when he ruled that the contract ought to be enforced by Kendall, the postmaster again declined to honor the agreement. The fact that the solicitor was a friend of the plaintiffs only deepened the partisan animosity evident in this dispute. The federal circuit court for the District of Columbia intervened by issuing a writ of mandamus ordering Kendall to fulfill the terms of the contract. Because Kendall had been appointed by Jackson to reform the post office (and to terminate some of the questionable practices of the previous postmaster), the case assumed the form of a conflict between the executive and judicial branches. Kendall presumably acted on Jackson's orders, and the president viewed the federal circuit court order as a direct challenge to the ordinary operation of the executive branch. Indeed, Kendall's attorney claimed before the Supreme Court that the court order unconstitutionally infringed on the powers of the executive.

A unanimous majority, with Justice Smith Thompson writing the opinion, sternly rebuked the former president (Jackson left office in 1837) and his postmaster. Thompson deemed Kendall's duty to honor the contract to be "of a mere ministerial character" and not subject to the control of the president (37 U.S. 524, 610). The majority particularly took issue with the postmaster's claim that he answered to Jackson alone, since the chief executive possessed the constitutional authority to enforce the laws. "This is a doctrine that cannot receive the sanction of this Court," Thompson wrote. "It would be vesting in the president a dispensing power which has no countenance for its support in any part of the Constitution, and is asserting a principle which, if carried out in its results to all cases falling within it, would be clothing the president with a power entirely to control the legislation of Congress, and paralyze the administration of justice" (37 U.S. 524, 613). Although the justices agreed on these basic questions pertaining to the separation of powers and the upholding of the contract, they disagreed about the authority of the circuit court to issue the writ of mandamus. A six-justice majority affirmed the power of the circuit court to issue the writ under the Judiciary Act of 1801, while three dissenters—Taney, Barbour, and Catron, Jackson's closest friends on the Court—argued that the circuit court lacked this authority under the statute.

Although Kendall lost the case and made the payment to Stockton and Stokes, the fight continued. At the urging of Kendall, who continued serving as postmaster general after Jackson left office, President Martin Van Buren called attention to the Court's decision and asked Congress to withdraw from the D.C. Circuit Court the power to issue writs of mandamus to executive officials. However, such legislation failed to pass both houses of Congress. Stockton and Stokes again brought suit against Kendall, this time for damages for the delay in the government's payment of what it had owed them. While the suit was pending, Kendall resigned his position as postmaster general to run Van Buren's 1840 reelection campaign. With partisan passions at their peak, a jury convicted Kendall and ordered him to pay $11,000 in damages. (The judge in the case had instructed the jury that Kendall could be held personally liable for his official acts if he had not acted in good faith.) Although a legal maneuver by his lawyer allowed Kendall a new trial, he again lost in court. It took another decision by the U.S. Supreme Court—*Kendall v. Stokes* (1845), in which the justices held that Stockton and Stokes had already received their remedy in the form of the initial writ of mandamus and could not subsequently sue for damages—to bring the dispute to an end.

Questions about the powers of the executive relative to the other branches of government were not the only separation of powers issues that confronted the Court. In a landmark case, *Luther v. Borden* (1849), the Court considered its own authority to issue rulings on matters deemed to be "political" in nature. Although the Marshall Court had vastly expanded the powers of the Supreme Court during the first three decades of the nineteenth century, there were limits to judicial power. Marshall himself thought so. In *Foster and Elam v. Neilson* (1829), for example, Marshall had deferred to Congress in a land dispute over whether a portion of West Florida belonged to Spain or the United States. In a dissenting opinion in *Rhode Island v. Massachusetts* (1838), a boundary dispute case between the two states, Taney took Marshall's judicial self-restraint a step further. "[T]he powers given to the courts of the United States by the Constitution are judicial powers," Taney asserted, "and extend to those subject, only, which are judicial in character, and not to those which are political" (37 U.S. 657, 752). Denying that the suit in question was a justiciable matter, Taney argued that the Court ought not issue a ruling in the case. "Contests for rights of sovereignty and jurisdiction between states over any particular territory, are not, in my judgment, the subjects of judicial cognizance and control, to be recovered and enforced in an ordinary suit," Taney wrote, "and are, therefore, not within the grant of judicial power contained in the Constitution" (37 U.S. 657, 753).

Taney fully developed this notion of nonjusticiable political questions in *Luther v. Borden*. This case arose out of the 1842 Dorr Rebellion in Rhode Island, a popular revolutionary movement aimed at dismantling the state's existing government. Longstanding constitutional problems lay at the heart of the rebellion. The state's constitution at the time was essentially the same as its original charter, granted by King Charles II, of England, in 1663. As Rhode Island industrialized and urbanized, this antiquated founding document failed to serve the demands of an increasingly democratically minded populace. Under the state constitution, power remained in the hands of rural areas at the expense of the expanding cities, and suffrage rights were accorded only to those who owned land. The document, moreover, lacked a bill of rights, failed to provide for the independence of the judiciary, and outlined no amendment process. When several efforts to reform the constitution failed during the 1830s, patrician reformer Thomas Dorr and his followers took drastic steps. After calling their own constitutional convention in 1841, the Dorrites established a rival government that claimed to rule in the name of the people. In June 1842, after the would-be government of Rhode Island failed in an attempt to take over the state arsenal, the militia—under the control of the established government—brought an end to the bloodless revolution. Imposing martial law and employing indiscriminate searches and mass arrests, Rhode Island authorities squelched the popular reform movement. Later that year, a Dorrite shoemaker named Martin Luther, whose home had been ransacked, brought a suit for trespass in federal circuit court against Luther Borden, a state militiaman. Luther based his case on the claim that the Dorr government was the legitimate government of the state of Rhode Island, and that Borden's violation of his home constituted a private act lacking legal authority. A jury in a federal circuit court rejected this argument and decided in favor of the legitimacy of the original government.

By the time the Supreme Court heard the appeal, in 1848, the questions presented in the case were practically moot. Five years earlier, Rhode Island had reformed its constitution and expanded suffrage rights. Only the theoretical matter of whether the people of a state retained a right to replace their government remained at issue. Over a period of six days, some of the nation's leading attorneys argued the case. Benjamin F. Hallet and U.S. Attorney General Nathan Clifford (later a Supreme Court justice) made the case for Luther, and John Whipple and Daniel Webster spoke for Borden and the established government. Hallet and Clifford claimed that the actions of the Dorr movement were consistent with the fundamental political and constitutional principles of the United States. Relying on the ideals outlined in the Declaration of Independence, Hallet and Clifford argued that the sovereign people institute governments and possess the right to alter or abolish them. The idea that legislation was necessary to change the government stood opposed to these republican precepts. Arguing for Rhode Island's established government, Whipple and Webster took the conservative Whig position regarding the notion of popular sovereignty. They emphasized the need for legal, legitimate change rather than mass revolutionary activity. Webster's most important contention concerned not abstract political theory, but the Court's jurisdiction in the case. The nation's foremost lawyer and orator claimed that determining the legitimate government of Rhode Island was not a proper judicial question for the Supreme Court. The state legislature determined the legitimacy of a state's constitution, and, under the U.S. Constitution, only the president and Congress possessed the power to intervene in a state's affairs, so as to guarantee that a state maintain a "republican form of government." The judicial branch, Webster argued, had no role in the process.

Chief Justice Taney agreed with Webster. Realizing the seriousness of the issues before the Court, Taney wondered aloud about the actual consequences of the Court declaring the established government of Rhode Island illegitimate. If the originally chartered government "had been annulled by the adoption of the opposing government, then the laws passed by its Legislature during that time were nullities; its taxes wrongfully collected; its salaries and compensation to its officers illegally paid; its public accounts improperly settled; and the judgments and sentences of its courts in civil and criminal cases null and void, and the officers who carried their decisions into operation answerable as trespassers, if not in some cases as criminals" (48 U.S. 1, 39). In part because of the far-reaching ramifications of such a decision, Taney concurred with Webster's suggestion that the matter was left to the other branches of government. According to Taney, state legislatures—not state courts—had always decided the legitimacy of a state's constitution. Rhode Island's high court had thus deferred the matter to the state legislature, and Taney's majority opinion took the same position. Federal courts, he argued, had no more right to decide such questions than state courts. "Undoubtedly the courts of the United States have certain powers under the Constitution and laws of the United States which do not belong to the State courts," he wrote. "But the power of determining that a state government has been lawfully established, which the courts of the state disown and repudiate, is not one of them" (48 U.S. 1, 40). The Court's refusal to venture into such matters marked the formulation of the "political questions doctrine," the idea that some issues are not appropriate for judicial resolution.

The majority opinion in *Luther v. Borden* also contained the Supreme Court's first interpretation of the Guarantee Clause of the Constitution. Followers of Dorr had relied on Article IV, Section 4, which states, "The United States shall guarantee to every State in this Union a Republican Form of Government." Webster argued that this clause had nothing to do with the judiciary and that only Congress and executive had the power to enforce this requirement on the states. Here, too, Taney agreed with Webster's position. "Under this article of the Constitution it rests with Congress to decide what government is the established one in a state," Taney wrote. "And when the senators and representatives of a state are admitted into the councils of the Union, the authority of the government under which they are appointed, as well as its republican character, is recognized by the proper constitutional authority. And its decision is binding on every other department of the government, and could not be questioned in a judicial tribunal" (48 U.S. 1, 42). In a dissenting opinion, Justice Levi Woodbury agreed that the matter was "not within our constitutional jurisdiction" but took issue with the majority's decision upholding Rhode Island's imposition of martial law (48 U.S. 1, 51).

Luther v. Borden ranks among the most significant decisions of the Taney era. On the one hand, the opinion constitutes one of the most important early examples of judicial self-restraint in the history of the Supreme Court. Many Democrats sympathetic to the Dorrites had hoped that the justices—themselves nearly all Democrats—would legitimize the actions of the Rhode Island reformers. The justices' refusal to do so demonstrated the Court's independence and neutrality in a politically charged atmosphere. On the other hand, in reality the Court had little room to maneuver in the case. A decision favorable to the Dorrites, years after the rebellion and after peaceful reform had occurred in the state, would have created innumerable problems in Rhode Island and brought political condemnation upon the Court. Had the Court overturned the state's constitution, the justices would in effect have nullified the reforms that had occurred in Rhode Island, as well as the policies pursued by President John Tyler during the Dorr Rebellion. (Tyler had supported the original government and offered the support of federal troops, although they were unnecessary.) The Court thus made the decision that it needed to make. Rhode Island's reformed government remained intact, the Court showed that it could rise above politics, and the justices wisely enunciated a new constitutional doctrine that prevented them from managing states' domestic affairs.

The Taney Court's other significant ruling regarding the separation of powers came during the Civil War. In April 1861, after the outbreak of hostilities at Fort Sumter, President Abraham Lincoln made the decision to blockade the major ports of the Confederate states. Congress was not in session at the time of the order, but in July it authorized the president to declare a state of insurrection, and in August it approved all of Lincoln's previous military actions. Under the blockade order, a variety of suits involving naval seizures of contraband came before federal district courts and, later, on appeal, before the Supreme Court. Collectively these were known as the *Prize Cases* (1863). Although the facts and circumstances varied widely among these disputes, all of the cases raised the issue of the relative powers of the president and Congress during wartime as well as the nature of the conflict between the Union and the Confederacy. Because these matters were very much intertwined, the *Prize Cases* posed a potential political minefield for the president. To put it simply, the existing rules of international and prize law implied that Lincoln's authority to wage war as commander in chief of the nation's armed forces depended on the sovereignty of the Confederacy, which the Lincoln administration refused to recognize. Conversely, a ruling that the war constituted a mere domestic insurrection threatened the president's legal power to blockade southern ports. Thus, the power of the president and the sovereignty of the Confederacy were both at issue.

For twelve days, lawyers on opposing sides debated these questions before the Court's nine justices, including three recent Lincoln appointees. Counsel for the owners of the vessels at the time of their capture argued against the president's power to blockade southern ports, and attorneys on the other side—representing either the claimants of the prizes or the U.S. government—took an expansive view of presidential power. James Carlisle, a prominent Washington lawyer who argued for the owners of the seized vessels, rested much of his argument on the fact that Congress had not declared war against the Confederate States at the time of the blockade order. Because it had not done so, a state of war—in a legal sense—did not exist. Without a state of war, a blockade could not be legitimate, especially since congressional authorization came after the president's actions. The president could not exceed his constitutional authority simply on the basis of necessity or emergency, Carlisle claimed. William M. Evarts and Richard H. Dana made the most compelling arguments on the government's side. They asserted that war was not a matter of law but of fact; war between the Union and the Confederacy existed, whether the U.S. Congress had declared so or not. The fact of war thus brought into play the laws of war, including the right to impose a naval blockade.

A majority of five justices accepted the government's arguments and ruled that Lincoln acted within his constitutional authority. Justice Robert Grier, who penned the majority opinion, held that the existence of war constituted a matter of fact rather than law. "As a civil war is never publicly proclaimed, *eo nomine* against insurgents," he wrote, "its actual existence is a fact in our domestic history which the court is bound to notice and to know" (67 U.S. 635, 637). The Union's refusal to recognize the sovereignty and independence of the Confederacy had no bearing on whether or not a state of war existed between them. "It is not necessary that the independence of the revolted province or state be acknowledged in order to constitute it a party belligerent in a war according to the law of nations," Grier contended. The justice buttressed his claim with evidence from the community of nations. As soon as news of the Battle of Fort Sumter and the organization of the Confederate government reached Great Britain, the Queen of England issued a neutrality proclamation, Grier noted. How could the owners of the seized vessels, who had brought suit in these cases, he wondered, "ask a court to affect a technical ignorance of the existence of a war, which all the world acknowledges to be the greatest civil war known in the history of the human race?" (67 U.S. 635, 669). This essential fact of war gave tremendous latitude to the president when it came to exercising his powers. As commander in chief of the Army and Navy of the United States, the president could legitimately exercise those powers in the face of a crisis like the one the nation confronted after the attack on Fort Sumter. Although acknowledging that only Congress could declare war, Grier argued that a president had no choice in such a situation but to take measures such as those taken by Lincoln. The president had a right, the majority of the justices concluded, to institute a blockade of Confederate ports prior to obtaining the approval of Congress.

Justice Samuel Nelson wrote a lengthy dissent, with which Justices Catron, Taney, and Clifford agreed. Nelson argued that the material fact of war meant nothing under the law, and by taking into account such matters the majority of the justices were asking the wrong questions. "Instead . . . of inquiring after armies and navies, and victories lost and won, or organized rebellion against the General Government, the inquiry should be into the law of nations and into the municipal fundamental laws of the government," Nelson wrote. "For we find there that to constitute a civil war in the sense in which we are speaking, before it can exist, in contemplation of law, it must be recognized or declared by the sovereign power of the state, and which sovereign power by our Constitution is lodged in the Congress of the United States" (67 U.S. 635, 690). Only congressional action, Nelson contended, could formally and legally initiate a war. Once Congress did enact legislation that authorized Lincoln to interdict trade with the South—on July 13, 1861, after the president's blockade proclamation—the blockade became lawful. Congress could not, however, Nelson argued, make its declaration apply retroactively, which it had attempted to do in order to legitimize Lincoln's actions.

Because the dissenters admitted that the war assumed lawful status after the act of July 13, the justices' decisions proved to be less contentious than the political rhetoric leading up to the case. Had the dissenting opinion been the majority ruling, the Court still would have upheld the legality of the blockade after Congress granted its approval.

Many Republicans and other supporters of the Union cause had feared that the justices might altogether deny the power to impose a blockade during a civil war. The Court's pro-Lincoln decision thus infused them with new hope. The *New York Times*, for example, praised the ruling and argued that the Court's broad interpretation of the executive's wartime powers meant that the recently issued Emancipation Proclamation would also pass constitutional muster. Although that issue never came before the justices, the Court's decision in the *Prize Cases* constituted an important political victory for Lincoln and a pivotal ruling in the development of presidential war powers. In granting the executive wide authority to act as commander in chief and in refusing to acknowledge the sovereignty of the Confederate States of America, the Court's ruling could not have been more favorable for the Lincoln administration's efforts to prosecute the war.

In cases involving the doctrine of separation of powers, in short, the Taney Court took bold and important steps. A Court composed almost entirely of Democrats, who owed their positions on the nation's highest tribunal to President Andrew Jackson, refused to accept his broad definition of the scope of executive power in *Kendall v. United States ex rel. Stokes* and affirmed a federal circuit court's power to issue a writ of mandamus. In the midst of national partisan debate over the Dorr Rebellion and the legitimacy of the government of Rhode Island, the same Democrat-dominated Court backed away from the constitutional dispute in *Luther v. Borden* and formulated the political questions doctrine—a self-imposed limitation on judicial power that remained important for more than a century. And in the Civil War's *Prize Cases*, the majority crafted a landmark decision that gave the president the power he needed to conduct the war without recognizing the legitimacy of secession or the Confederacy. That decision marked the first time the Court had affirmed a broad definition of executive power, and it foreshadowed the tremendous expansion of presidential authority to conduct foreign policy and war during the twentieth century.

Commercial Regulation and Admiralty Jurisdiction

Disputes arising out of government regulation of commercial activity, whether on land or sea, figured prominently in the work of the Supreme Court during the middle of the nineteenth century. Article I, Section 8 of the Constitution, which enumerated the powers of Congress, empowered the legislative branch to "regulate commerce with foreign Nations and among the Several States." These nine words possessed potentially extraordinary power and provoked considerable debate among the justices, especially in light of the fact that the Tenth Amendment reserved to the states those powers "not delegated to the United States by the Constitution." Thus, more than the Contract Clause, the Commerce Clause raised the issue of the relative degree of powers possessed by the national government and the states.

Given that Congress would regulate interstate commerce, numerous questions remained. What exactly did the word "commerce" encompass? Was it merely the exchange of goods, or would it be defined more broadly? What if Congress enacted no legislation regarding a particular area of commercial activity? Was congressional power over interstate commerce total and complete, thus prohibitive of any state regulation, or were states free to exercise their own regulatory powers in the absence of congressional action? The existence of slavery, of course, only complicated matters. White southerners refused to admit that Congress possessed any authority to regulate slavery in the southern states, so they usually took a narrow view of the Commerce Clause. Chief Justice John Marshall's leading opinion on the subject shed little light on these problems. In *Gibbons v. Ogden* (1824), Marshall had held that a steamboat monopoly granted by the state of New York violated a federal coasting license statute. Although Marshall defined commerce broadly to include steamboat navigation, he avoided interpreting the commerce power as exclusive to Congress. In other words, Marshall's opinion left open the subject of the proper boundaries between national and state regulation. This critical question plagued the Court for much of the Taney period.

Another facet of commercial activity—admiralty law—also took center stage during Taney's years as chief justice. Admiralty law acquired its name from the Lord High Admiral in England, under whose courts the law of seagoing vessels was administered. A form of international law, admiralty law ensured that uniform rules applied to the ships of all nations. Because by nature it required uniformity, the framers of the Constitution granted admiralty jurisdiction to the federal courts. Article III, Section 2 of thc Constitution provided that federal judicial power extended "to all cases of admiralty and maritime jurisdiction." In accordance with this provision, in the Judiciary Act of 1789 Congress gave to the U.S. District Courts original jurisdiction in all civil cases involving admiralty and maritime law. The act provided for appellate jurisdiction in the Circuit Courts when the amount involved exceeded $300 and further appellate jurisdiction in the Supreme Court when the amount involved exceeded $2,000.

The most important admiralty cases to reach the Supreme Court during the Taney period involved the scope and definition of federal jurisdiction. During the Marshall era, the justices carefully adhered to existing English common law rules regarding admiralty. In *The Thomas Jefferson* (1825), the Court limited federal admiralty jurisdiction to cases involving vessels on the high seas and on waters within the ebb and flow of the tide. This rule arose out of the peculiar maritime environment in England, for that nation contained no navigable inland waters to speak of when this doctrine was formulated. Rapid economic expansion and the transportation revolution during the middle of the nineteenth century afforded the Taney Court the opportunity to amend these long-standing common law principles, although advocates of state sovereignty staunchly resisted any expansion of federal judicial power. The Court's evolving interpretation of both the Commerce Clause of Article I and the Admiralty Clause of Article III thus responded to the economic changes that transformed mid–nineteenth-century America. And because both clauses held the potential for greatly augmenting national power at the expense of the states, the Court's decisions in such cases often thrust the tribunal to the forefront of national debate.

The Court's first significant ruling regarding the commerce power occurred during Taney's initial term as chief justice in *New York v. Miln* (1837). In 1824, New York had passed a law aimed at restricting the flow of paupers into the state. The legislation required the masters of all vessels arriving in the Port of New York from foreign countries or from other states to provide, within twenty-four hours of arrival, the name, place of birth, age, and occupation of all passengers on board. In addition, the law mandated that the master of the vessel provide bond for each foreigner brought to port and to remove any such passenger deemed likely to become a ward of the city. When the master of the ship *Emily* failed to comply with the statute, the city of New York brought suit for $15,000 in penalties against George Miln, the merchant who was to receive the ship's nonhuman cargo. A resident of another state, the defendant removed the case to the U.S. Circuit Court for the Southern District of New York, and when the circuit judges were unable to arrive at a decision, the case went to the U.S. Supreme Court.

Although on its face *Miln* seemed to present a rather uncontroversial question—whether the Commerce Clause prevented New York from enacting such a law—the issue of controlling the entry of undesirables raised the slavery issue in the minds of many white southerners. In 1823, in the aftermath of a slave insurrectionary panic, the state of South Carolina had passed the Negro Seaman Act, a law that required free black sailors to remain on their vessels while docked in South Carolina's harbors on penalty of imprisonment and forced enslavement. Over the next several years, other coastal slave states enacted similar laws restricting the entry of black sailors into southern ports, to which the international community responded with shock and outrage. Despite a U.S. Circuit Court ruling to the contrary, two of Andrew Jackson's attorneys general—one of which was Taney, who served from 1831–1833—claimed that the police powers of the states superseded the federal treaty power and that the laws were constitutional. Keenly aware of the implications of any U.S. Supreme Court ruling for their attempts to police slave society, white southerners thus viewed *New York v. Miln* as an important case.

Aware of its importance, counsel vigorously argued the respective sides of the case. Lawyers for the city argued that the tremendous flow of people into the port necessitated some degree of legal control over immigration. They viewed the law in question as a simple police regulation that in no way collided with the authority of Congress under the Commerce Clause. Even if the New York law could be deemed a regulation of commerce, the prosecution contended, the commerce power was not exclusive in nature; states, therefore, retained the power to pass laws relating to commerce, provided they did not interfere with national legislation. Moreover, with neither a federal treaty nor an act of Congress at stake in this case, the city claimed, New York had acted well within its legal and constitutional authority. Defense counsel, in contrast, argued that the law clearly violated the Constitution's Commerce Clause.

Under the precedent established by the Marshall Court in *Gibbons v. Ogden* (1823), commerce encompassed navigation, including the transport of goods and passengers. Such was the subject of the New York statute. Just because a law was a police regulation, moreover, did not mean that it was constitutional. Any police regulation that interfered with interstate or foreign commerce, the defense contended, overstepped state authority and treaded on congressional prerogative.

Justice Philip Pendleton Barbour crafted a narrowly drawn opinion that upheld the New York statute. Purposely avoiding the larger question presented by the dispute—whether the power to regulate commerce rested exclusively with Congress—the majority held simply that the New York law constituted an ordinary police regulation. "We shall not enter into any examination of the question whether the power to regulate commerce be or be not exclusive of the states," Barbour wrote, "because the opinion which we have formed renders it unnecessary: in other words, we are of opinion that the act is not a regulation of commerce but of police; and that being thus considered, it was passed in the exercise of a power which rightfully belonged to the states" (36 U.S. 102, 132). Barbour attempted to distinguish *Miln* from previous Commerce Clause decisions by noting that persons—rather than goods—were the subjects of the regulation in question. Persons could not be articles of commerce, he claimed, and any discussion of the New York law as a regulation of commerce defied reason. Instead, the majority opinion focused on the state's traditional powers to provide for the general welfare of its citizenry. "We think it as competent and as necessary for a state to provide precautionary measures against the moral pestilence of paupers, vagabonds, and possibly convicts," the majority concluded, "as it is to guard against the physical pestilence which may arise from unsound and infectious articles imported, or from a ship, the crew of which may be laboring under an infectious disease" (36 U.S. 102, 142–143). Viewing the matter in this way—as an issue of health, safety, and welfare—the Court ruled that New York had acted well within the bounds of its authority. Indeed, Barber's majority opinion went so far as to argue that state power over such matters was "complete, unqualified, and exclusive" (36 U.S. 102, 139). This bold assertion shocked even some of his colleagues, who during conference reportedly had not decided on such a position.

Justice Story expressed particular dismay at Barbour's definition of the state's police power. In a dissenting opinion, Story unhesitatingly admitted that states possessed the power to enact legislation regulating health, implementing quarantines, or preventing the immigration of paupers. What irked the justice was the majority's contention that the law in question fell into one of these categories—that it was, in other words, a simple police regulation. Story saw the law as much more. He argued that the New York statute acted on subjects beyond the state's territorial limits and that it thus interfered with congressional authority over commerce. "Suppose the act had required that the master and owner of ships should make report of all goods taken on board or landed in foreign ports, and of the nature, qualities, and value of such goods; could there be a doubt that it would have been a regulation of commerce? If not, in what essential respect does the requirement of a report of the passengers taken or landed in a foreign port or place, differ from the case put?" Story answered his own question: "I profess not to be able to see any" (36 U.S. 102, 157). Upon concluding that the New York law did constitute a regulation of commerce, Story asserted that the power to regulate commerce lay exclusively with Congress. Representing another strain of thought on the commerce power, Justice Smith Thompson issued a concurring opinion, in which he claimed that the state regulation was valid only because it conflicted with no federal enactment. This question—whether congressional power was exclusive—dominated the justices' debates over the Commerce Clause for the next decade and a half.

The issue next arose in the *License Cases* (1847), the collective name for three disputes involving state regulation of alcohol. Temperance proved to be one of the most successful reform movements of the antebellum era, with several states enacting statutes governing the sale, transportation, or consumption of liquor at the behest of religious and otherwise idealistic reformers. *Thurlow v. Massachusetts* and *Fletcher v. Rhode Island* both dealt with laws that required state licenses for retailers of imported liquor in less than bulk quantity, and *Pierce v. New Hampshire* pertained to a statute that mandated a license for selling liquor, either wholesale or retail, regardless of quantity. In all the cases, the justices faced the question of whether these state laws treaded on federal power under the Commerce Clause, given that Congress had authorized the importation of liquor.

Again, because debates over the regulation of commerce had implications for the slavery issue, the *License Cases* attracted great attention. Daniel Webster, representing a retailer convicted under the Massachusetts statute, argued passionately that these laws violated the Commerce Clause, which he believed gave to Congress exclusive and plenary power over the subject. An ardent nationalist, Webster refused to concede any ground to those who championed states' rights, and he especially feared that the South would make good use of any pro–states' rights doctrine that issued from the case. Webster contended that prohibiting the sale and consumption of liquor, as Massachusetts had, stood in direct opposition to the tariff laws of the United States, which authorized the importation of spirits. Webster's chief opponent in the case, John Davis, contended that the regulations in question were mere expressions of the states' police authority. In particular, he attempted to show that excessive drinking led to poverty and crime. Therefore these laws, Davis argued, constituted regulations of public health and safety.

The Court unanimously upheld all three of the statutes in question. Although the justices agreed on the decision, they could not agree on the law: six justices wrote nine separate opinions. Justice McLean wrote a different opinion for each of the three cases, Justice Catron wrote two opinions, and Taney, Daniel, Grier, and Woodbury each wrote opinions that applied to all three cases. No consensus emerged on the larger issue at stake—the extent to which congressional regulation of commerce precluded state control over the subject. On this crucial point, in fact, the justices seemed more divided than ever. Justice McLean, who believed in the exclusivity of federal power under the Commerce Clause, nevertheless drew a distinction between the regulation of commerce and the mere licensing of liquor sellers. The power to license lay within a state's legitimate police powers, he claimed. The Methodist McLean, moreover, looked with favor on the motives of the state legislators who had enacted the measures and viewed the licensing effort as a "great moral reform" (46 U.S. 504, 488). For his part, Taney upheld the Massachusetts and Rhode Island laws on the basis of the "original package doctrine," which Chief Justice Marshall had formulated in *Brown v. Maryland* (1827). In that case, the Court had ruled that states could not tax imported goods so long as they remained in their original package. Once those items had been mixed with other property, though, a state was free to tax or regulate them within the bounds of the state. Since the Massachusetts and Rhode Island laws dealt with small quantities of retail liquor, Taney argued, the statutes in question posed no threat to congressional authority under the Commerce Clause. The New Hampshire law was different, for it required licensing regardless of the quantities sold. In his discussion of this law, Taney expressed his belief in a state's concurrent power to regulate commerce, provided that no conflict existed between state and federal laws. In such an instance, congressional legislation was "controlling and supreme," he argued (46 U.S. 504, 579).

The other members of the Court held diverse views. Justice Daniel challenged Taney's reliance on the "original package" notion by noting that many commodities—such as "a steam engine, a piano, a telescope, or a horse"—could be shipped without ever being in a "package" per se (46 U.S. 504, 612). Daniel's ideological commitment to states' rights underlay his reasoning. Justice Catron believed that the obvious disagreement over the meaning of *Gibbons v. Ogden* and *Brown v. Maryland* meant that the question of whether Congress possessed exclusive power over commerce remained an open one; Justice Grier agreed and did not see any reason for the Court to decide the matter in this instance. Justice Woodbury's opinion, meanwhile, presaged the direction the Court would take later when he suggested that the question of exclusivity of congressional power rested on whether national uniformity of regulation was necessary in a particular case. As for the license laws, he upheld them because he simply did not view them as regulations of commerce. In sum, the justices had agreed on nothing in the case, except that the laws in question were constitutional.

A few years later, the *Passenger Cases* (1849) provided the Court with another opportunity to develop a coherent doctrine regarding commercial regulation. But the justices found that task to be more difficult than ever. Encouraged by the Court's earlier ruling in *New York v. Miln*, the states of New York and Massachusetts had enacted new legislation taxing immigrant passengers arriving at their ports and excluding those who were diseased or mentally incompetent. Revenue from the taxes in New York went toward financing hospitals, and in Massachusetts the money was used for the support of the poor. These measures generated immediate controversy. Proponents viewed the laws as necessary to prevent an influx of paupers and "lunatics" from inundating their cities, while opponents charged that passage of the statutes constituted an unwarranted and unconstitutional exercise of state power. In the background, again, stood the slavery question. What were the implications for slavery, if southern states could not regulate those using their ports? The *Richmond Enquirer*, a leading southern newspaper and an advocate of states' rights, framed the question this way: "What becomes of the power to keep the citizens of New York from stealing our property and refusing to give it up or those who stole it, if we cannot pass such a bill as may authorize us to search their vessels, or to demand bond and security for the indemnity of masters, whose slaves may be stolen, by every kidnapper?" (Warren 1928, 170). Each of the *Passenger Cases*, individually known as *Norris v. Boston* and *Smith v. Turner*, was argued before the Court three times. (Vacancies and absences on the high court during the late 1840s were frequent and prolonged, thus making reargument necessary.) Daniel Webster, the only lawyer to participate in all these arguments, made his last major appearance before the justices in the *Passenger Cases*, and his passionate and eloquent opposition to the legislation convinced a bare majority.

The divisions among the justices, though, were so great that no meaningful doctrine arose from the decision. Members of the Court particularly disagreed over what the Court had decided in *Gibbons v. Ogden* and *New York v. Miln*, while the issue of whether congressional power under the Commerce Clause was exclusive continued to divide the justices. The Court's two most nationalistic justices on matters of commercial regulation, McLean and Wayne, ruled against the state enactments on the grounds that Congress possessed absolute and exclusive power over commerce. Both men believed that *Gibbons* had settled that question. Wayne's opinion, moreover, particularly addressed southern whites' anxiety about a broad interpretation of the federal commerce power. "The fear expressed, that if the states have not the discretion to determine who may come and live in them, the United States may introduce into the southern states emancipated Negroes from the West Indies and elsewhere, has no foundation," he wrote (48 U.S. 283, 428). Because the southern states had entered into the Union with slavery, Wayne reasoned, only state legislation could govern the operation of the South's "peculiar institution." Avoiding the possible implications for slavery, Justices Catron and Grier took a more narrow view of the cases at hand. They emphasized that the state measures contradicted federal immigration legislation and violated existing treaties with Great Britain. Moreover, they explicitly disagreed with McLean and Wayne about the question of the exclusivity of congressional power. The third position represented among the majority was that of Justice John McKinley, who contended that Article I, Section 9 of the Constitution provided that only Congress could regulate "migration and importation." This constitutional provision, which most understood as applying primarily to the slave trade, had not even been mentioned by the lawyers arguing the case. In the *Passenger Cases*, the Court thus arrived at no consensus regarding the proper balance between the state and national governments when it came to the regulation of commerce.

The Taney Court's most significant Commerce Clause decision came in the case of *Cooley v. Board of Wardens of the Port of Philadelphia* (1852), in which the justices reached a general agreement about the relationship between federal and state power over commerce. The Board of Wardens provided pilots for vessels entering and leaving the Port of Philadelphia. Under a state law of 1803, masters of vessels who refused to employ pilots provided by the board still had to pay half the pilotage fee, which went into a state fund "for the relief of distressed and decayed pilots, their widows and children." Because the law affected interstate and foreign commerce, it potentially ran afoul of the Commerce Clause. Like the statutes at issue in the *Passenger Cases*, which the Court had invalidated, the Pennsylvania statute imposed a tax to be used for the relief of a particular class of persons. Unlike those previous cases, though, the pilotage law did not regulate articles of commerce—the passengers or commodities on board—nor did it seem to conflict with existing federal law. Indeed, counsel for the Board of Wardens pointed to an act of Congress of 1789 that specifically authorized states to regulate "all pilots in the bays, inlets, rivers, harbors, and ports of the United States." Opposing counsel contended that the Pennsylvania law violated three distinct provisions of the Constitution: Article I, Section 10's prohibition on state-imposed "imposts or duties on imports or exports"; Article I, Section 9's ban on preferences being given "by any regulation of commerce or revenue, to the ports of one state over those of another"; and Article I, Section 8's grant of authority to Congress to "regulate commerce with foreign nations and among the several states" (the Commerce Clause).

In a landmark decision, the recently arrived Justice Benjamin R. Curtis upheld the Pennsylvania law. With only cursory analysis, Curtis dismissed the first two constitutional objections to the state pilotage fee. The prohibition on state "imposts or duties" did not apply in this instance, he argued, because that provision "was intended to operate upon subjects actually existing and well understood when the Constitution was formed." "Imposts and duties on imports, exports, and tonnage" Curtis claimed, "were then known to the commerce of a civilized world to be as distinct from fees and charges for pilotage, and from the penalties by which the commercial states enforced their pilot laws, as they were from charges for wharfage or towage, or any other local port charges for services rendered to vessels or cargoes."

Moreover, the law in question gave no "preference" to the Port of Philadelphia, as counsel had asserted. If the pilotage fee had any effect on commercial activity there, Curtis claimed, the measure served to inhibit incoming traffic.

Curtis devoted most of the majority opinion to the issue that had divided the justices ever since the *Miln* decision—the question of whether power to regulate commerce rested exclusively with Congress. The majority's new position, outlined by Curtis in *Cooley,* was that the extent of federal power over commerce depended on the subject of the regulation. "Now, the power to regulate commerce embraces a vast field, containing not only many, but exceedingly various subjects, quite unlike in their nature," Curtis explained, "some imperatively demanding a single uniform rule, operating equally on the commerce of the United States in every port, and some, like the subject now in question, as imperatively demanding that diversity, which alone can meet the local necessities of navigation" (53 U.S. 299, 319). To argue either that congressional power over commerce was exclusive or that states possessed a concurrent power was shortsighted, Curtis claimed. Both positions neglected to take the subject of the regulation into account. "Whatever subjects of this power are in their nature national, or admit only of one uniform system, or plan of regulation," Curtis wrote, "may justly be said to be of such a nature as to require exclusive legislation by Congress" (53 U.S. 299, 319). Pilot regulations did not fall into this category. Despite establishing this new rule for testing state statutes that governed commercial activity, the Court went no further. Curtis did not venture to explain which subjects might be national in scope and which might be left to states; that question the Court would address on a case-by-case basis.

This new doctrine formulated by the Court in *Cooley v. Board of Wardens* was known as "selective exclusiveness." Although the majority reached more of a consensus than it had in a Commerce Clause case since 1837, three justices continued to hold fast to doctrinaire positions. Justices McLean and Wayne, convinced of the exclusivity of federal power over commerce, made their argument in dissent. (Even after the ruling in *Cooley,* McLean in a circuit opinion continued to assert the exclusivity of federal power over commerce.) Justice Daniel, the Court's most vociferous advocate of states' rights, expressed his own differences with the majority's middle-of-the-road holding in the case. In a concurring opinion, he agreed that the Pennsylvania statute was constitutional but declined to concede anything to the national government when it came to commercial regulation. Daniel described pilot laws as stemming from "an original and inherent power in the states, and not one to be merely tolerated, or held subject to the sanction of the federal government" (53 U.S. 299, 326). Selective exclusiveness, a pragmatic—though indefinite—solution to the problem of regulating commerce, signaled a departure from the Court's earlier, more categorical approach to the issue. The support of five justices for this doctrine seemed the greatest level of agreement the Court could muster.

Admiralty jurisdiction proved to be a somewhat less divisive matter. Although the Court operated for many years under *The Thomas Jefferson* (1825), a Marshall-era precedent that restricted federal jurisdiction to those waters within the ebb and flow of the tide, rapid economic growth and technological change necessitated legal reform. By the 1840s, the completion of the Erie Canal triggered a rapid expansion of steamboat traffic on the Great Lakes and the nation's rivers. By the middle of the 1840s, half the total tonnage of steamboat cargo was in this western traffic, rather than along the eastern seaboard. With increasing numbers of cases involving steamboats burdening the state courts, in 1845 Congress moved to enact legislation expanding federal admiralty jurisdiction. To do so, Congress turned to Justice Joseph Story, the author of the Court's opinion in *The Thomas Jefferson*. Story drafted a measure that extended admiralty jurisdiction to federally licensed vessels employed in interstate commerce on the Great Lakes and connecting waterways. Because many proponents of the legislation doubted whether Congress could modify a constitutional grant of judicial power, the 1845 statute constituted only a beginning step in the dramatic expansion of federal admiralty jurisdiction. In a series of cases during the 1840s and 1850s, the Supreme Court addressed the issue and augmented federal control over this increasingly important element of commerce.

The first of these cases, *Waring v. Clark* (1847), originated with a collision on the Mississippi River between two steamboats, the *De Soto* and the *Luda*. When the vessels smashed into each other at night about ninety-five miles above New Orleans—the *De Soto* allegedly lacked warning lights or a lookout—the *Luda* sank. The master of the *Luda*, Thomas Clarke, brought suit against the owners of the *De Soto* in the U.S. District Court in New Orleans. Because the collision took place before the congressional legislation of 1845, which applied only to the Great Lakes and connecting rivers anyway, the question of federal jurisdiction remained open. The District Court decided that it did have jurisdiction in the case, based on the notion that where the collision occurred, the river was affected by the tide. When the case reached the Supreme Court, the justices had to consider whether to adhere to *The Thomas Jefferson* and English rules regarding admiralty or to stake out new ground on the issue.

Writing for the majority, Justice James Wayne held that English principles were not controlling in American admiralty law. "The grant of admiralty power to the courts of the United States was not intended to be limited or to be interpreted by what were cases of admiralty jurisdiction in England when the Constitution was adopted," he wrote. At best, common law could provide "analogies" to help American judges decide cases. This was a bold argument, for English common law principles had always guided American courts on the subject. Still, Wayne's majority opinion proceeded no further down this path. Instead of crafting a new, more expansive U.S. doctrine regarding admiralty jurisdiction, Wayne simply agreed with a lower court that the site of the collision lay within the ebb and flow of the tide. In other words, although he asserted that U.S. courts did not have to adhere to English principles, Wayne proceeded to apply English principles. He simply upheld federal jurisdiction in the case on the basis of the location of the collision.

In a lengthy dissent, Justice Levi Woodbury, joined by Justices Daniel and Grier, reiterated the traditional common law understanding of admiralty and adhered to the Court's previous ruling in *The Thomas Jefferson.* Tracing the history of admiralty in England, Woodbury questioned how the U.S. Constitution or American law had altered the long-standing doctrine that jurisdiction came only in cases in which vessels were within the ebb and flow of the tide. Woodbury and the other dissenters particularly took issue with the majority's opinion on two grounds: their ruling extending the federal courts' admiralty jurisdiction undermined the right to trial by jury, which did not exist in admiralty courts, and threatened local and state control over maritime matters. "If we disclaim jurisdiction here, what evil can happen? Only that our citizens in this class of cases will be allowed to be tried by their own state courts, state laws, and state juries," Woodbury asserted. "While, if we do the contrary, the powers of both states and juries will be encroached on, and just dissatisfaction excited, and the harmonious workings of our political system disturbed" (46 U.S. 441, 495–496). In the end, Woodbury concluded that the federal courts lacked jurisdiction over a collision that occurred ninety-five miles above New Orleans. As "it is hardly possible that a regular tide from the ocean should be felt there," he claimed, the federal court should not hear the matter (46 U.S. 441, 498).

The Court's willingness in *Waring v. Clarke* (also known as *The De Soto*) to question the applicability of English principles and to accept the notion that a wreck so distant from the high seas actually fell within the ebb and flow of the tide brought the Court a step closer to overturning *The Thomas Jefferson.*

A year after *Waring,* the Court considered another case that raised similar questions about the extent of federal admiralty jurisdiction. *New Jersey Steam Navigation Co. v. Merchant's Bank of Boston* (1848) involved the burning of a passenger- and freight-carrying steamboat, the Lexington, which caught fire after bales of cotton had negligently been placed too close to a hot chimney. Compounding the chaos on board was the fact that the vessel's fire hoses were missing, as were the boat's heaving lines for the fire buckets. All but two of the ship's 140 passengers perished in the conflagration, which occurred in Long Island Sound, about fifty miles out of New York. The Lexington, which was en route to Providence, Rhode Island, also contained a shipment of gold and silver coins owned by the Merchant's Bank of Boston. Despite a contractual agreement that the bank shipped its valuable cargo at its own risk, the bank brought suit against the steamboat company in the federal district court for Rhode Island for gross negligence. After the district court dismissed the case for lack of jurisdiction, the U.S. Circuit Court ruled in the bank's favor and awarded damages.

The New Jersey Steam Navigation Company thereupon appealed to the Supreme Court.

By a 6–2 vote, the Court decided in favor of the bank. In the first part of the majority opinion, Justice Samuel Nelson held that because the Lexington failed to meet the fire safety standards set by federal law and because the crew negligently stowed the cotton next to the chimney, the steamboat company was liable for the loss of the specie. This holding was especially significant in light of the contract stipulating that the steamboat transported the treasure at the risk of the bank. According to the Court, such a contract could not relieve a common carrier from liability in a case of gross negligence. The rest of the majority opinion pertained to the jurisdiction of the federal courts. Counsel for the steamboat company had claimed that English common law provided that cases involving contracts came within admiralty jurisdiction only when they applied to such things as seamen's wages or other contracts made and executed on the high seas. Nelson's opinion took a much broader view of admiralty jurisdiction and concluded that the subject matter of the contract—not the location where it was made—was the determinative factor. Any cause of action that arose out of a maritime transaction fell within the purview of the admiralty jurisdiction of the federal courts. The scope of American admiralty jurisdiction would, in other words, not be subject to the limitations of English common law.

The culmination of this line of cases expanding admiralty jurisdiction came in *Genesee Chief v. Fitzhugh* (1852), one of the half dozen most significant rulings of the Taney era. A collision between the schooner *Cuba*, which was transporting wheat from Ohio to New York via Lake Erie, and the steamboat, the *Genesee Chief*, produced a lawsuit in the District Court for the Northern District of New York. Suing under the 1845 act that extended admiralty jurisdiction to the Great Lakes, the owners of the *Cuba* alleged that the negligence of the *Genesee Chief* caused the accident. Counsel for the *Genesee Chief* blamed the *Cuba* and contended that the incident occurred within New York's waters, outside the reach of federal jurisdiction. When the district court ruled in favor of the *Cuba* and the circuit court subsequently affirmed the decision, the case came before the Supreme Court. Although the Court found the steamboat at fault for lacking a proper lookout, the key constitutional question in the case was whether the case properly belonged in the federal courts. For the first time, the Court interpreted the 1845 statute and, in doing so, assessed whether *The Thomas Jefferson* remained a valid precedent.

Chief Justice Taney's majority opinion upheld the statute, overturned *The Thomas Jefferson*, and established a broad new definition of federal admiralty jurisdiction. According to Taney, the 1845 act expanding the admiralty jurisdiction to the Great Lakes fell within Congress's power to control the jurisdiction of the federal courts. "If this law, therefore, is constitutional," he argued, "it must be supported on the ground that the lakes and navigable waters connecting them are within the scope of admiralty and maritime jurisdiction, as known and understood in the United States when the Constitution was adopted" (53 U.S., 443, 453). Here the chief justice launched into a lengthy discussion of the issue that had plagued the Court ever since the growth of steamboat transportation: whether admiralty jurisdiction could be restricted to tidal waters. "Now there is certainly nothing in the ebb and flow of the tide that makes the waters peculiarly suitable for admiralty jurisdiction, nor anything in the absence of a tide that renders it unfit . . . and if the distinction is made on that account, it is merely arbitrary, without any foundation in reason; and, indeed, would seem to be inconsistent with it" (53 U.S. 443, 454). Taney proceeded to demonstrate how the distinction had been formulated in the first place. In England, he explained, nearly every navigable stream and river fell within the ebb and flow of the tide. Because tidewaters and navigable waters were synonymous, English admiralty jurisdiction was confined to "public navigable waters," rather than private waters. The same applied to the United States at the time of the founding. But years of legal debate about the nature of admiralty law only confused the issue. "[T]he public character of the river was in process of time lost sight of, and the jurisdiction of the admiralty treated as if it was limited by the tide," he wrote. "The description of a public navigable river was substituted in the place of the thing intended to be described."

Taney's brilliant argument undermined the authority of *The Thomas Jefferson*, and the chief justice easily dismissed the precedent as an "erroneous decision." The real problem presented by that case was that it was decided in 1825, at a time when no one could have foreseen the enormous expansion of commerce in the western portion of the United States. Sounding a practical note that echoed the Court's famous *Charles River Bridge* decision, Taney concluded that technological advancement required that *The Thomas Jefferson* be overturned. "It is evident that a definition that would at this day limit public rivers in this country to tide-water rivers is utterly inadmissible. We have thousands of miles of public navigable water, including lakes and rivers in which there is no tide." All such waters came within the admiralty and maritime jurisdiction of the federal courts.

The majority opinion in the *Genesee Chief* case marked a significant expansion of federal judicial power and an important step in establishing uniform federal admiralty principles. Only Justice Peter Daniel, a die-hard advocate of states' rights, dissented, and even he acknowledged that many deemed his views on the subject to be "contracted and antiquated" (53 U.S. 443, 465). Taney's opinion represented a reasonable interpretation of the Constitution and a practical realization that commercial development necessitated abandoning existing precedent. Subsequent decisions affirmed and expanded this ruling. Whereas the *Genesee Chief* case had considered the constitutionality of the 1845 statute, which dealt only with the Great Lakes, in *Jackson v. Steamboat Magnolia* (1858) the justices ruled that a collision on the Alabama River, above the ebb and flow of the tide, was properly before the federal courts. After *Genesee Chief*, the justices found themselves free from having to use the tidal flow of a waterway as the determinative factor in whether the federal courts possessed jurisdiction. One of the most nationalistic rulings of the Taney era, the *Genesee Chief* decision represented a bold departure from Justice Story's earlier attempt to deal with the admiralty question. "Marshall, who never liked the Jefferson decision," according to one historian, "would surely have congratulated his successor" (Newmyer 1968, 112).

Slavery

In the slavery question, Taney and his colleagues met their most difficult challenge. The framers of the Constitution had left most questions regarding slavery open to interpretation. Although the nation's founding document referred to the "peculiar institution" in at least three places—the Fugitive Slave, Three-Fifths, and Slave Trade Clauses—the Constitution never used the words "slavery" or "slave." Instead, the document referred to a fugitive slave as a "person held in service or labour," while the portion of the Constitution providing that slaves count as three-fifths of a person for purposes of taxation and representation referred to bondspeople simply as "other persons." These textual ambiguities allowed for considerable interpretive variation. Proslavery southerners as well as prominent abolitionists such as William Lloyd Garrison saw the Constitution as an overtly proslavery document that provided for the return of fugitives and the codification of black inferiority in the Three-Fifths Clause. Some antislavery activists, however, made much of the fact that every time the Constitution mentioned slaves it referred to them as "persons." This fact, coupled with the Fifth Amendment's guarantee that "no person . . . be deprived of life, liberty, or property, without due process of law" inspired these antislavery champions to claim that the Constitution was on their side. Such persons included Salmon Chase, a lawyer who would later become chief justice, as well as black abolitionist Frederick Douglass. Although debate over slavery had occasionally arisen in national politics before the 1840s, most notably during the crisis over Missouri's admission to the Union, the Marshall Court had avoided having to render an opinion in a significant slavery case. Taney was not so fortunate. As the nation experienced political convulsions over the slavery question during the two decades before the Civil War, Taney's Supreme Court found itself in the middle of controversy in a number of instances.

The first of these famous disputes arose in 1841 in the *Amistad* case. In 1839, the Spanish schooner *Amistad*, carrying a load of Africans to be sold into slavery, had set sail from Havana on its way to Principe, another Cuban port. The Africans revolted and killed all but two of the crew members. Demanding to return to their native land, the mutineers ordered the crew of two to take the ship to Africa, but the

Spanish sailors instead steered the vessel northward. When the *Amistad* landed in Long Island Sound between New York and Connecticut, a four-way legal dispute arose over the fate of the ship's human cargo. The crew members filed suit in federal court for the return of the ship and the Africans, and the American naval officer who recovered the ship filed a salvage claim. President Martin Van Buren and his administration, seeking to appease the government of Spain, sided with the Spanish sailors and sought the return of the vessel and its cargo to them, whereas American abolitionists, sensitive to the plight of the Africans, sought their freedom and return to Africa. Although this complicated dispute thus involved the interpretation of treaties under international law as well as the law of salvage, for most Americans the case raised the simple issue of whether the Africans deserved to be freed. After hearing the various claims, a federal district judge in New York ordered that the Africans be returned to their homeland. Because Spanish law prohibited the slave trade in its imperial possessions, the capture of the Africans had been illegal in the first place, and the two slavers had no legal right to hold them. With President Van Buren intent on preventing conflict with Spain, the U.S. government appealed to the Supreme Court.

With arguments before the Court lasting eight days, the case attracted national and international attention. Roger Baldwin, a Connecticut lawyer who later served as governor and senator, led the legal effort to free the *Amistad* Africans, and seventy-four-year-old former president John Quincy Adams assisted in arguing the case. Adams, in particular, offered a forceful critique of the Van Buren administration's eagerness to appease the Spanish and focused on the moral imperative of freeing the kidnapped Africans. Known for his irascible temperament, Adams delivered a bitter and sarcastic argument that stood in stark contrast to that of Baldwin, who addressed the international legal questions with reason and aplomb. In the end, the Court ruled that the Africans deserved their freedom. In an 8–1 decision, with Justice Henry Baldwin in dissent, the justices held that the *Amistad* Africans be returned to their homeland, which they were. Strangely, a series of American presidents refused to accept the Court's ruling as final. Presidents John Tyler, James K. Polk, Franklin Pierce, and James Buchanan all recommended that the United States pay reparations to Spain to compensate for its loss, although Congress never appropriated any such funds. Historians speculate that presidential eagerness to remain on good terms with Spain had much to do with the ongoing interest of the United States during this period in annexing Cuba, which was at that time still held by Spain. The case's impact, therefore, was more political than doctrinal.

More significant than the much-publicized *Amistad* ruling was the Court's decision in *Groves v. Slaughter* that same year. This case involved a provision of the Mississippi constitution of 1832 that declared that "the introduction of slaves into this State as merchandise or for sale shall be prohibited from and after the first day of May, 1833." By introducing such a provision, the state hoped to stop an influx of undesirable and potentially dangerous slaves coming in from other states, halt the outflow of capital that paid for them, control the size of the state's black population, and perhaps keep the price of slaves in Mississippi from dropping as a result of an excess of supply. (The state constitution made an exception for new settlers who wanted to bring their own slaves into the state.) When Moses Groves refused to pay out-of-state slave trader Robert Slaughter for the slaves he received on the grounds that such transactions were illegal, the dispute came into a federal court. The court ruled that this provision of the state constitution was not self-executing and that because the transaction occurred before the legislature passed a statute enforcing the prohibition, the sale was lawful. Groves subsequently appealed to the Supreme Court.

Groves v. Slaughter was the first instance in which the Supreme Court considered the respective powers of the state and national governments with regard to the interstate movement of slaves. The enormous national implications of the dispute drew some of the country's most talented counsel to the case, including Henry Clay and Daniel Webster, who represented Slaughter in opposition to the state restriction. Argument continued for seven days. Debate among the lawyers centered on whether, in light of the Constitution's Commerce Clause, a state could restrict commerce with other states and whether the Mississippi constitutional provision violated Slaughter's right of property in slaves.

Despite the potentially explosive nature of the case, the Court chose the least controversial resolution of the matter. Writing for the majority, Justice Smith Thompson avoided the relationship between the Mississippi constitutional provision and the Commerce Clause and instead ruled simply that the state's ban on imported slaves was not self-executing. In other words, because the state legislature had not yet enacted legislation implementing the constitutional provision at the time of the sale (it did not do so until 1837), the ban was not valid. The Court thus upheld the lower court's decision that the sale of the slaves was legal and binding. Thompson's opinion represented only his and Justice Wayne's views; the other members of the Court, in a series of concurrences, saw fit to announce their own views on the subject. Justice McLean staked out a bold position in the case, the first instance in which he articulated his belief in the exclusive nature of federal power under the Commerce Clause. The regulation of slavery, though, he deemed an exception to this power, for every state maintained the power to exclude slaves from its borders. Chief Justice Taney affirmed his commitment to state power over the "peculiar institution," and Justice Baldwin wrote an extensive opinion proclaiming his belief in the absolute property rights of southern slaveholders. Justices McKinley and Story dissented without opinion. Justice Catron, who was ill, wrote no opinion in the case. Such diversity of opinions became the rule in later disputes involving the relationship between commerce and slavery, particularly the *License Cases* and the *Passenger Cases.*

The effects of the *Groves* decision were felt in both the legal and political arenas.

Legally, the Supreme Court issued a subsequent ruling reinforcing its decision, in the process claiming a tremendous amount of power for the federal judiciary. In *Rowan v. Runnels* (1847), the Court turned aside the Mississippi Supreme Court's interpretation of the state constitution's ban on the importation of slaves from other states. Even though the state high court ruled that the constitutional provision was self-executing, Chief Justice Taney's majority opinion in *Runnels* reaffirmed the *Groves* ruling and upheld contracts for the purchase of slaves made in good faith. Thus, in essence, the Supreme Court rejected the notion that a state court constituted the highest authority on matters of state law. Politically, the *Groves* ruling ultimately served as the basis for arguments put forth in Congress in favor of popular sovereignty—the right of the occupants of a territory to decide for themselves whether their jurisdiction would be slave or free. Although the majority opinion in *Groves* had ignored the issue of state control over slavery, proponents of the spread of slavery relied on Taney's and Baldwin's reasoning to claim that settlers in the territories gained in the Mexican-American War should decide for themselves whether it would be lawful to hold slaves. By not addressing the issue of state control over slavery, the majority's vague ruling had the unintended consequence of subsequently sanctioning "squatter sovereignty," as it was sometimes called.

Whereas the significance of *Groves* lay in its application in the long term, the effects of the Court's decision in *Prigg v. Pennsylvania* (1842) were immediate and substantial. The first case to interpret directly one of the Constitution's provisions regarding slavery, *Prigg* involved the Fugitive Slave Act of 1793 and the Fugitive Slave Clause on which it rested. For many years, the easy passage of fugitive slaves from Maryland into Pennsylvania and the efforts of professional slave catchers to track them down had been a source of contention between the two states. Pennsylvania's personal liberty law of 1826 stood at the center of this conflict. The law aimed to prevent the kidnapping of free blacks in Pennsylvania by making it more difficult for slave catchers to take possession of fugitives and return them to bondage. The Pennsylvania act prohibited judges from acting solely on a slave catcher's oath when authoring seizure and made the owner's oath of ownership inadmissible in removal hearings. Such regulations irritated slaveholding Marylanders, who wanted the rendition process to be as easy as possible. In order to resolve the ongoing dispute between the two states, Maryland and Pennsylvania agreed to find a test case to come before the U.S. Supreme Court.

A dispute involving fugitive Margaret Morgan would be that case. Margaret, a slave in name only whose master had always allowed her to live as if she were free, moved from Maryland to Pennsylvania in 1832 after her marriage to a free black man. On the death of Margaret's master in Maryland, the heiress of the estate hired a slave catcher, Edward Prigg, to locate Margaret and bring her back. Even though she had lived for years unmolested by her previous owner, she was still a slave under Maryland law. After obtaining an arrest warrant from a Pennsylvania justice of the peace, Prigg found Margaret and seized her. The couple had an unspecified number of children, at least one who had been born in Pennsylvania. In keeping with the terms of the 1826 act, as well as the federal Fugitive Slave Law of 1793, Prigg brought Margaret and her children before the justice of the peace in order to obtain a certificate of removal. At this point, the justice refused to participate further in the case, a right he possessed under the 1826 law. Prigg then forced Margaret and her children back to Maryland without the certificate, which was required under the 1826 state law. Because Prigg had violated the Pennsylvania statute, a county court brought kidnapping charges against him, and Maryland extradited him to stand trial. Under an agreement between the two states, if Prigg were convicted, appeals would be expedited so as to facilitate the case's coming before the U.S. Supreme Court. As expected, the local court convicted Prigg, the Pennsylvania Supreme Court upheld the conviction, and the case came before the justices in early 1842. For the first time, lawyers argued the controversial questions surrounding the recapture of fugitive slaves before the nation's highest judicial tribunal. Counsel for Prigg contended that the power to return fugitives rested exclusively with the national government, while lawyers for the state of Pennsylvania argued that the issue was best left to states.

In an 8–1 decision, the Supreme Court reversed Prigg's conviction. More important, in the process of doing so, the Court made a number of important rulings on the fugitive slave issue. Justice Joseph Story's majority opinion held that the Constitution's Fugitive Slave Clause guaranteed to slaveholders "the complete right and title of ownership in their slaves, as property, in every State in the Union into which they might escape from the State where they were held in servitude" (41 U.S. 539, 611). No legislation—either state or national—was necessary for the provisions of the clause to be put into action. It was entirely self-executing. Under the Fugitive Slave Clause, masters or slave catchers could remove fugitives from free states without any judicial oversight, so long as these actions were carried out "without any breach of the peace or any illegal violence" (41 U.S. 539, 613). Story added, moreover, that the clause had been absolutely necessary for the formation of the Union. The right of recapture, he claimed, "was so vital to the preservation of [the South's] domestic interests and institutions, that it cannot be doubted that it constituted a fundamental article, without the adoption of which the Union could not have been formed" (41 U.S. 539, 611). Here Story, either knowingly or not, distorted the truth. In fact, southerners at the Constitutional Convention had introduced the idea of incorporating a fugitive slave clause into the document near the end of the proceedings, and scarcely any debate ensued. The rendition of fugitives certainly had not been a major compromise of the Convention, as northerners at Philadelphia expressed no reservations about the clause. Story's revisionist account of the founders' activities served the purpose of portraying the clause—and the right of recapture—as essential ingredients of the federal Union.

The majority's broad reading of the Fugitive Slave Clause included the notion that Congress possessed exclusive power over the rendition of runaway slaves. It made no sense, according to Story, that slaveholding states would leave to nonslaveholding states the power to regulate fugitives within their own borders. This would practically destroy the rights of slave owners and create chaos in the rendition process. Only Congress, the majority held, could enact legislation regulating the return of fugitives. Such an interpretation of the Fugitive Slave Clause had a number of implications. First, the exclusive nature of congressional power on the subject, coupled with the fact that the clause included no reference to state enforcement, meant that states could in no way be required to aid in the return of fugitives. This constituted the one significant element of Story's opinion that ultimately served an antislavery purpose. Second, because the power to control the return of fugitives lay with Congress, the Court upheld the Fugitive Slave Act of 1793. On this point, Story responded to critics who questioned the act's constitutionality, based on the fact that the power to return fugitives was not included among Congress's enumerated powers. Employing a loose construction of the Constitution, Story argued that congressional authority could not be confined to a specific list of powers. Rather, the authority of Congress to deal with fugitive slaves fell within its obligation "to provide for the ordinary exigencies of the national government, in cases where rights are intended to be absolutely secured, and duties are positively enjoyed by the Constitution" (41 U.S. 539, 620). Third, Story's interpretation of the Fugitive Slave Clause allowed him to rule the Pennsylvania personal liberty law unconstitutional. That law, he held, "purports to punish as a public offense against that state, the very act of seizing and removing a slave by his master, which the Constitution of the United States was designed to justify and uphold" (41 U.S. 539, 626). Story's decision, it seemed, thus put the national government squarely on the side of slaveholders.

Although Story's opinion was deemed that of the majority, by no means did the justices all agree on these issues. Chief Justice Taney, along with Justices Thompson and Daniel, agreed with every part of the decision except Story's ruling that federal power over fugitives was exclusive in nature. In particular, they opposed Story's claim that states had no role in enforcing federal fugitive slave legislation. Exaggerating and even misrepresenting Story's reasoning, Taney wrote that "according to the opinion just delivered, the State authorities are prohibited from interfering for the purpose of protecting the right of the master and aiding him in the recovery of his property" (41 U.S. 539, 627). (Story had in fact only claimed that states *were not obliged* to assist the federal government in the rendition process, but he specifically stated that states could exercise their powers to aid in the return of fugitives.) The chief justice asserted that it had never been decided that individual rights secured in the Constitution could not be maintained or enforced by the states. "[I]t has always been held to be the duty of the States to enforce them," Taney wrote, "and the action of the general government has never been deemed necessary except to resist and prevent their violation" (41 U.S. 539, 628). Taney feared that northern states, acting in accordance with the *Prigg* decision, would refuse to assist in the rendition process, to the detriment of slaveholding interests. The lone dissenter in the case, Justice McLean, argued that the Pennsylvania law served to prevent the kidnapping of free African Americans and should be upheld.

The complicated and contested nature of the Court's holding in *Prigg* made its impact and legacy ambiguous. Abolitionists immediately condemned the ruling for strengthening the hand of slaveholders in the rendition process and for apparently sanctioning the kidnapping of free blacks in the North. The fact that one of Margaret's children had been born in Pennsylvania and was thus free under that state's law—which Story ignored—made the case all the more offensive on a human level. As a matter of doctrine, Story's decision particularly upset abolitionists because it denied alleged fugitives the right to a jury trial before their removal to the South. One abolitionist best summed up the opposition to *Prigg* by condemning it for establishing "the principle of slavery as the law of the whole Union, on the ruins of state sovereignty, habeas corpus, and jury trials" (Wiecek 1978, 47). As time passed, however, antislavery lawyers seized on Story's assertion that states were not required to assist in the return of fugitives. Story's argument, along with Taney's misrepresentation of it, gave antislavery lawmakers grounds for enacting legislation explicitly banning state officials from in any way assisting in the rendition process. Massachusetts, Vermont, Connecticut, New Hampshire, Pennsylvania, and Rhode Island all did so between 1843 and 1848. Some northern state judges refused to hear fugitive slave cases altogether, on the basis of Taney's claim that the majority opinion held that they lacked jurisdiction. Thus, even though the majority decision undoubtedly established the positive right of slaveholders to recapture escaped slaves, a portion of Story's opinion formed the basis of considerable northern antislavery opposition to the rendition process. By the end of the 1840s, southern slaveholding interests demanded stronger national legislation that would create a federal bureaucracy of sorts to carry out the rendition process. These demands later resulted in the passage of a new, tougher federal law enacted as part of the Compromise of 1850.

Prigg's mixed legacy became apparent as early as 1847, when the Court felt the need to hear another challenge to the constitutionality of the Fugitive Slave Act of 1793. This case involved Ohio resident John Van Zandt, who concealed and harbored fugitives belonging to Wharton Jones, a citizen of Kentucky. Nine of Jones's slaves, who lived in Kentucky just a few miles south of Cincinnati, escaped into Ohio in April 1842 and began their journey northward. Van Zandt, a "conductor" on the Underground Railroad, picked them up in his covered wagon while traveling on a road leading out of Cincinnati. Van Zandt hid inside the wagon with eight of the fugitives, while he let the ninth drive the wagon. Two white Ohioans, eager to receive rewards offered for the capture of fugitives, chased the wagon and succeeded in seizing all but one of the slaves. The two men received a hefty reward for their actions. Van Zandt, in contrast, went to federal court, where he was charged with harboring and concealing escaped slaves, in violation of the Fugitive Slave Act of 1793. Arguments in the case centered on whether Van Zandt's actions constituted harboring and concealing, as well as the larger moral questions involving slavery and natural rights. Justice John McLean and District Judge H. H. Leavitt, who heard the case in the federal circuit court in Cincinnati, thought the questions involving the federal act were best left to the U.S. Supreme Court. They therefore issued a certificate of division in the case, on the pretense that differences of opinion existed between them (a common practice at the time), and the dispute came before the Supreme Court.

Attorneys for the defendant in *Jones v. Van Zandt* (1847) attempted to turn the dispute into a debate over the morality of the return of fugitives. Leading antislavery lawyers Salmon Chase and William Seward donated their services and argued the case for Van Zandt. Of course, they addressed the issue of whether transporting fugitives in a wagon constituted "harboring" and "concealment" in violation of the federal statute. Still, they developed many of their arguments with an eye toward the larger abolitionist cause, as they invoked the Declaration of Independence, the Bill of Rights, and natural law in opposition to slavery and the return of fugitives. Chase, in addition, put forth a novel interpretation of the Article IV's Fugitive Slave Clause—that it served as a mere article of compact among the states and did not constitute a source of congressional regulatory power. According to this position, because the power to return fugitives was not included among the enumerated powers of Article I, Congress lacked authority to pass any legislation regarding fugitives. The law of 1793 was therefore unconstitutional. Together these arguments made up about 140 pages, which Chase and Seward circulated widely in antislavery circles both in the United States and abroad.

The Court, however, showed little interest in the broad issues of slavery and natural rights raised by counsel. In a unanimous opinion written by Justice Levi Woodbury, the Court confined itself to the facts of the case and affirmed the constitutionality of the Fugitive Slave Act of 1793. The decision relied heavily on Story's opinion in *Prigg v. Pennsylvania.* In that case, Woodbury wrote, the justices "were fortified by the idea that the Constitution itself, in the clause before cited, flung its shield, for security, over such property as is in controversy in the present case, and the right to pursue and reclaim it within the limits of another state." Citing the great English jurist William Blackstone, Woodbury continued, "This was only carrying out . . . the clear right of every man at common law to make fresh suit and recapture of his own property within the realm" (46 U.S. 215, 229). Declining to address "theoretical opinions" regarding the compromises made at the founding on the slavery issue, Woodbury declared that the Court's duty was to the Constitution and the laws.

The justices thus upheld the fugitive slave law, as well as Van Zandt's conviction under it.

Again demonstrating the disputed legacy of *Prigg v. Pennsylvania*, the Court heard one more case in which the nature of federal and state power to regulate fugitive slaves was at issue. In *Moore v. Illinois* (1852), the justices considered an Illinois statute that made it a misdemeanor with a penalty of up to six months in jail to "harbor and secret a Negro slave." This time Chase—again arguing the antislavery side—took the opposite tack from his position in the Van Zandt case. Instead of challenging the *Prigg* decision, as he had in the previous instance, Chase contended that because the Fugitive Slave Act of 1793 had been upheld in *Prigg* and because *Prigg* had ruled that federal power over the regulation of fugitive slaves was exclusive, the Illinois statute could not stand. The two laws conflicted with each other, and the state regulation had to give way. Convicting a defendant under both would constitute double jeopardy, which the Fifth Amendment prohibited. Because the Illinois law did not pass constitutional muster, the defendant's conviction under the statute, Chase contended, had to be overturned.

The justices upheld the conviction and let stand the Illinois law. Writing for the majority, Justice Robert C. Grier rejected Chase's arguments and held that the statute in question constituted a legitimate exercise of the state's police power. Nothing in the measure conflicted with the Constitution or federal legislation on the return of fugitives, according to Grier. Rather, the state law represented an attempt to maintain peace and order for the public benefit. Grier went on to argue that the act of assisting fugitives proved detrimental to the Union. "Experience has shown . . ." he contended, "that the results of such conduct as that prohibited by the statute in question are not only to demoralize their citizens who live in daily and open disregard of the duties imposed upon them by the Constitution and laws, but to destroy the harmony and kind feelings which should exist between citizens of this Union, to create border feuds and bitter animosities, and to cause breaches of the peace, violent assaults, riots, and murder." By enacting a law prohibiting such activities, the state sought simply to "defend itself against evils of such magnitude, and punish those who perversely persist in conduct which promotes them" (55 U.S. 13, 18). The majority also rejected Chase's contention that conviction under the Illinois law and the federal statute constituted double jeopardy, as Grier carefully distinguished the wording of the two measures in an attempt to show that the defendant was not being tried for the same crime twice.

Most significant, in *Moore v. Illinois* the Court for the second time reiterated its holding in *Prigg v. Pennsylvania*. Contradicting Chase's claim that any state law regarding fugitive slaves ran afoul of the Fugitive Slave Clause and the federal fugitive slave law, Grier explained that only state legislation that interfered with the return of fugitives was void. "[A]ny State law or regulation which interrupts, impedes, limits, embarrasses, delays, or postpones the right of the owner to the immediate possession of the slave, and the immediate command of his service, is void," he wrote (55 U.S. 13, 21). Laws that supported the constitutional rights of slave owners by aiding in the return of fugitives did not violate the Constitution. On this point, Grier extensively quoted Story's opinion that states could exercise their police power to assist in the rendition of fugitives. The Court's decision in *Moore* significantly curtailed the attempts of antislavery activists to rely upon *Prigg* for support.

Meanwhile, with the constitutionality of the Fugitive Slave Act settled and the holding in *Prigg* clarified, the Court turned its attention to another important issue having to do with slavery—the status of slave sojourners. In 1851, the justices heard *Strader v. Graham*, a case involving a group of slave musicians from Kentucky. After being taken more than once to perform in Ohio, the slaves were returned to their native state. Later, they ran away to Canada with the aid of sympathetic whites in Kentucky, whereupon the slave owner sued for $3,000 in damages those who had abetted the escape. Attorneys for the defendants charged that their clients could not be held liable for assisting fugitive slaves, because the musicians were not in fact slaves at the time that they absconded. Rather, by virtue of their time in Ohio, counsel contended, the blacks were free men, who had achieved this status immediately upon stepping foot on Ohio soil. This claim rested on the Northwest Ordinance of 1787, which at the time of its passage banned slavery in the territories north of the Ohio River. The Kentucky Court of Appeals rejected this argument, and the case came before the U.S. Supreme Court.

In a unanimous opinion, the Court denied that it had any jurisdiction in the case. Writing for his colleagues, Chief Justice Taney held that only the laws of Kentucky controlled the status of the slave musicians who had traveled into Ohio. Nothing in the laws of Ohio or of the United States undermined the legal authority of Kentucky in this case. The Northwest Ordinance, Taney claimed, was no longer in force in Ohio and had no bearing on the status of the slaves in question. The Court, therefore, refused to hear the case since no question of federal law was at issue, and the ruling of the Kentucky court stood. Although short and straightforward, the Supreme Court's opinion in *Strader* was an important one. Presumably, it left to the slave states the power to determine the status of their black residents, regardless of whether they had traveled to free territory. This holding essentially supported the legal doctrine of reversion—the idea that a slave taken into a free state, though free from the control of the master while on free soil, nevertheless reverted to the status of a slave on returning to a slave state. It was a variation of this question that confronted the Court in the *Dred Scott* case.

The Dred Scott *Case and Its Aftermath*

In 1846, Dred Scott, a slave living in St. Louis, filed suit in a Missouri state court for his freedom. The cause alleged that he, his wife, and their two daughters, by virtue of their residence in the free state of Illinois and the free territory of Wisconsin, were entitled to be free. Scott's owner, an army surgeon named John Emerson, had taken his slave with him to Fort Armstrong in Illinois, where Scott resided from December 1833 until May 1836. Later, when the army evacuated Fort Armstrong, Dr. Emerson had relocated to Fort Snelling in present-day Minnesota, where Scott had remained for nearly two years and married a slave woman, Harriet Robinson. At the time, Fort Snelling lay in Wisconsin Territory, where Congress had forever prohibited slavery in the Missouri Compromise. The Wisconsin Enabling Act of 1836, creating the new territory, also specifically had banned slavery there. Scott thus possessed a strong claim to freedom under Missouri law based on his lengthy residence in free territory. After his stay in the North, he and his wife spent a brief time with Emerson in Louisiana before returning to St. Louis. In 1843 Dr. Emerson died, whereupon Dred Scott and his family became the property of Emerson's widow, Irene. After being rented out to various whites, Scott tried to purchase freedom for himself and his family from Irene Emerson. When she refused, Scott filed suit for his freedom in 1846. The sympathetic sons of Scott's former master, Peter Blow, probably assisted him in initiating the litigation. (Emerson had purchased Scott from Blow's estate after Blow's death in the early 1830s.)

Dred Scott's case followed a complicated and unlikely path to the U.S. Supreme Court. Legal technicalities and delays prevented the case from coming to trial in a St. Louis circuit court until 1850. In this initial trial, the judge charged the jury that if Scott had in fact resided in a free state, he could no longer be held as a slave. This charge relied on a string of Missouri precedents stretching back to the 1820s, which had consistently held that slaves who left the state and resided in free territory could not be returned to slavery in Missouri. Although not unique, the state's policy in this regard was among the most liberal of the slave states. Not surprisingly, given the charge and the law that lay behind it, the jury ruled in favor of granting Scott his freedom. But not wanting to lose her four slaves, Mrs. Emerson appealed to the Missouri Supreme Court. There Scott and his cause found a less sympathetic audience. The state's highest court, which included two judges recently elected in 1851, ignored eleven previous decisions granting freedom to slaves in similar situations. In a two-to-one decision, Judge William Scott declared that "times are not now as they were when the former decisions on this subject were made" and ruled that Scott was still a slave.

In 1854 the case entered a new phase. Scott's lawyers filed suit in a federal court against John A. Sanford, Irene Emerson's brother, who was a citizen of New York. This move marked a new legal strategy on the part of counsel. Had Scott appealed the Missouri Supreme Court's decision directly to the U.S. Supreme Court, the justices probably would have denied jurisdiction, just as they had in *Strader v. Graham*. In that case, Chief Justice Taney had held that each state could decide for itself whether a slave's sojourn in free territory had any effect on his status as a slave. Filing a new lawsuit thus gave the Scott and his wife another chance for freedom, as their case would be heard in a federal court, where the *Strader* precedent would not necessarily apply. Sanford, misspelled "Sandford" in the official record of the case, managed many of Emerson's affairs from New York. His residency in another state opened the federal courts to Scott, based on diversity jurisdiction. But Scott's move to the federal court required that he be a citizen, because only citizens of different states could sue each other in federal court under diversity jurisdiction. Sanford's counsel responded by filing a plea in abatement—a legal device intended to end the case by denying jurisdiction, based on the argument that Scott lacked citizenship. The federal judge ruled Scott eligible to bring the suit as a resident of Missouri, but he refused to offer a constitutional definition of citizenship. On the merits of the dispute, the judge instructed the jury that Scott's residence on free soil had no bearing on his status as a slave, and the jury decided in favor of Sanford. Scott and his family remained in bondage.

At a time when concerns over slavery and sectionalism dominated the political landscape, the appeal of Dred Scott's case to the U.S. Supreme Court initially drew surprisingly little attention. In contrast to other Taney-era cases, the dispute did not attract the nation's top attorneys. Montgomery Blair, a well-connected lawyer and free-soil Democrat from Missouri, offered to argue Scott's case for free (Scott's patrons, the Blows, were unable to afford the appeal), but Blair failed to enlist another prominent attorney to join him. Meanwhile, Sandford secured the services of proslavery U.S. Senator Henry S. Geyer of Missouri, as well as attorney (later senator) Reverdy Johnson, of Maryland. Of the three lawyers, only Johnson, a close friend of Chief Justice Taney's, possessed the level of reputation that had come to mark the argument of great cases before the nation's highest court. Most observers undoubtedly thought the justices would reject Scott's claim to freedom on narrow grounds and that the case would establish no new precedent.

But as both sides made their arguments in February 1856, one particular contention immediately changed the tenor of the case and drew renewed attention to the decade-old dispute. Counsel for Sanford claimed that Scott had not become free during his stay in federal territory because the law that had forbidden slavery there—the Missouri Compromise—was unconstitutional. Were the Court to accept this argument, vast areas where slavery had been prohibited might be opened to slaves. At the height of sectional tension over the future of slavery in Kansas, this argument on behalf of Sanford had the potential to augment greatly the significance of the Court's ruling by raising the issue of slavery in the territories. In a charged political atmosphere, the justices postponed making a decision and ordered reargument at the end of the year, after the presidential election. After the lawyers presented their cases a second time, there were deep divisions among the justices about whether to confine themselves to narrow issues or deliver a sweeping opinion on the nature of black citizenship and the constitutionality of the extension of slavery. Believing that the plea in abatement was not before the Court, because it had not been part of the appeal, Justice Nelson, of New York, favored a limited ruling that would focus only on Scott's status, rather than on the question of citizenship. The southern justices, in contrast, sought a decision that would deny black citizenship and grant broad authority to slaveholders to take their human property into the territories. After some discussion, on February 14, 1857, the majority agreed that it would follow the *Strader v. Graham* precedent and rule that Scott's case was governed by Missouri state law and not properly before the federal courts. Justice Nelson received the assignment to write a limited opinion along these lines.

But within a few days, the Court changed its position and decided to rule on the constitutionality of the Missouri Compromise. Two of the northern justices, McLean and Curtis, indicated that they planned to dissent and declare Scott free under the terms of the Missouri Compromise, and the majority felt a need to respond to their arguments. Other members of the Court believed that the justices had a duty, once and for all, to resolve in a broad opinion the great political issue of slavery in the territories that had vexed the nation for at least the past decade. In the meantime, president-elect James Buchanan influenced the deliberation process. Justice Catron, of Tennessee, who had a reputation for meddling in politics, corresponded regularly with the president-elect that winter. Catron particularly urged Buchanan to lean on Justice Grier, who, like the incoming president, hailed from Pennsylvania. Buchanan and Catron believed that the broadest possible decision delivered by the greatest number of justices would have the most potent effect in resolving the issue of slavery in the territories. Grier notified Buchanan that he planned to concur with the lengthy opinion that Taney had begun writing, which would address the issues of black citizenship and slavery in the territories. In his inaugural address on March 4, 1857, President Buchanan—who knew what the Court was about to decide—stated that he would "cheerfully submit" to the Court's opinion in the case, "whatever this may be" (Stampp 1990, 93).

Two days later, on March 6, 1857, Chief Justice Taney and his eight colleagues filed into the justices' courtroom in the basement of the Senate chamber to render the Court's decision in *Dred Scott v. Sandford.* A packed room watched and listened as the seventy-nine-year-old chief justice read the opinion of the Court with trembling hands and fading voice. Taney held that the question of citizenship was legitimately before the Court, and he went on to devote close to half of his opinion to the issue. Addressing the matter from the perspective of the original intent of the framers, Taney ruled that neither slaves nor free blacks could claim citizenship under the Constitution. "[T]he legislation and histories of the times, and the language used in the

Declaration of Independence," Taney wrote, "show, that neither the class of persons who had been imported as slaves, nor their descendants, whether they had become free or not, were then acknowledged as a part of the people, nor intended to be included in the general words used in that memorable instrument." Taney continued by claiming—in one of the most oft-quoted passages in Supreme Court history—that they "had no rights which the white man was bound to respect" (60 U.S. 393, 407). The existence of antimiscegenation statutes, according to the chief justice, showed that the founders regarded free blacks and slaves as equally inferior to whites under the law. Two clauses of the Constitution, moreover, specifically singled out the black race as a separate category excluded from citizenship: the Slave Trade Clause, which referred "unquestionably," in Taney's words, to "persons of the race of which we are speaking," and the Fugitive Slave Clause, which mandated the delivering up of escaped slaves. "[C]ertainly these two clauses were not intended to confer on [slaves] or their posterity the blessings of liberty, or any of the personal rights so carefully provided for the citizen," the chief justice asserted (60 U.S. 393, 411). Taney rested his views on black citizenship squarely on what he believed to be the intentions of the framers of the Constitution. Because the framers had deemed blacks inferior to whites, African Americans—whether slave or free—had no legitimate constitutional claims to citizenship.

The second half of Taney's opinion dealt with the scope of congressional power over slavery in the territories. Although scholars have long debated whether this issue was properly before the Court and whether Taney's statements on the question were mere obiter dicta, the chief justice seemed determined to address the subject. Taney held that Congress possessed no power to regulate slavery in the territories. His argument rested on two contentions. First, the chief justice took a restrictive view of the Territories Clause. Article IV, Section 3 of the Constitution provided that "Congress shall have Power to dispose of and make all needful Rules and Regulations respecting the Territory or other Property belonging to the United States." Based on this clause, Congress had, beginning in 1787 with the Northwest Ordinance, enacted a series of legislative measures pertaining to slavery in territories, including the Missouri Compromise and the Kansas-Nebraska Act. Taney put forth an unorthodox and dubious interpretation of this clause, arguing that it applied only to those territories that were part of the United States at the time of the drafting of the Constitution. Second, Taney relied on the Fifth Amendment to assert that congressional legislation on slavery in the territories violated the rights of slaveholders to do with their property as they wished. Under the amendment, no person could "be deprived of life, liberty, or property, without due process of law." Taney argued that Congress could in no way restrict the right to hold slave property—a right "distinctly and expressly affirmed in the Constitution" (60 U.S. 393, 451). Neither could a territorial legislature, he contended, enact legislation interfering with the right of slaveholding. In this way, Taney took a swipe at the notion of popular sovereignty, the idea that the people of a territory could decide its status with regard to slavery. This principle lay at the heart of both the Compromise of 1850 and the Kansas-Nebraska Act.

All of the other justices in the majority wrote opinions in the case, although few had substantial disagreements with the chief justice. On the issue of citizenship, most agreed with Taney's conclusion, and on the question of Scott's status all but two members of the Court held that he remained a slave. Justice Nelson, for his part, wrote a narrow opinion—the one that originally was to be the majority opinion—denying the jurisdiction of the federal courts and ruling that Scott was still a slave. McLean and Curtis issued their dissents, both of which argued for the constitutionality of the Missouri Compromise and attacked Taney's outright rejection of black citizenship. Curtis's opinion, the lengthier and better reasoned of the two, quickly became an important document of the antislavery cause and a campaign tract for the Republicans. His dissent made the compelling point that before the adoption of the Constitution, five states recognized blacks as citizens and granted them suffrage. Curtis used this evidence to contradict directly Taney's claim that blacks could not be counted as members of the political community at the time of the founding. Curtis's dissent went so far as to state that the majority opinion lacked judicial force, as he asserted that the chief justice's denial of Scott's citizenship meant that the Court lacked jurisdiction over the case. A disagreement between Taney and Curtis over the timing of the release of the dissent prompted Curtis's resignation from the bench soon after the announcement of the decision.

The *Dred Scott* decision had a huge impact on the already deeply divided nation. Taney's opinion struck at the heart of the newly formed Republican Party, for it declared the principle on which the party had been founded—the nonextension of slavery into the territories—to be unconstitutional. In this way, the opinion served as a convenient foil for the party's political candidates, and Abraham Lincoln, of Illinois, made the ruling central to his 1858 campaign for the U.S. Senate against Stephen Douglas. The decision, by initiating such a powerful backlash on the part of abolitionists and opponents of slavery's extension, boosted Republican strength. Previously indifferent or skeptical northerners took notice when Lincoln and others charged that the opinion resulted from a conspiracy on the part of the southern slave power. In his famous "House Divided" speech, Lincoln noted that "Stephen [Douglas], Franklin [Pierce], Roger [Taney], and James [Buchanan] all understood one another from the beginning and all worked upon a common plan or draft drawn up before the first lick was struck" (Delbanco 1992, 94). Although Lincoln had no evidence that the Pierce administration's Kansas policy, Buchanan's election, Taney's decision, and the ruling's endorsement by the leading proslavery politicians of the day had all been worked out in advance to as to cause the spread of slavery, the argument certainly made sense to many northern voters.

Democrats generally applauded the Court's decision. Many northern Democrats saw the ruling as the final resolution of the territories issue, and Taney's denunciation of the notion of black citizenship certainly resonated with the racial views of most Democrats. Still, Taney's opinion discredited Democrat Stephen Douglas's notion of popular sovereignty as much as it did the Republican principle of nonextension of slavery. In this way, the decision put the Illinois senator on the defensive against Lincoln, harmed Douglas's presidential ambitions, and eventually destroyed Democratic Party unity. No decision of the Taney era so dramatically affected the politics of the day. In an ironic twist of fate, a dispute over the actual ownership of Dred Scott led to his transfer to another master and his eventual manumission in May 1857, just a few months after the Court announced its decision. Scott lived in freedom for only sixteen months, as he died in September 1858.

Dred Scott v. Sandford was not the Taney Court's last word on the slavery issue. Two important postscripts to the decision demonstrated the extent to which sectional politics shaped the relationship between proslavery constitutionalism and federal power. *Ableman v. Booth* (1859), a case involving the Fugitive Slave Act of 1850, brought about an ironic convergence of nationalism and proslavery jurisprudence at the end of the Taney era. In 1854, Missouri slave owner Benjamin Garland traveled to Wisconsin to recapture a runaway slave named Joshua Glover. Invoking the federal fugitive slave law, Garland filed the appropriate complaint before the U.S. commissioner in Milwaukee, who issued a warrant for the arrest of the fugitive. Acting on this authority, a deputy marshal forced his way into Glover's cabin, bound him, and carried him off to the Milwaukee jail. A large public rally denounced the seizure of Glover and vowed to release him, while abolitionist editor Sherman Booth secured a writ of habeas corpus for Glover from a local judge. When the federal marshal and the county sheriff denied that the state habeas corpus proceeding had any legal authority over the federal prisoner, the crowd broke into the jail and freed Glover, who was never recaptured. Federal authorities arrested Booth and charged him with violating the Fugitive Slave Act. Before his case could be heard, however, Booth appealed to the Wisconsin Supreme Court for a writ of habeas corpus. The state court ordered his release on the grounds that the fugitive slave law violated the Constitution, whereupon Stephen Ableman, the federal marshal, appealed to the U.S. Supreme Court. In a clash between the state and federal judicial power, the Wisconsin Supreme Court asserted that it would not have to carry out a judicial order of the U.S. Supreme Court.

In a 9–0 decision, the U.S. Supreme Court ruled that the state court had no grounds to defy federal authority. Chief Justice Taney's majority opinion flatly denied that the state court possessed any of the power it claimed. Taking a page from John Marshall's book, Taney cited the Supremacy Clause of the Constitution and maintained that federal judicial supremacy constituted an essential element of the general supremacy of the national government. No state court could, he argued, refuse to abide by or interfere with a federal judicial decision. "[N]o power is more clearly conferred by the Constitution and laws of the United States, than the power of this court to decide, ultimately and finally, all cases arising under such Constitution and laws; and for that purpose to bring here for revision, by writ of error, the judgment of a State court, where such questions have arisen, and the right claimed under them denied by the highest judicial tribunal in the State," Taney wrote (62 U.S. 506, 525). The absence of federal judicial authority would lead only to legal chaos and uncertainty, as individual state courts would interpret federal law as they chose. Although Taney conceded that state courts could inquire into any imprisonments through its habeas corpus authority, once it was determined that a prisoner was held under federal authority the state court had no grounds to proceed further. Although in the abstract a forceful statement of judicial power, in practice the decision in *Ableman v. Booth* provided further protection to the interests of slaveholders.

The second case involving slavery to follow the *Dred Scott* opinion came in early 1861, just as the secession crisis was unfolding. *Kentucky v. Dennison* involved Willis Lago, a free black from Ohio, who helped a Kentucky slave girl escape to freedom as she traveled with her master through Ohio on the way to Virginia. Kentucky indicted Lago for theft, and the state's governor Beriah Magoffin asked Ohio governor William Dennison to extradite Lago. After consulting with his attorney general on the matter, Dennison concluded that Lago had violated no law for which he needed to be extradited. Kentucky thereupon petitioned the U.S. Supreme Court to take the case under its original jurisdiction and to issue a writ of mandamus to Dennison ordering him to surrender Lago. In a unanimous opinion, Chief Justice Taney held that a writ of mandamus constituted the appropriate means for dealing with the situation and that, for the purposes of extradition, the demanding state governed the definition of crimes. Moreover, the chief justice criticized Ohio's governor for attempting to decide on his own which offenses should be classified as criminal. Although Taney in every way expressed his dissatisfaction with Ohio's actions, the chief justice faced a major dilemma. As the Court delivered the opinion in March 1861, the southern states were in the process of seceding from the Union. Taney, sympathetic to the seceding states, could not bring himself to rule that the governor could be coerced to return the fugitive, as this seemed to lend too much credence to national supremacy. Although federal law authorized governors to extradite fugitives, federal power, Taney ruled, could not be used to coerce or punish them for their refusal to do so. Abolitionist Willis Lago thus remained in Ohio.

Conclusion

Despite the starkly Jacksonian Democratic makeup of the Taney Court, which even in its early years contained few holdovers from the Marshall era, the years from 1836 to 1864 produced no revolution in U.S. constitutional development. The Taney Court neither destroyed the nation that Federalists had created, nor did it undermine the power of the Supreme Court that Marshall had so carefully crafted. Rather, in most areas—particularly contract and commercial cases—Taney and his colleagues exhibited a balanced pragmatism that served as a mild corrective to Marshall's grand, idea-driven decision making. As the republic expanded and the economy exploded, Taney and his colleagues confronted real-life economic and social situations that Marshall could scarcely have imagined during his early years on the Court. During the Taney years, states did gain more power to regulate than Marshall would have liked or permitted, but for the most part the national government retained its authority, and the federal courts even expanded their reach. Slavery jurisprudence, of course, was the one big difference between the tenures of the two chief justices. The Taney Court's unswerving devotion to slaveholding interests constituted a serious blot on an otherwise solid—even outstanding—judicial record.

References and Further Reading

Baxter, Maurice G. *Henry Clay the Lawyer.* Lexington: University Press of Kentucky, 2000.

———. *Daniel Webster and the Supreme Court.* Amherst: University of Massachusetts Press, 1966.

Conron, Michael A. "Law, Politics, and Chief Justice Taney: A Reconsideration of the *Luther v. Borden* Decision." *American Journal of Legal History* 11 (1967): 377–388.

Currie, David P. *The Constitution in the Supreme Court: The First Hundred Years.* Chicago: University of Chicago Press, 1985.

Delbanco, Andrew, ed. *The Portable Abraham Lincoln.* New York: Viking Penguin, 1992.

Ely, James W., Jr. *The Guardian of Every Other Right: A Constitutional History of Property Rights.* New York: Oxford University Press, 1992.

———. "The Scope of Admiralty Jurisdiction." In John W. Johnson, *Historic U.S. Court Cases: An Encyclopedia.* 2nd ed. New York: Routledge, 2001, pp. 436–438.

Fehrenbacher, Don E. *The Dred Scott Case: Its Significance in American Law and Politics.* New York: Oxford University Press, 1978.

Finkelman, Paul. *Dred Scott v. Sandford: A Brief History with Documents.* Boston: Bedford Books, 1997.

———. "*Prigg v. Pennsylvania* and Northern State Courts: Anti-Slavery Use of a Pro-Slavery Decision." *Civil War History* 25 (1979): 5–35.

———. "*Prigg v. Pennsylvania:* Understanding Justice Story's Proslavery Nationalism." *Journal of Supreme Court History* (1997): 51–64.

Frankfurter, Felix. *The Commerce Clause under Marshall, Taney, and Waite.* Chapel Hill: University of North Carolina Press, 1937.

Fritz, Harry W. "The *Right* of Revolution v. the Right of *Revolution.*" In John W. Johnson, ed., *Historic U.S. Court Cases: An Encyclopedia.* New York: Routledge, 2001, pp. 239–242.

"From Judicial Grant to Legislative Power: The Admiralty Clause in the Nineteenth Century." *Harvard Law Review* 67 (1954): 1214–1237.

Hall, Kermit L., ed. *The Oxford Companion to the Supreme Court of the United States.* New York: Oxford University Press, 1992.

Horwitz, Morton J. *The Transformation of American Law, 1780–1860.* Cambridge: Harvard University Press, 1977.

Hyman, Harold M., and William M. Wiecek. *Equal Justice Under Law: Constitutional Development, 1836–1875.* New York: Harper and Row, 1982.

Irons, Peter. *A People's History of the Supreme Court.* New York: Penguin Books, 1999.

Kutler, Stanley I. *Privilege and Creative Destruction: The Charles River Bridge Case.* Baltimore: Johns Hopkins University Press, 1971.

Lewis, Walker. *Without Fear or Favor: A Biography of Chief Justice Roger B. Taney.* Boston: Houghton Mifflin, 1965.

Newmyer, R. Kent. *The Supreme Court Under Marshall and Taney.* Arlington Heights, IL: Harland Davidson, 1968.

Schwartz, Bernard. *A History of the Supreme Court.* New York: Oxford University Press, 1993.

Stampp, Kenneth. *America in 1857: A Nation on the Brink.* New York: Oxford University Press, 1990.

Streichler, Stuart A. "Justice Curtis's Dissent in the Dred Scott Case: An Interpretive Study." *Hastings Constitutional Law Quarterly* 24 (1997): 509–544.

Swisher, Carl Brent. *History of the Supreme Court of the United States*, vol. 5, *The Taney Period, 1836–64.* New York: Macmillan, 1974.

———. *Roger B. Taney.* New York: Macmillan, 1936.

Warren, Charles. *The Supreme Court in United States History*, vol. 2. Boston: Little, Brown, 1928.

Wiecek, William. *The Guarantee Clause of the U.S. Constitution.* Ithaca, NY: Cornell University Press, 1972.

———. "Slavery and Abolition Before the United States Supreme Court, 1820–1860." *Journal of American History* 65 (1978): 34–59.

4

Legacy and Impact

Because few chief justices in the Supreme Court's history have dominated their times like Roger B. Taney, any evaluation of the Taney Court must rely heavily on an assessment of Taney himself. No chief justice has had a more disputed and controversial legacy. At the time of Taney's death, as many rejoiced, it seemed, as mourned. Best known as the author of the opinion in the *Dred Scott* case, Taney's passing elicited no sorrow from those who viewed the decision as a part of southern slaveholders' attempts to nationalize their "peculiar institution." So vociferous were some of Taney's critics that they successfully blocked what would have been a routine appropriation of federal money for a bust in his honor. This hostility to Taney reflects one school of thought, both at the time of the chief justice's death and even today among some scholars. Still, Taney had—and has—his admirers. During the late nineteenth century, Taney's friends and Democratic allies did their best to defend the deceased chief justice's reputation. Since that time, Taney has won the most acclaim for his decisions regarding contracts and commerce, and in the first decades of the twentieth century his standing among legal scholars and historians reached its peak. Although generally regarded today as a "great" chief justice, this evaluation rests entirely on Taney's opinions in cases having to do with economic issues and the separation of powers. To some extent, therefore, Taney remains the villain of the *Dred Scott* case.

The Disputed Reputation of Roger B. Taney

The Civil War and Reconstruction Era

After spending much time during the Civil War years in ill health while living in a rented home in the nation's capital, Roger B. Taney died on October 12, 1864, at the age of eighty-seven. Three days later, a group of family members, friends, dignitaries, and onlookers gathered at Taney's Washington, D.C., residence to pay their last respects. President Lincoln and three cabinet officers, including Secretary of State

Seward, were in attendance. Afterward, a train took Taney's body to Frederick, Maryland, where the funeral service took place in the town's Catholic church, which Taney had helped to build.

At once, the partisan struggle to interpret Taney's judicial work began. Some Republican newspapers vilified the chief justice for the *Dred Scott* ruling, for his sympathy toward the Confederacy, and for his supposed abuses of judicial power. "The Nation can feel little regret at his removal from an office which, in his hands, has been so promiscuously used," wrote the *Philadelphia North American*. "It is fortunate for the interests of humanity that the President and Senate who must fill the vacancy are devoted to the interests of republican liberty and will suffer no man of that school of politics to which Taney belonged to intrude into the judicial robes of which death has deprived him" (Warren 1928, 391). Democratic newspapers, in contrast, lavished praise on the deceased jurist. The *National Intelligencer*, for example, claimed that he had "a reputation as much distinguished by the superior dignity of his character as by the extraordinary vigor of his intellect" (Warren 1928, 393).

A few months later, the debate over Taney spilled onto the floor of the U.S. Senate. On February 23, 1865, Senator Lyman Trumbull, a Republican of Illinois, introduced a bill, already passed by the House of Representatives, providing for the placement of a marble bust of Taney in the Supreme Court's chamber, where busts of the previous chief justices were already displayed. Senator Charles Sumner, of Massachusetts, rose in opposition. "I object to that; that now an emancipated country should make a bust to the author of the *Dred Scott* decision," he stated. Trumbull responded that Taney had presided over the Court for more than a quarter century and trusted that a bill to honor a man who "had added reputation to the character of the judiciary of the Unites States throughout the world is not to be hooted down by an exclamation that the country is to be emancipated." This comment provoked a sharp retort from Sumner. "[T]he name of Taney is to be hooted down the page of history," Sumner announced. "Judgment is beginning now; and an emancipated country will fasten upon him the stigma which he deserves. . . . He administered justice at last wickedly, and degraded the judiciary of the country, and degraded the age."

Sumner's comments provoked a forceful response from Senator Reverdy Johnson, of Maryland, an eminent lawyer and a lifelong friend of Taney's. Expressing his doubt that Sumner would fare as well among future historians as would Taney, Johnson offered a spirited defense of his friend. "Sir, the decisions of that learned jurist are now quoted with approbation everywhere, and there is not a judge upon the bench now, three or four of them having been selected by the present incumbent of the presidential office, who will not say at once that a brighter intellect never adorned the judicial station." Johnson's assessment of the justices' views was correct, for during his last years Taney had succeeded in winning the personal respect of every one of Lincoln's appointees. Still, Johnson's words were to no avail. Republican Senators

John P. Hale, of New Hampshire (who had favored abolishing the Court and appointing a new one in 1861), Henry Wilson, of Massachusetts, and Benjamin F. Wade, of Ohio, all spoke out against the allocation of $1,000 for the marble bust. Wade, most pointedly, remarked that his Ohio constituents "would pay $2,000 to hang this man in effigy rather than $1,000 for a bust to commemorate his merits" (*Congressional Globe*, Senate, 38th Congress, 2nd Session, 1012, 1016). With such staunch opposition from leading Republicans, the appropriation bill failed to pass the Republican-controlled Senate.

The debate on the Senate floor constituted only the opening round of a barrage of criticism. During the same month as the controversy over the bust, with northern victory imminent and the demise of slavery on the horizon, the *Atlantic Monthly* published a lengthy piece on the late chief justice's opinions in slavery cases. This extensive and careful analysis of Taney's decisions on the slavery question, which was probably written by Boston lawyer Charles M. Ellis, began with statements Taney had made while he was attorney general under Andrew Jackson and concluded with the *Dred Scott* opinion. "By this record will the world judge Chief Justice Taney," the author predicted (*Atlantic Monthly*, February 1865, 159). Taney's other efforts and achievements as chief justice paled in comparison to his slavery opinions, the article asserted, and only for the latter would he be remembered: "[T]he slaveocrats' revolution of the last two generations, and the Secession war, and the triumph of Liberty, will be the theme of the world; and he, of all who precipitated them, will be most likely, after the traitor leaders, to be held in infamous remembrance; for he did more than any other individual—more than any President, if not more than all—more in one hour than the legislature in thirty years—to extend the Slave Power" (*Atlantic Monthly*, February 1865, 159). Asserting that Taney had perverted the meaning of the Declaration of Independence and the Constitution, the article compared Taney unfavorably even with the infamous Lord Chief Justice George Jeffreys of England, the much-reviled persecutor of Protestants during the late seventeenth century. Because the United States professed to hold a higher standard of justice than England, according to the article, the depths of Taney's cruelty reached lower than even those of Jeffreys.

The most vitriolic of the posthumous attacks on Taney came in an anonymous sixty-six-page pamphlet, "The Unjust Judge, A Memorial of Roger Brooke Taney," published that same year. Like the *Atlantic* article, the pamphlet accused Taney of the worst abuses of judicial power and asserted that the *Dred Scott* opinion alone would shape Taney's reputation. "From that hour [of the decision] it ceased to be remembered that he had ever made any other decision; nor so long as the remembrance of these times may endure will it be forgotten that he made that one" ("Unjust Judge," 1865, 5). Indeed, the author dismissed Taney's other judicial work as "a long series of opinions, too trite even to be quoted, and too dull to be read, which would not confer distinction upon a judge of the most inferior judicatory in the land" ("Unjust Judge," 1865, 7).

Much of the pamphlet argued that the framers had been antislavery in their outlook and that the Constitution embodied the spirit of the Declaration of Independence, particularly its assertion that all men are created equal. The author of "The Unjust Judge" took particular satisfaction in showing how Taney, early in his career, viewed slavery as incompatible with the Declaration, a position that he later repudiated in the *Dred Scott* case. As a young lawyer in Frederick County, Maryland, Taney had defended Jacob Gruber, an antislavery Methodist minister accused of disturbing the peace and inciting rebellion, and in the process had cited the Declaration of Independence in support of his antislavery views. "At forty, Mr. Taney had responded to the call of the Revolution, 'insisted on the principles contained in that venerated instrument,' the Declaration . . . ," the author of "The Unjust Judge" wrote. "At eighty, clothed with the power and prerogative of the most potential place in the nation, on an occasion when he might have promoted, essentially, a consummation for which the whole earth was panting, he proved false to himself, false to the hope and charities he had once cherished, false to the liberal principles he had eulogized, and to a Free Constitution he had sworn to support" ("The Unjust Judge," 1865, 47). The pamphlet drew heavily from Justice Benjamin Curtis's dissent in the *Dred Scott* case, in an attempt to demonstrate that many African Americans, contrary to Taney's assertion, had enjoyed the rights of citizenship at the time of the founding.

But more than an academic criticism of Taney's reasoning in the *Dred Scott* opinion, "The Unjust Judge" constituted a rhetorical assault on the character of the nation's fifth chief justice. The author excoriated Taney as a "malevolent old man" engaged in "the most nefarious of purposes," a man as untrue to the principles of the Christian religion as he was to the ideals of the Constitution. In his perversion of the law and misuse of judicial power, Taney equaled the infamous Jeffreys "in his worst moods, in his worst days." Moreover, the author contended, "in the character and dimension of his crime against humanity," Taney exceeded Jeffreys. "As a Jurist, or, more strictly speaking, as a Judge, in which character he will be most remembered, he was, next to Pontius Pilate, perhaps the worst that ever occupied the seat of judgment among men," the pamphlet stated ("The Unjust Judge," 1865, 65). The exceedingly harsh tone of "The Unjust Judge," as well as its constitutional arguments regarding slavery, prompted one scholar to assert that Charles Sumner was the author of the polemic. The views expressed certainly coincided with those of the abolitionist senator from Massachusetts. Regardless of its authorship, though, the pamphlet showed the degree of animosity toward Taney over the *Dred Scott* decision at a time when the nation was experiencing the rush of Union victory and emancipation.

Taney's friends and defenders refused to let such attacks go answered. In 1872, Samuel Tyler, a longtime intimate of the chief justice and member of the bar of Frederick County, Maryland, published his *Memoir of Roger Brooke Taney* in an effort to vindicate the chief justice. Two years before his death, Taney had asked Tyler to commence work on this volume, which ended up being a 659-page account of Taney's life and labors. Taney penned a portion of the book himself—the part relating to his early life—and Tyler wrote the rest after examining letters and documents relating to the chief justice's public and private life. From beginning to end, of course, the *Memoir* lauded Taney's accomplishments and made a case for his greatness. The first few chapters detailed his life at the bar in Frederick County and Baltimore as well as his service under President Andrew Jackson, and subsequent chapters covered his work on the Supreme Court.

In the chapter covering the period of the *Dred Scott* controversy, Tyler described at length the rise of a "radical" movement to abolish slavery in the United States. Writing in 1872, in the midst of Reconstruction, Tyler's critique of "radical" abolitionism no doubt resonated with an American public that was beginning to grow weary of the relatively "radical" constitutional reforms of the day. The Fourteenth and Fifteenth Amendments, ratified in 1868 and 1870 respectively, had recently established the citizenship of African Americans and had prohibited infringement on their right to vote. When Tyler criticized the abolitionists as "radicals," in other words, his audience understood him as well to be critiquing the Reconstruction policies of the day. "Radicalism belongs rather to the instincts of man than to his reason," Tyler wrote. "It is philanthropic rather than patriotic. It moves to its ends through paths of destruction; and always terminates by an inevitable recoil of society to save itself from anarchy in a military despotism" (Tyler 1872, 341–342).

In portraying the abolitionists as radicals, Tyler set the tone for his interpretation of Taney's slavery decisions and for his defense of the chief justice's overall judicial record. From Tyler's perspective, the ideals of Taney's critics represented a drastic departure from the American political and constitutional mainstream, whereas Taney acted squarely within established constitutional norms. Tyler defended *Dred Scott* as a correct decision, despite being overruled by the recently concluded Civil War. He took issue with Justice Curtis's dissenting opinion by calling into question the basic assumptions on which it rested. In the dissent, Curtis had asserted that slavery was "contrary to natural right" and "created only by municipal law." On the basis of this argument, Curtis had contended that a citizen could not take his slaves into a territory in which slavery was forbidden. Tyler strongly disagreed. "The doctrine that slavery was created by municipal law," he wrote, "is one of the most extraordinary aberrations from a great fundamental principle of public law to be found in the history of judicial administration" (Tyler 1872, 363). Tyler went on to argue that slavery had been recognized by the law of nations for centuries and that "natural right" constituted ambiguous grounds for asserting that slaves could not be taken into the new territories. Although he professed no love of slavery, Tyler saw it as his "duty" to clarify the historical record on such matters.

Tyler's attempt to dismiss the opposition to *Dred Scott* as driven by radical politics was also evident in how he dealt with the charge that the decision resulted from a slave power conspiracy. Many Republicans had picked up on New York Senator William Seward's charge in 1858 that a whispered exchange between the chief justice and incoming President James Buchanan on the inaugural platform in 1857 had demonstrated that a conspiracy had existed between the president and the justices. According to Seward, the case had been cooked up by proslavery interests who sought a ruling allowing slavery to spread all over the country. Kansas, in particular, at that time was a bloody battleground over the future of slavery, and the *Dred Scott* decision prompted Buchanan in 1858 to refer to Kansas as a slave state. Tyler dismissed charges of such a conspiracy by obtaining letters from Justices John A. Campbell and Samuel Nelson, two of the three members of the Court when the *Dred Scott* decision was issued who were still living at the time Tyler was writing. (Curtis was the other one.) Campbell's and Nelson's letters, which Tyler included in the book, stated that they knew of no collusion between Buchanan and members of the Court. Tyler, moreover, published the full text of a speech Reverdy Johnson delivered in 1858, in which he had refuted Seward's charges. Johnson had noted that Dred Scott had himself initiated the suit and that the case had begun making its way through Missouri state courts well before the passage of the Kansas-Nebraska Act. Tyler blasted Seward as "a man of crooked ways" and derided the conspiracy charge as "an unmitigated calumny from beginning to end, invented by a bad man to serve in his machinations for the Presidency" (Tyler 1872, 379). Taney had held the New York senator in such contempt, according to Tyler, that had he won the Republican nomination and the presidential election in 1860 the chief justice would have refused to administer to him the oath of office.

While he portrayed the chief justice's critics as radicals and scoundrels, Tyler compiled numerous testimonials praising Taney's private benevolence and professional achievements. In an effort to humanize the deceased chief justice—depicted by his opponents as a judicial monster—Tyler devoted a whole chapter to Taney's private life, much of which extolled him for his religious devotion. Tyler included a laudatory sermon about Taney that was delivered by the pastor of the Protestant Episcopal Church in Lincoln's hometown of Springfield, Illinois, as well as Justice Peter V. Daniel's account of his inadvertently interrupting the chief justice while Taney was on his knees in prayer. "He made an apology as soon as possible for the intrusion, which the Chief Justice accepted," Tyler wrote, "with the remark that it was his custom, before he began the duties of the day, to seek divine guidance through prayer" (Tyler 1872, 478). A man of sincere religiosity, in short, Taney was no Pontius Pilate—or even a Jeffreys. The deceased chief justice, Tyler attempted to show, combined the qualities of a Christian gentlemen with those of a learned jurist. Tyler chose former Justice Benjamin Curtis—a successful lawyer in the postwar period—to provide the final bit of evidence for the case he was building, for Tyler reprinted the admiring remarks Curtis had delivered on the occasion of Taney's death. Tyler must have been satisfied that his *Memoir* achieved its purpose of rehabilitating the much-maligned Taney. In 1873, a year after the *Memoir*'s publication, Taney's successor Salmon P. Chase died, and Congress—without debate—appropriated money for marble busts of both of the deceased chief justices.

From the Late Nineteenth to the Mid-Twentieth Century

As contemporaries of Taney and of the *Dred Scott* ruling passed on, and as partisan feelings over the issues of slavery and Civil War faded away, the harsh criticism of Taney and the intense debate over his reputation subsided. During the late nineteenth and early twentieth centuries, as American race relations reached their lowest ebb, Taney's slavery decisions figured less prominently in evaluations of his judicial record than before. During the 1890s, northern political leaders basically abandoned the cause of black civil rights, thus giving a free hand to southern states to deal with African Americans as they wished. White southerners enacted Jim Crow laws mandating the separation of the races in public facilities and implemented laws disfranchising African Americans. At the same time, white mobs lynched black men in record numbers. Over the course of the next few decades, moreover, American popular culture denigrated blacks in literature, film, and art. During an era marked by little or no progress in the area of black civil rights, historians and legal scholars largely ignored or excused the *Dred Scott* decision and began to view Taney and his colleagues in a more favorable light.

The pinnacle of Taney's early twentieth-century rehabilitation came during the 1930s, when the nation's leading judges and scholars lavished praise on him. In 1931, Chief Justice Charles Evans Hughes traveled to Frederick, Maryland, to celebrate the unveiling of a bust of Taney. Hughes's remarks on this occasion, subsequently published in the *American Bar Association Journal*, summarized nearly forty years of scholarly writing on Taney and set the tone for the next two decades of interpretation. Hughes portrayed Taney as a serene and dignified leader in an age of partisan strife as well as a fitting successor to the great Chief Justice Marshall. In particular, Hughes celebrated Taney's firm devotion to the nationalistic principles established by Marshall. Hughes cited *Holmes v. Jennison* (1840), for example, where Taney emphasized the exclusive power of the national government in the realm of foreign relations, as well as *Genesee Chief v. Fitzhugh* (1852), in which Taney extended the admiralty jurisdiction of the federal courts to all navigable waters.

Most pointedly, Hughes took issue with those who focused undue attention on Taney's record on slavery. "It is unfortunate that the estimate of Chief Justice Taney's judicial labors should have been so largely influenced by the opinion which he delivered in the case of *Dred Scott*," Hughes observed. Hughes dismissed again the charges of conspiracy raised by contemporaries of the decision and hailed "the sincerity of the action of the Chief Justice, who thought he was rendering a national service." Blaming the furor surrounding the decision on "the temper of the times," Hughes downplayed the importance of the *Dred Scott* case because of its "negligible influence upon the development of constitutional jurisprudence" (Hughes 1931, 787). Ironically, Hughes described Taney's opinion in *Ableman v. Booth* (1859), in which the Court asserted the supremacy of the federal judiciary over state tribunals, as "the crown of the judicial career of Chief Justice Taney." Hughes focused on the nationalistic nature of the holding in the case, rather than the fact that the opinion protected slavery by thwarting the Wisconsin Supreme Court's effort to nullify the federal fugitive slave law. As Samuel Tyler had done in his biography of Taney, Hughes concluded his article by quoting Justice Curtis's eulogy, after which Hughes offered his own definitive assessment of his predecessor: "He was a great Chief Justice" (Hughes 1931, 790). Five years later, in 1936, confirmation of the once-disgraced Taney's rehabilitation came with the commissioning of a U.S. Coast Guard cutter named in honor of the nineteenth-century chief justice. (The cutter *Taney*, the Guard's largest ship at the time of its commissioning, went on to fight at Pearl Harbor in Hawaii as well as in Korea and Vietnam.)

In 1937, Harvard law professor and future Supreme Court justice Felix Frankfurter seconded Hughes's appraisal. More than any twentieth-century scholar, Frankfurter was responsible for Taney's rehabilitation. In *The Commerce Clause Under Marshall, Taney, and Waite*, Frankfurter traced Taney's contributions to the evolution of the commerce power. Frankfurter looked favorably on the Taney Court's willingness to grant wide latitude to states to engage in commercial regulation, particularly Taney's idea that the Commerce Clause, in the absence of federal legislation, posed no barrier to state regulation. Although he differed with Marshall on this question, Taney did not arrive at this position out of a doctrinaire commitment to states' rights. On the contrary, according to Frankfurter, Taney's willingness to allow states to engage in such regulatory activities arose out of his "conception of the judicial function, . . . his unwillingness to open the door to judicial policy-making wider than the Constitution obviously required" (Frankfurter 1937, 54).

Overall, Frankfurter attempted to disassociate Taney from the South and to discredit the idea that he was the "leader of a band of militant 'agrarian,' 'localist,' 'proslavery' judges" who represented a sharp break with Marshall (Frankfurter 1937, 48). Frankfurter believed that much of Taney's jurisprudence flowed out of the precedents established by Marshall and that ultimately a series of compromises yielded a sound and pragmatic approach to the issue of commercial regulation. Frankfurter went to great lengths to demonstrate that Taney's jurisprudence lay within the mainstream of American constitutional development—that it represented opposition to "financial concentration" rather than agrarianism, "legislative freedom for the states" rather than "localism." "Least of all was he a 'pro-slavery' man in any invidious sense," Frankfurter contended. "[H]e was merely concerned lest the Union be broken by extreme action, and the South become the economic vassal of northern capitalism" (Frankfurter 1937, 49). Frankfurter seemed passionately concerned with exalting Taney's judicial achievements. "The mists of prejudice are only gradually lifting from Taney's reputation," Frankfurter wrote. "Eventually, one hopes, it will become intellectually disreputable to see him predominantly as the judicial defender of slavery" (Frankfurter 1937, 66). Although acknowledging that Marshall would forever overshadow his successor, Frankfurter concluded that Taney stood second in American constitutional history only to the great Marshall.

This favorable view of Taney continued to hold sway into the mid-twentieth century. In a 1941 essay, leading constitutional scholar Beryl Harold Levy took previous interpretations of Taney, especially with regard to slavery, a step further. Whereas Tyler had attempted to justify the *Dred Scott* ruling and Frankfurter had downplayed its importance, Levy portrayed Taney's decision as an exception in his judicial record and one that was in conflict with his private beliefs. According to Levy, Taney's entire Supreme Court career exemplified his commitment to judicial restraint. Only in *Dred Scott* did the Taney Court overturn a federal statute, and it did so, according to Levy, only because Justice John McLean had insisted on issuing a dissenting opinion in the case. This dissent forced the majority, led by Taney, to draft a more expansive opinion that dealt with the issue of congressional control over slavery in the territories. Levy, moreover, made much of Taney's antislavery statements during his early legal career, his support for the colonization movement, and his manumission of his own slaves, in an effort to demonstrate that the *Dred Scott* decision failed to conform to Taney's own beliefs. In short, Levy articulated a remarkably positive interpretation of Taney, even with regard to the slavery issue.

Perhaps the capstone of this celebratory view of Taney came in a speech delivered in 1954 by Chief Justice Earl Warren. Like Hughes in 1931, Warren made the pilgrimage to Frederick, Maryland, to honor the memory of Taney—this time to dedicate a new monument—and his speech drew heavily on the ideas of the Marylander's earlier defenders. Warren announced that the tribute to Taney helped redress a wrong and "erase the calumny which Taney's enemies had hurled at him during his lifetime and which superficial historians preserved as gospel truth for a time after his death" ("Address of Earl Warren," 1954, 3). Warren lamented that Taney had been viewed for so many years simply as a champion of provincial interests and the institution of slavery. "But, by and large, with the passing of time and the cooling of passions," Warren observed, "that characterization has been discredited and the true Taney has emerged." Warren went on to praise Taney for his development of the notion of police powers, his expansion of admiralty jurisdiction, his advocacy of federal judicial supremacy over the states, and his commitment to judicial restraint. Taking his cues from Frankfurter and Levy, Warren portrayed Taney "as one who personally detested slavery but who detested even more the prospect of violent disunion." Echoing Hughes's assessment, Warren deemed his nineteenth-century predecessor "a great Chief Justice" ("Address of Earl Warren," 1954, 3).

Recent Interpretations

Not until the 1970s did this view of Taney come under wholesale attack. With the civil rights movement of the 1950s and 1960s came advances in the constitutional rights of African Americans and a greater sensitivity to America's troubled racial past. In light of these contemporary developments, historians in particular took another look at the *Dred Scott* decision and Taney's record with regard to slavery. In 1978, the historian Don E. Fehrenbacher published the first comprehensive study of the decision and the politics and law of slavery that lay behind it. Fehrenbacher spared no criticism in his evaluation of Taney. He at length dispelled what he saw as the myth of the antislavery Taney and instead portrayed the chief justice as fanatically committed to "southern life and values, which seemed organically linked to the peculiar institution and unpreservable without it" (Fehrenbacher 1978, 559). Taney's majority opinion in *Dred Scott*, according to Fehrenbacher, revealed the chief justice's pride in the South, his fear of slave uprisings, and his bitter indignation at the abolitionists' denunciations of the region and its peculiar institution. "The Dred Scott opinion, defensive in substance but aggressive in temper," Fehrenbacher concluded, "was the work of an angry southern gentleman" (Fehrenbacher 1978, 561).

Most recently, in a 1994 essay, legal historian Paul Finkelman offered an even more forceful critique of Taney. Examining Taney's views on slavery from his days as President Andrew Jackson's attorney general through his years of service as chief justice, Finkelman argued that the *Dred Scott* decision was no aberration. On the contrary, the decision embodied Taney's career-long commitment to slavery and white supremacy. From *Prigg v. Pennsylvania* (1842) to *Kentucky v. Dennison* (1861), Taney's opinions demonstrated a single aim on the part of the chief justice—to protect and preserve the "peculiar institution." States' rights concerns, according to Finkelman, were secondary for Taney. When slavery stood to benefit, Taney allowed the states, for example, to determine the status of those who resided within their borders. But in *Dred Scott* the chief justice denied that states could determine questions of citizenship because he did not want northern free blacks to bring suits into federal courts. "[Taney] was uninterested in constitutional principles; only in proslavery and pro-southern results," Finkelman claimed (Finkelman 1994, 98). For this reason—and particularly because of Taney's narrow views of citizenship and congressional power over territories in the *Dred Scott* opinion—Finkelman declared that "greatness" was not among Taney's attributes. His successes in other areas of constitutional jurisprudence cannot obscure his denial of "fundamental liberty and human rights to millions of Americans." "However we admire Taney's personal grace, his clever opinions on commercial issues, and his sometimes brilliant analysis of constitutional issues," Finkelman summarized, "his racism, proslavery dogmatism, and secessionist sentiments will remain his legacy" (Finkelman 1994, 100).

Thus, for almost 140 years, ever since Taney's death in 1864, journalists, political leaders, judges, legal scholars, and historians have argued over how Taney ought to be remembered. At the center of the debate has stood the *Dred Scott* decision, as those on both sides have wrangled over its meaning and its significance. Litigation involving slavery, of course, constituted a minuscule portion of the Taney Court's overall caseload and of Taney's judicial record. Still, as the central issue of the mid-nineteenth century and as an important component of twentieth-century debates about racism, civil rights, and affirmative action, slavery matters a great deal in any assessment of Taney's reputation and legacy. In our own time, no one contends that *Dred Scott* or Taney's slavery jurisprudence was unimportant, but some do claim that it ought to be emphasized to a lesser degree than other components of Taney's judicial record.

The Constitutional and Political Legacy of the Taney Court

Any evaluation of Taney and his Court must take these 140 years of debate into consideration. On the one hand, Taney's historical defenders have made an important point: that his Court's decisions in economic regulation cases proved decisively important in their own time and afterward in fostering the economic development of the United States. On the other hand, Taney's detractors make an irrefutable case as well: that he and his colleagues must be held responsible for the *Dred Scott* decision—a gross misinterpretation of the legal rights of American blacks at the time of the founding and a blatant expansion of the rights of slaveholders. Still, because the constitutional impact of *Dred Scott* was so short-lived, that decision might best be understood in terms of its political—rather than legal—effects. Thus, the dispute over Taney's reputation perhaps offers a means for understanding the overall legacy and impact of the Court's decisions during this period. In light of the subsequent evolution of constitutional doctrine, the Taney Court's legacy was most evident and significant in three general areas: economic regulation, federalism, and the separation of powers. But the Court's impact was also felt politically. By placing the Court squarely on the side of slaveholders with its poorly reasoned decision in *Dred Scott*, the Taney Court helped bring about the Civil War.

Economic Regulation

Rapid economic development and technological change thrust economic issues to the forefront of U.S. constitutional development during the mid-nineteenth century. Business expansion manifested itself in everything from the growth of internal improvements—roads, canals, and railroads—to the rise of corporations. Taney and his colleagues confronted critical questions about the government's role in regulating and promoting economic development, and in general they dealt with these matters in a pragmatic and innovative fashion. In contrast to Marshall, who developed a grand style of judging that emphasized the formulation of constitutional doctrine, the Taney Court worked to accommodate the Constitution to the changing needs of U.S. society. Early in U.S. history, at a time when the nation needed defining, Marshall sought to clarify the intentions of the framers, to establish the supremacy of the national government, and to create a national market that unleashed creative enterprise. Taney's aims and contributions, though less grand, were no less significant.

Nowhere was the Taney Court's judicial creativity and accomplishment greater than in its contract decisions. Taney and his colleagues inherited Marshall's ruling in *Dartmouth College v. Woodward* (1819), in which the Court had protected corporate charters from state regulation, as well as its more moderate decision in *Providence Bank v. Billings* (1830), in which the Court held that states could tax corporations to protect the public interest. The Taney Court, sensitive to the legal demands of economic progress and technological change, expanded the ideas established in *Billings*. Taney held in *Charles River Bridge v. Warren Bridge* (1837) that corporate charters—and corporate privilege—ought to be narrowly defined. Because, as Taney put it, "the object and end of all government is to promote the happiness and prosperity of the community," the notion of the public interest underlay the Court's opinion in the case. The *Charles River Bridge* decision not only rested on a firm constitutional foundation in light of *Billings*, the ruling also constituted an appropriate response to the economic growth and popular democracy of the age. The public good, in other words, triumphed over private rights.

The Taney Court's subsequent contract decisions proved equally important, although perhaps less attuned to the public will. Although *Charles River Bridge* limited the rights of corporations, Taney and his colleagues were careful not to go too far in restricting corporate privilege. To do so would have harmed the investment climate and the nation's economy. But neither did the Court yield to investors' desires to create a virtually unregulated economic order, for excessive corporate privilege stood in stark opposition to the basic Democratic philosophy of Taney and his colleagues. Instead, the Court took a moderately procorporate position. In *Bank of Augusta v. Earle* (1839), the Court held that states possessed the power to regulate corporations but only in explicit ways; restrictions on business activity could not be implied in state statutes or constitutions. In *Bronson v. Kinzie* (1843), the Court thwarted a state attempt to help debtors by restricting mortgage foreclosure sales as a violation of the Contract Clause. And in a series of cases, the Taney Court opened the federal courts to corporations on the basis of diversity of citizenship. All of these decisions affirmed the importance of protecting property rights, showed sensitivity to contemporary trends in business activity, and helped the nation down the path of economic development. At the same time, by using the Contract Clause to protect business transactions from state interference, the Taney Court set a precedent for the future. During the late nineteenth century, after the Fourteenth Amendment placed limits on the states' powers to restrict liberty without due process of law, the Supreme Court frequently invalidated minimum wage, maximum hours, and other workers' health and safety legislation enacted by states. Because the Taney Court had put the Contract Clause to a similar use, Taney and his colleagues must shoulder some of the blame for the laissez-faire excesses of those who succeeded them. Still, in general the Taney Court proved remarkably able to deal with a host of complicated issues involving contracts.

Taney and his colleagues proved equally successful in their approach to the Commerce Clause. Marshall left an ambiguous legacy with his vaguely nationalistic opinion in *Gibbons v. Ogden* (1824), in which the Court had struck down a New York steamboat monopoly as a violation of a federal coastal licensing act. In the decision, Marshall had hinted that the grant of power to Congress over commerce would have been sufficient to invalidate the state monopoly even in the absence of federal legislation. The slavery issue only complicated matters. If congressional control over commerce was exclusive, as Marshall implied, then states potentially lacked the authority to regulate the movement of slaves or the migration of free blacks. With the slavery issue always looming in the background, the Taney Court struggled to figure out just exactly how far states could go in controlling commercial activity. In some instances, the Court upheld state regulatory measures, as in the *License Cases* (1847), while in other instances, as in the *Passenger Cases* (1849), it did not. In the process of dealing with the issue, however, the Court gave new life to the notion of state police power, an idea that had yet to be developed at the time of Taney's appointment. Particularly when it affirmed state regulatory measures, such as in *New York v. Miln* (1837) and the *License Cases*, the Court articulated the notion that states possessed the power to legislate in the public interest—to pass laws that protected public health, safety, welfare, and morals. Ultimately, the justices did resolve the larger question of whether the commerce power rested exclusively with Congress, when, in *Cooley v. Board of Wardens* (1852), the Court held that some matters required local regulation while other necessitated national control.

Despite the tortured journey toward the conclusion reached in *Cooley*, the Taney Court proved proficient in defining and interpreting the Commerce Clause. The

Court's unevenness and inconsistency in addressing the issue was ultimately both politically shrewd and legally successful. By refusing to articulate a definitive position on whether congressional control over commerce was exclusive, the Court avoided being drawn into the debate over slavery in its Commerce Clause decisions. At the same time, the Taney Court's rulings in this area provided a workable constitutional framework for state legislative experimentation without narrowing the scope of federal power. The Taney Court's moderation and pragmatism fit the changing needs of the mid–nineteenth century economy and society. As R. Kent Newmyer argued, "The Marshall Court had painted with broad strokes. The new age needed a lighter touch and more subtle shading. . . . A delicate interpretation of the commerce power was needed, one which would please both North and South and, at the same time, would encourage national commerce" (Newmyer 1968, 101–102). Taney and his colleagues provided this "subtle shading" and in the process maintained an appropriate balance between state and national power.

Federalism

At the time of Taney's appointment, nationalists feared that the Marshall Court's great decisions establishing the supremacy of the national government were in jeopardy. Beginning with *Fletcher v. Peck* (1810), in which the Court first overturned a state statute, and *Martin v. Hunter's Lessee* (1816), in which the justices overruled a state court decision, the Marshall Court had followed a clearly nationalistic trajectory. Any state action—either a statute or a court decision—that violated the Constitution yielded to Marshall's forceful assertion of national judicial power. The Marshall Court's nationalistic interpretation of the commerce power—evident in *McCulloch v. Maryland* (1819) and *Gibbons v. Ogden*—and the Court's broad definition of contractual rights in *Dartmouth College v. Woodward* (1819) had also imposed strict limits on the states. In the latter three cases, Marshall and his colleagues invalidated a Maryland tax on the National Bank, struck down a New York steamboat monopoly, and thwarted New Hampshire's attempted takeover of Dartmouth College. Marshall's contributions to the creation of a national economic order and a national government seemed in jeopardy when Taney joined the Court. Best known at the time of his appointment as the man who had engineered the death of the national bank during the Jackson administration, Taney had earned a reputation as an opponent of centralized power.

To some degree, the record of the Taney Court confirmed this early perception of the chief justice. Decisions such as *Charles River Bridge v. Warren Bridge* and *West River Bridge v. Dix* (1848), in which the Court held that state eminent domain proceedings were not subject to review by the federal courts, certainly shifted more power to the states than Marshall would have allowed. Moreover, a certain strain of thought also emerged from the Taney Court's commerce power decisions that emphasized the inherent power and sovereignty of the states. In *New York v. Miln* (1837), for example, Justice Philip P. Barbour's majority opinion referred to the "complete, unqualified, and exclusive" power exercised by states within their own spheres, and a minority of the Court continued to assert such views in Commerce Clause cases throughout the Taney era (36 U.S. 102, 139). Still, despite occasional victories by this pro-South, pro–states' rights wing of the Court, the overall thrust of the Court's economic regulation decisions embraced the middle-of-the-road position laid down in *Cooley v. Board of Wardens.* By granting to states the power to regulate within their own domains, the Taney Court developed the notion of the police power without interfering with the need for national commercial legislation where necessary. No doctrinaire advocate of states' rights, Chief Justice Taney gave more latitude to the states to regulate than Marshall had, but he prevented the Court from adopting an inflexible position on federal-state relations.

In some areas, the Taney Court exhibited even more nationalism than its predecessor. This was especially true when it came to cases involving the federal judiciary, which greatly expanded its power and jurisdiction during Taney's tenure. The Court demonstrated nationalistic principles in, for example, *Swift v. Tyson* (1842), in which it held that national uniformity was desirable in the rules that applied in commercial cases in the federal courts. Rejecting the notion that state court decisions governed interstate commercial transactions, *Swift* pointed toward the development of a federal commercial common law. In a series of decisions culminating in *Genesee Chief v. Fitzhugh* (1852), moreover, the Taney Court abandoned the accepted common law understanding of admiralty law—the idea that the jurisdiction of admiralty courts extended only to waters within the ebb and flow of the tide. Instead, Taney and his colleagues held that any public navigable waterway came within the admiralty jurisdiction of the federal courts. The Court also augmented the jurisdiction of the federal courts with regard to corporations. In *Louisville v. Letson* (1844) and *Marshall v. Baltimore and Ohio Railroad Company* (1854), the justices gave corporations greater access to federal tribunals by revising the requirements for achieving "diversity of citizenship." Perhaps the most forceful pronouncement of federal judicial power came in *Ableman v. Booth* (1859), in which a unanimous Court thwarted a state court's refusal to abide by a Supreme Court decision. Taken together, these decisions constituted a significant expansion of federal judicial authority.

To be sure, Taney's nationalistic sentiments did not rise to the level of Marshall's. But one particular case surely demonstrates the extent of Taney's nationalism, however surprising it was to contemporaries. *Holmes v. Jennison* (1840) raised the issue of whether the governor of Vermont could extradite a fugitive to Canada, where he was charged with murder. On a writ of habeas corpus, Taney's opinion not only affirmed the Supreme Court's jurisdiction in the case, it also held that the governor could not enter into an agreement with a foreign head of state to surrender a fugitive. Taney contended that the Constitution explicitly reserved foreign affairs to the national government. The opinion shocked Democratic Senator James Buchanan, who indignantly described the opinion as "latitudinous and centralizing beyond anything I ever read, in any other judicial opinion" (Swisher 1974, 176). Although surprising to Democratic partisans, Taney's judicial record in some respects built on Marshall's legacy in aiding the growth of national power.

Separation of Powers

The Taney Court confronted important questions having to do with the relative powers of the three branches of government. In this respect, Taney differed somewhat from his predecessor, for on the whole, Marshall's decisions had a greater impact on federalism than on the separation of powers. If national supremacy was one of the hallmarks of Marshall's judicial record, an expanded role for the federal judiciary constituted an important component of Marshall's vision for the nation. Taney, of course, fully subscribed to the notion of judicial review—the idea that the Court possessed the authority to review legislative acts—and his decisions increased the power and jurisdiction of the federal courts in many ways. Still, Taney also placed limits on the exercise of the Supreme Court's power by developing the doctrine of nonjusticiable political questions, the idea that certain matters were best left to the political branches of the government. The Civil War, meanwhile, raised other separation of powers questions that Marshall had not confronted, particularly relating to executive power during wartime.

The political questions doctrine, put forth in *Luther v. Borden* (1849) stands as one of the Taney era's most important legacies. By refusing to decide which of two governments constituted the legitimate authority in Rhode Island, the Court indicated its unwillingness to involve itself in certain disputes, particularly those arising under the Guarantee Clause of the Constitution. Although the Court "should always be ready to meet any question confided to it by the Constitution, it is equally not its duty to pass beyond its appropriate sphere of action," Taney claimed (48 U.S. 1, 47). Since *Luther*, this doctrine has provided the Court with a discretionary device for exercising judicial restraint when confronted with issues that it would rather avoid. Immediately after the Civil War, congressional reliance on the Guarantee Clause as the basis for Reconstruction legislation helped prevent a showdown with the Supreme Court over the constitutionality of these measures. During much of the twentieth century, moreover, the political questions doctrine kept the federal courts from examining and supervising the reapportionment of state legislatures. In *Baker v. Carr* (1962), however, the Court held that such matters were in fact justiciable, and the rise of judicial activism during this era thus signified a decline in the significance of the political questions doctrine. In *United States v. Nixon* (1974), for example, the Court rejected President Richard Nixon's claim that a special prosecutor's subpoena for taped Oval Office conversation constituted a nonjusticiable political question. Still, the notion remained important in U.S. constitutional law, as some scholars contend that the political questions doctrine lay behind the reluctance of federal courts during the 1960s and 1970s to take up constitutional challenges to the Vietnam War.

In the area of presidential power, the Taney Court upheld President Abraham Lincoln's actions during the Civil War, thus setting an important precedent for the expansion of presidential power during wartime. The *Prize Cases* (1863) presented the Court with an opportunity to affirm or to halt Lincoln's blockade of Confederate ports. By taking Lincoln's side, the justices broadly interpreted the portion of Article II, Section 2 of the Constitution that designates the president as "Commander in Chief of the Army and Navy of the United States." During the twentieth century—a century marked by major wars and global conflict—presidents claimed greater authority to act in the realm of foreign policy and even to send U.S. forces into combat without a congressional declaration of war. The expansion of the power of the president as commander in chief owes much to the Taney Court's approval of Lincoln's blockade.

Slavery

As the debate over Taney's reputation reveals, the slavery issue looms large in the legacy of the Taney Court. More than any single decision, *Dred Scott v. Sandford* (1857) defined the Supreme Court during the mid-nineteenth century. In the same way that *Marbury v. Madison* (1803) forever fixed John Marshall's reputation as the progenitor of judicial review, so did *Dred Scott* firmly establish Taney's reputation as the foremost judicial advocate of slavery in American history. Indeed, the comparison is even more apt when considering that both rulings were forceful statements of judicial power and that the decisions were the first two in which the Supreme Court declared acts of Congress to be unconstitutional. But the parallel ends there. Marshall's 1803 decision stirred up relatively little political controversy, whereas Taney's opinion played a significant role in bringing about the Civil War. *Marbury v. Madison* assumed greater significance over time, as subsequent justices cited the decision as precedent and used it to justify the expansion of federal judicial power. *Dred Scott*'s impact, in contrast, proved to be both immediate and powerful.

The *Dred Scott* decision exacerbated northern fears that a "Slave Power conspiracy" had taken hold of the national government, thus contributing to the sectional polarization of political debate and causing northern sentiment to shift decidedly against the South. The ruling led to the rapid rise of Abraham Lincoln of Illinois, a key opponent of the decision, and practically destroyed the political career of Illinois Senator Stephen Douglas, who had been positioning himself for a run at the presidency for years. Lincoln earned a national reputation by debating Senator Douglas, the incumbent, during their 1858 contest for a U.S. Senate seat. In their debates, Lincoln posed a series of difficult questions to Douglas about his stance on slavery and whether it conformed to the Court's ruling. Did Douglas really agree with Taney that the Constitution prevented Congress or a territorial legislature from making laws regarding slavery in new territories? Such questions put Douglas on the defensive, as he sought to respond in such a way as to win votes in Illinois as well as to maintain his standing as a presidential candidate with appeal to southern voters. Although Douglas won the Senate race, Lincoln had made his mark. Northerners, who viewed the Supreme Court and its proslavery decision with increasing alarm, cast their votes for Lincoln in 1860. Lincoln's hostility to the *Dred Scott* decision only confirmed southern fears that the election of a Republican president would bring about the abolition of slavery. Secession and war followed. A suit for freedom filed by an unknown slave litigant in Missouri had, in a sense, helped speed the sectional disintegration that culminated in the Civil War.

If the political results of *Dred Scott* were monumental, the constitutional and legal impact of the decision was minimal. As a matter of law, the opinion had a short life. Five years after the decision, in 1862, both Congress and President Lincoln took steps to invalidate the opinion—or at least to act as though the ruling had never been made. In June of that year, Congress passed a law banning slavery in all federal territories, and Lincoln quickly signed it. A few months later, Attorney General Edward Bates issued an official decision declaring free men of color born in the United States to be citizens. The attorney general, taking his cue from Curtis's dissent, claimed that *Dred Scott v. Sandford* lacked the force of law. On January 1, 1863, the Emancipation Proclamation announced the end of slavery in those areas still in rebellion against the United States, and two years later, after the Civil War had ended, Congress passed the Thirteenth Amendment to the Constitution. The Thirteenth Amendment, ratified by the required three-fourths of the states by the end of the year, abolished slavery in the United States. The following year, Congress explicitly overruled the *Dred Scott* decision in the Civil Rights Act of 1866, which granted citizenship to all persons born in the United States. Two years later, the Fourteenth Amendment made this guarantee of citizenship part of the Constitution. In short, although it had helped bring about the Civil War, the *Dred Scott* decision had had virtually no effect on American constitutional law.

In the final analysis, the Taney Court must be remembered both for its contributions to American constitutionalism and its role in exacerbating the sectional crisis. Many of its decisions with regard to economic regulation, federalism, and the separation of powers stand as landmarks of American constitutional history—cases that cannot be ignored when evaluating the overall legacy and impact of the Taney Court. A more dynamic economic order, a more balanced federalism, and a clearer delineation of the proper roles of the various branches of government all came about during the Taney period. In some respects, these results served effectively to counterbalance the work of the Marshall Court. Still, the Taney Court must bear the burden of its infamous slavery opinions, for America's troubled history of race relations owes much to the decisions made by its political and judicial leaders during the Civil War era. Although in many ways a great chief justice, Taney will never be—and should never be—deemed the greatest.

References and Further Reading

"Address of Earl Warren, Chief Justice of the United States, on the Occasion of the Dedication of the Late Chief Justice Taney Monument, Second Annual Pilgrimage of Chief Justice Taney General Assembly, Fourth Degree Knights of Columbus, Frederick, Maryland, October 24, 1954."

Fehrenbacher, Don E. *The Dred Scott Case: Its Significance in American Law and Politics.* New York: Oxford University Press, 1978.

Finkelman, Paul. "'Hooted Down the Page of History': Reconsidering the Greatness of Chief Justice Taney." *Journal of Supreme Court History* (1994): 83–102.

Frankfurter, Felix. *The Commerce Clause Under Marshall, Taney, and Waite.* Chapel Hill: University of North Carolina Press, 1937.

Hughes, Charles Evans. "Roger Brooke Taney." *American Bar Association Journal* 17 (December 1931): 785–790.

Hyman, Harold M., and William M. Wiecek. *Equal Justice Under Law: Constitutional Development, 1835–1875.* New York: Harper and Row, 1982.

Levy, Beryl Harold. *Our Constitution: Tool or Testament?* Port Washington, NY: Kennikat Press, 1941; reprint edition, 1965.

Lewis, Walker. *Without Fear or Favor: A Biography of Chief Justice Roger Brooke Taney.* Boston: Houghton Mifflin, 1965.

Newmyer, R. Kent. *John Marshall and the Heroic Age of the Supreme Court.* Baton Rouge: Louisiana State University Press, 2001.

———. *The Supreme Court Under Marshall and Taney.* Arlington Heights, IL: Harland Davidson, 1968.

Palmer, B. W. *Marshall and Taney: Statesmen of the Law.* New York: Russell and Russell, 1939; reprint edition, 1966.

"Roger Brooke Taney." *Atlantic Monthly* 15, no. 88 (February 1865): 151–161.

Stern, Robert L. "Chief Justice Taney and the Shadow of *Dred Scott.*" *Journal of Supreme Court History* (1992): 39–52.

Swisher, Carl B. *History of the Supreme Court of the United States*, vol. 5, *The Taney Period, 1836–1864.* New York: Macmillan, 1974.

Tyler, Samuel. *Memoir of Roger Brooke Taney, LL.D., Chief Justice of the Supreme Court of the United States*. Baltimore: John Murphy, 1872.

"The Unjust Judge: A Memorial of Roger Brooke Taney, Late Chief Justice of the United States." New York: Baker and Godwin, 1865.

Warren, Charles. *The Supreme Court in United States History*, vol. 2. Boston: Little, Brown, 1928.

Wiecek, William. *Liberty Under Law: The Supreme Court in American Life*. Baltimore: Johns Hopkins University Press, 1988.

Winitsky, Marvin Laurence. "Roger B. Taney: A Historiographical Inquiry." *Maryland Historical Magazine* 69 (1974): 1–26.

PART TWO

Reference Materials

Key People, Laws, and Events

Abolitionism

The movement to abolish slavery in the United States gained strength throughout the early and mid-nineteenth century and played a pivotal role in shaping American politics and policy during this period. Abolitionism had religious roots. Young New England Protestants, influenced by the wave of revivals of the day, took the lead in advocating immediate and unconditional emancipation. Evangelicals such as Theodore Dwight Weld, Arthur and Lewis Tappan, and William Lloyd Garrison viewed slavery as a sin—a violation of the Biblical teaching that "God is no respecter of persons" and Christ's command to love one's neighbor as oneself. Though they often rejected political parties, abolitionists formed antislavery societies, preached sermons describing the horrors of bondage, and published newspapers, tracts, and other antislavery literature. The most famous abolitionist newspaper was *The Liberator*, which Garrison began publishing on January 1, 1831.

Abolitionism should be distinguished from other antislavery movements and activities. The colonization movement, for example, favored the removal of American slaves to Africa, and the political antislavery movement, which did not gain strength until the 1850s, put forth mostly an economic and social critique of the extension of slavery. *See Free Soil Movement* and *Republican Party*

Anti-Masons

Anti-masonry was a short-lived political movement in the United States during the late 1820s and early 1830s. As the name implies, Anti-masons opposed the power and influence of the Freemasons, or Masons, a popular all-male fraternal order known for its secret rituals. Many Americans, particularly evangelical Christians, increasingly perceived the Masons as an aristocratic, exclusive, anti-Christian organization that thought itself above the law. Moreover, during an era of economic uncertainty and dislocation, many viewed Masons as concerned only about protecting and helping each other. Anti-masonry thus became a significant political force. Anti-masons formed their own political party and held a convention in 1830, and two years later they nominated well-known lawyer William Wirt as the party's candidate for the presidency.

Black, Jeremiah S.

Black was a prominent member of the nation's legal community during the mid-nineteenth century and the sixth reporter of the Supreme Court. Born in Pennsylvania in 1810, he served as chief justice of the Pennsylvania Supreme Court and later as attorney general of the United States under President James Buchanan. In that role, he assisted in enforcing the federal fugitive slave law and in formulating the administration's position during the secession crisis. Rejected as a nominee for the Supreme Court during Buchanan's last month in office, Black was elected by the justices to serve as Supreme Court reporter in 1861. As reporter, he produced the two-volume *Black's Reports*. He resigned his position in 1864 to pursue a lucrative private law practice, and he argued several post–Civil War cases before the Supreme Court. Black died in 1883.

Calhoun, John C.

The foremost spokesman for the interests of the South in the national government, particularly during the 1830s and 1840s, John C. Calhoun figured prominently in the major political and constitutional disputes of the period. Born in 1782 in the District of Ninety-six (later Abbeville), South Carolina, Calhoun graduated from Yale and subsequently studied law in Charleston as well as at the Litchfield Law School in Connecticut. Elected to the U.S. House of Representatives, he served from 1811 to 1817, during which time he held nationalistic views and expressed particular enthusiasm for the War of 1812. He later accepted the post of secretary of war under President James Monroe (1817–1825). Calhoun served as vice president under both John Quincy Adams and Andrew Jackson, but a rift with President Jackson over the tariff and Calhoun's efforts to nullify it led him to resign from the vice presidency in 1832. Elected to the U.S. Senate from South Carolina, Calhoun emerged as a champion of southern interests and a vocal defender of slavery. He described the institution as a "positive good," used the theory of state sovereignty to justify state prohibitions on abolitionist literature, and argued that the Constitution's Fifth Amendment protected the property rights of slaveholders. He died in 1850, just before the passage of the Compromise of 1850.

Chase, Salmon P.

Chase argued a series of fugitive slave cases during the 1840s and 1850s, sought the Republican presidential nomination in 1860, and ultimately succeeded Taney as chief justice of the Supreme Court. Born in New Hampshire in 1808, he graduated from Dartmouth and practiced law in the nation's capital before settling in Cincinnati. A deeply religious man, Chase accepted abolitionist assumptions about the immorality of slavery, and he helped transform the abolitionist movement into a political force in the North during the 1850s. Central to this transformation was Chase's contention that the framers of the Constitution had opposed slavery and had actually crafted an antislavery constitution. Chase argued that wealthy slaveholding interests—whom he deemed the "Slave Power"—had subverted the framers' Constitution and were conspiring to dominate the national government. Chase claimed that the Constitution had established slavery solely as the creature of local law and that the Congress therefore lacked authority to regulate the return of fugitive slaves. In arguing the antislavery side in *Jones v. Van Zandt* (1847) and *Moore v. Illinois* (1852), Chase earned the nickname "attorney general for fugitive slaves." Having served briefly as a U.S. senator (1849) as well as Ohio governor (1855–1861), Chase unsuccessfully sought the Republican nomination for the presidency in 1860. President Abraham Lincoln attempted to keep an eye on his ambitious political rival by appointing Chase as secretary of the treasury, in which capacity he served until his resignation 1864.

On December 6, 1864, Lincoln appointed Chase to the chief justiceship, which had become vacant on Taney's death a few months earlier. Chase presided over the Court during the difficult years of Reconstruction, when the Court confronted challenges to various wartime and postwar policies of the national government. His major opinions came in *In re Turner* (1867), in which he upheld the constitutionality of a postwar civil rights measure, and in *Texas v. White* (1869), in which he sustained congressional Reconstruction policy that reorganized the states. As chief justice, Chase presided over the 1868 impeachment trial of President Andrew Johnson, the first such trial in U.S. history. After suffering a series of strokes in 1870, Chase's health declined, and he died in 1873.

Clay, Henry

One of the great national political leaders of the day, Henry Clay earned the nickname "the Great Compromiser" for his repeated efforts to save the Union. Born in 1777 in Hanover County, Virginia, Clay studied law with Virginia's famous Chancellor George Wythe (who also taught Thomas Jefferson and John Marshall), gained admission to the bar in 1797, and later moved to Lexington, Kentucky. Entering politics soon after his arrival there, he served in the state legislature and, briefly, in the U.S. Senate (1806–1807, 1810–1811). He became most famous for his service in the U.S. House of Representatives, where he won the post of Speaker of the House and transformed the job into a position of real power. Serving in this capacity during six Congresses, Clay made important contributions to the early republic. He argued forcefully for the need for war with England in 1812 and afterward helped negotiate the peace; he advocated the "American System," which included a protective tariff, internal improvements, and a national bank; and he fashioned the Missouri Compromise, which established relative sectional harmony for nearly three and a half decades by allowing slavery in Missouri but prohibiting it in the future anywhere north of Missouri's southern border (latitude 36 degrees, 30 minutes). In addition to his years in the House, Clay held the position of secretary of state (1825–1829), again served in the U.S. Senate (1831–1842), and helped pass a compromise tariff in the aftermath of the Nullification Crisis. In 1850, his attempts to enact yet another sectional compromise initially failed, although his proposals formed the basis of what eventually became the Compromise of 1850. Although a central figure in American politics for four decades, Clay never won the presidency. As a major candidate, he lost the elections of 1824, 1832, and 1844, and he failed to win his party's nomination in 1840 and 1848. Clay died in 1852.

Compromise of 1850

The Compromise of 1850 attempted to resolve the increasingly bitter sectional divisions that emerged as northerners and southerners debated the extension of slavery into new territories gained in the Mexican-American War. After the introduction of the Wilmot Proviso of 1846, which threatened to abolish slavery in these areas altogether, some southerners believed secession from the Union was the only way to protect the rights of slaveholders. With the Union imperiled, Senator Henry Clay, of Kentucky, unsuccessfully attempted in 1849 to pass a compromise bill. Two important factors altered the political landscape and allowed for its subsequent passage. First, the mysterious death in 1849 of President Zachary Taylor, who had opposed the bill, led to Vice President Millard Fillmore's accession to the presidency; the new president fully supported the measure. Second, Senator Stephen Douglas successfully maneuvered the compromise measure through Congress by splitting Clay's original bill into five separate bills, for which Douglas was able to cobble together distinct majorities that favored each of its provisions. Under the terms of the Compromise, California entered the Union as a free state; Utah and New Mexico Territories were organized, and the settlers there had the opportunity to decide for themselves whether to permit slavery; the present-day boundaries of Texas were established, and the state's enormous debts were assumed by the federal government; the slave trade was abolished in Washington, D.C.; and a new fugitive slave law was enacted. This last provision proved most controversial of all, and the 1850s witnessed a series of conflicts over the rights of fugitive slaves. On the whole, the Compromise failed to end, or even diminish, the sectional tensions unleashed by territorial expansion.

Democratic-Republicans

In contrast to the Federalists, their rivals during the early national period, the Democratic-Republicans viewed the Constitution as an outline of the specific powers granted to the new national government. If the Constitution did not explicitly grant power to the national government, that obligation or duty remained with the states. Democratic-Republicans (sometimes called simply "Republicans") thus emphasized the Tenth Amendment to the Constitution, which held that "the powers not delegated to the United States by the Constitution, nor prohibited by it to the States, are reserved to the States respectively, or to the people." Republicans, particularly their leader, Thomas Jefferson, emphasized the virtues of agricultural cultivation and the need for local governance. They feared the corrupting influence of government when it became too distant and detached from the people, and they looked warily on commercial and industrial activity, which they viewed as harmful to the preservation of the common good and the welfare of the republic. This party gradually evolved into the organization that would come to be identified most closely with President Andrew Jackson during the nineteenth century, by which time it had become known as the Democratic Party. *See also National Republicans; Old Republicans.*

Federalist Party

The Federalists began as a political faction led by Alexander Hamilton, who served as the secretary of the treasury under President George Washington during the 1790s. Federalists thought that the Constitution had created a strong national government with many more powers than under the old Articles of Confederation. They saw the Constitution as a flexible document that could be loosely interpreted, particularly with regard to the powers of Congress. Article I, Section 8 of the Constitution contained a clause granting Congress the power "to make all Laws which shall be necessary and proper for carrying into Execution the foregoing powers, and all other Powers vested by this Constitution in the Government of the United States." Therefore, Federalists believed, if the Constitution did not explicitly prohibit the new national government from exercising some power, the Necessary and Proper Clause most likely granted that power to the new government. The best example of this interpretation was the creation of the national bank, the Bank of the United States, which Congress established in 1791 to centralize the nation's financial structure. Federalists hoped to use national power to initiate and promote U.S. economic development, along the lines of the Industrial Revolution that was occurring in Europe, particularly in England. They believed in the inherent goodness of commercial activity and industrial development, which they saw as essential to building a great and powerful nation.

Free Soil Movement

The free soil movement, which gained particular strength in the North during and after the Mexican-American War, sought to block the extension of slavery to new territories in the West. Free Soilers made economic and social—rather than moral—arguments against slavery, and they seemed more concerned with how slavery adversely affected whites than how it harmed blacks. Viewing the southern planter aristocracy as an affront to American democratic ideals and slaves as a threat to the livelihood of free white laborers, Free Soilers hoped to prevent both the spread of slavery and the migration of free blacks to the West. The movement drew support from both Whigs and Democrats, and Free Soilers formed a separate political party in 1848. They nominated Democratic ex-president Martin Van Buren for the presidency and former Whig Charles Francis Adams for the vice presidency. Although they polled 14.4 percent of the popular vote in the free states in 1848, antislavery elements in the established parties were hesitant to join the new movement, and by 1852 the Free-Soil Party had all but collapsed. As sectional tensions increased during the next few years, the free soil movement grew and eventually evolved into the Republican Party. *See also Republican Party.*

Fugitive Slave Act of 1793

In 1793 Congress enacted a fugitive slave law in accordance with Article IV, Section 2 of the Constitution, the Fugitive Slave Clause. This clause stated that any "person held to service or labour" who escaped from one state into another "be delivered up on claim of the party to whom such service or labour may be due." The federal law provided that a slave owner or his agent could seize a runaway slave, after which the slave would be brought before a federal or state judge or a local magistrate. On receiving satisfactory proof that the fugitive was owned by the claimant, the judge or magistrate issued a certificate of removal to the owner or his agent. Anyone interfering with this rendition process, under the federal law, could be sued by the slave owner for $500. The owner also possessed the right to initiate a separate lawsuit for "injuries" caused by interference with this process. In *Prigg v. Pennsylvania* (1842), the Court upheld the Fugitive Slave Law of 1793, and the Compromise of 1850 included a modified—and stricter—version of this measure. *See also Compromise of 1850.*

Howard, Benjamin C.

Howard served as the fifth Supreme Court reporter, during the period 1843–1861. Born in Maryland in 1791, Howard studied at Princeton, practiced law in Maryland, and held a variety of public offices, including a seat in Congress for four terms. While in Congress, he chaired the House Foreign Relations Committee from 1835–1839. In 1843, at the urging of a group of justices dissatisfied with reporter Richard Peters, the Court hired Howard as Supreme Court reporter. Although he did not actively seek the job, Howard's long association with Justice Wayne—whom he knew from their days at Princeton—certainly helped him obtain the position. Howard generally got along better with the justices than Peters had, but errors in his reports of decisions also made him subject to occasional criticism. In September 1861, Howard resigned as reporter in order to run for governor of Maryland, in which he was unsuccessful. Although Taney tried to persuade Howard to retain his position, the chief justice received no support in the matter from his colleagues, and Jeremiah S. Black replaced Howard in December 1861. Howard died in 1872.

Johnson, Reverdy

Johnson was a leading lawyer of the Civil War era and a close friend of Chief Justice Taney. Born in Maryland in 1796, Johnson served in the War of 1812, and in 1817 he established a law practice in Baltimore. During the 1840s he served in the U.S. Senate and, beginning in 1849, as attorney general under President Zachary Taylor. An active member of the Baltimore bar for six decades, Johnson argued many cases before the Supreme Court. These included, most notably, *Waring v. Clarke* (1847), *Pennsylvania v. Wheeling and Belmont Bridge* (1852), *Seymour v. McCormick* (1857), and *Dred Scott v. Sandford* (1857). A moderate on the sectional issues that divided the country, Johnson attended the Washington Peace Conference of 1861, which attempted to work out a compromise to avoid civil war. He helped keep Maryland in the Union during the Civil War and returned to the U.S. Senate to serve from 1863 to 1868. After Taney's death in 1864, Johnson became a staunch defender of the deceased chief justice's reputation. Johnson died in 1876.

Kansas-Nebraska Act

Enacted by Congress in 1854, the Kansas-Nebraska Act played a critical role in the national struggle over the issue of slavery in the territories during the years before the Civil War. Senator Stephen Douglas, of Illinois, originally introduced the measure because he hoped for the construction of a transcontinental railroad that would benefit his home state. Only if these new territories were organized would it be possible to extend rail lines through the vast open lands of the Great Plains. The most controversial part of the legislation opened up the new territories of Kansas and Nebraska to slavery, on the basis of the principle of popular sovereignty—the idea that the settlers there would decide for themselves whether to allow slavery. Although Congress had employed this same language with regard to Utah and New Mexico Territories in the Compromise of 1850, the extension of this principle to Kansas and Nebraska overturned the Missouri Compromise, which had forbidden slavery in most of the territory originally known as the Louisiana Purchase. Because the Missouri Compromise had helped prevent the slavery issue from dividing the Union ever since 1820, the overturning of this sectional agreement had profound political implications. The passage of the Kansas-Nebraska Act led to the founding of the Republican Party, the primary tenet of which was opposition to the extension of slavery in the West.

Know-Nothing Party

Formally known as the American Party, the Know-Nothings briefly emerged during the mid-1850s as a powerful force in American politics. As the United States encountered an influx of immigrants during the 1840s, most of them Irish Catholic, many native-born white Protestants expressed alarm. This antiforeign, anti-Catholic sentiment lay at the heart of Know-Nothingism, or nativism. In 1854, nativists formed a political organization marked by secrets and rituals. Each member pledged never to vote for a foreign-born or Catholic candidate for elective office. If questioned about the organization, they were to respond by saying simply, "I know nothing." The Know-Nothings won a series of victories, particularly in the northern states, during the 1854–1855 elections, and it seemed as though anti-Catholicism might rival antislavery as the dominant political and social cause of the day. There was in fact much overlap between the two movements, as much of the rural, Protestant population of the North proved sympathetic to antislavery ideas as well as to anti-Catholicism. Ultimately, antislavery movements had a greater appeal in the North, and a series of national events—including the Kansas-Nebraska Act, the *Dred Scott* decision, and John Brown's raid—kept slavery at the center of national political debate. By 1856, the Republican Party replaced the American Party as the Democrats' chief competitor when John C. Fremont outpolled nativist presidential candidate Millard Fillmore by almost a half million votes. Most nativists eventually joined the Republicans.

Marshall, John

Born in Virginia in 1755, Marshall fought in the American Revolution, held a seat in the Virginia House of Burgesses, and during the late 1780s emerged as a passionate advocate of a new constitution that would create a stronger national government. Virginia's leading Federalist by the end of the eighteenth century, Marshall served as secretary of state under President John Adams before his nomination to the Supreme Court in 1801. Under Marshall's leadership, the Court emerged as a key player in the new nation. It was by no means inevitable that the Court would play such a role. Article III of the Constitution was brief and vague in its delineation of the high court, and the three men who had held the chief justiceship before Marshall, during the Court's first decade, had done little to make the tribunal's presence felt on the national stage. Marshall changed all that. Beginning with his assertion in *Marbury v. Madison* (1803) that it was "emphatically the province of the judicial department to say what the law is," the Court assumed power to rule on the constitutionality of legislative acts. This assertion of the power of judicial review became the primary means by which Marshall transformed the role of the Court. On another level, Marshall changed the Court's method of decision making. Marshall, often by the sheer force of his personality, succeeded in persuading his judicial colleagues of the need for unanimity among the justices. Under his leadership, the Court spoke with one voice when rendering its most important constitutional decisions, and usually that voice belonged to Marshall. Separate concurring opinions were rare, and dissents even more so.

Most of the Marshall Court's significant decisions came in two areas of constitutional law—contracts and commerce. In *Fletcher v. Peck* (1810), Marshall and his colleagues overturned a Georgia statute that rescinded land grants previously made by the state legislature. The rescinding act, the Court held, violated the Contract

Clause of the Constitution, which prohibited the states from making any law "impairing the obligation of contracts." Similarly, in *Dartmouth College v. Woodward* (1819), the Court invalidated New Hampshire's attempt to bring Dartmouth College under state control. In that case the Court defined the college's original charter as a contract, thus making it subject to the protections of the Constitution's Contract Clause.

Commerce Clause cases typically involved the question of precisely how much power the clause granted to Congress. *McCulloch v. Maryland* (1819), a landmark decision involving the state of Maryland's attempt to levy a tax on the national bank, resolved the long-debated question of whether the Commerce Clause authorized Congress to create a bank. Marshall ruled the state tax unconstitutional, upheld the constitutionality of the national bank, and fashioned a broad interpretation of the commerce power. Several years later, in *Gibbons v. Ogden* (1824), Marshall further expanded Congress's power to regulate commerce when he reversed a New York court decision that had allowed a state-granted steamboat monopoly on the Hudson River. In the process, he held that congressional control over commerce was "plenary," or complete in every respect.

The work of the Marshall Court was profoundly important in the early history of the United States. Marshall made the Court a powerful force in national life, for his decision in *Marbury* ensured that the tribunal would be the arbiter of major constitutional questions. His work in the area of contracts protected the interests of property holders and investors, thus creating a commercial economic order favorable to investment and credit. Marshall's opinions in Commerce Clause cases such as *McCulloch* and *Gibbons* expanded the powers of Congress at the expense of the states, thereby asserting the supremacy of the national government in matters of commerce. These decisions mirrored Marshall's deeply held political beliefs. As a Federalist, he hoped to strengthen the national government and encourage the economic development of the new republic. He died in 1835.

National Republicans

The National Republicans were a faction within the Democratic-Republican Party (the party that had its origins with Thomas Jefferson) that eventually evolved into the Whig Party. By the 1810s, the influence of the Federalist Party had diminished on the national political scene, and an era of dominance by the Democratic-Republican Party began. Soon, however, factions developed among Democratic-Republicans, particularly after the controversial presidential election of 1824. The House of Representatives elected John Quincy Adams president after no candidate received an electoral majority. Andrew Jackson, who had won the most popular votes in the contest, became a sharp critic of the administration. Those who supported Adams assumed the label "National Republicans" to distinguish themselves from the followers of Jackson, who took more of a states' rights position. By the 1830s, the National Republicans evolved into a formal political party of their own, the Whigs, based on their common opposition to Jackson, who succeeded Adams as president. *See also Whig Party.*

Nullification Crisis

The Nullification Crisis was a dispute between South Carolina and the federal government over the high tariff enacted in 1828. South Carolinians, particularly those with a stake in the cotton-export economy, opposed the tariff for two reasons. First, they believed that Congress had increased the tariff as a way to protect and promote industry in the United States by steeply increasing the price paid for imported goods—textiles, shoes, furniture, firearms, and other manufactured items. Taxing these imports offered no help to agricultural interests and in fact meant that they, and all U.S. consumers, paid higher prices for goods made in the United States. Second, the high tariff restricted free trade and thus served as an encouragement to foreign nations to erect trade barriers of their own, which would hurt cotton exports from the South. For these reasons, South Carolina, led by John C. Calhoun, argued that states, as sovereign entities, ought to have the power to nullify federal laws if they believed them to be contrary to their interests. Calhoun articulated the theory in the "South Carolina Exposition and Protest" in 1828. In 1832, after he and President Andrew Jackson clashed on the issue, he resigned the vice presidency and led South Carolina to issue an Ordinance of Nullification. The state even threatened to secede. President Jackson responded by pledging to keep South Carolina in the Union by force, if necessary. In 1833, Congress enacted a compromise tariff measure that gradually lowered tariff rates over a period of several years, and the crisis thus came to an end.

Old Republicans

Like the National Republicans, the Old Republicans were a faction that developed from the Democratic-Republicans, the party founded by Thomas Jefferson. During the decade or so after the War of 1812, the Old Republicans championed what they believed to be the true principles of the Constitution and their party's founder: states' rights, agrarianism, and a limited national government. Virginians from plantation areas particularly embraced this position, and they articulated their vision for the nation through the *Richmond Enquirer.* Old Republicans strongly opposed national legislation establishing tariffs, banks, and internal improvements, for they feared that such measures would help commercial and industrial interests, undermine agricultural interests, centralize power in the national government, and lead to corruption and moral decline.

Peters, Richard

Peters served as the fourth reporter of the Supreme Court, during the years 1828–1843. He is best known for *Wheaton v. Peters* (1834), the Court's first copyright case, in which he successfully defended his condensed published version of many of the Court's earliest decisions. Despite this legal victory, he was often at odds with members of the Court, who frequently complained about his handling of their opinions. Justice Catron, who criticized Peters for omitting his dissent in *Kendall v. United States* from the reports, became Peters's leading opponent. In January 1843, with two of the justices absent because of illness, Justices Catron, Wayne, Baldwin, and Daniel joined to bring about Peters's dismissal, despite the objections of Chief Justice Taney. Bitter about how he had been treated, Peters attempted to continue publishing reports of the Court's decisions for profit, without being employed by the government, but the venture failed. He died in 1848.

Republican Party

The Republican Party was founded in 1854 by a group opposed to the passage of the Kansas-Nebraska Act and the spread of slavery to new western territories. An exclusively northern party, the Republicans became a political home for a variety of activists and movements: abolitionists, who viewed slavery as morally wrong; former Whigs, who advocated high tariffs, internal improvements, and economic development; Know-Nothings, whose rural and evangelical outlook often translated into opposition to slavery; and disgruntled northern Democrats, who believed their party had been taken over by southern slaveholding interests. What bound these diverse interests together was a common belief in the notion of free labor—an essential belief in the dignity of labor and the idea that hard work would ultimately result in upward mobility. Because slavery stood in stark opposition to these ideals, Republicans advocated an end to the spread of slavery. Most within the party forsook moral antislavery arguments for the sake of an economic and social critique of the "peculiar institution."

The party's first presidential candidate, John C. Fremont, did surprisingly well in the 1856 election, and Republicans succeeded in winning the presidency when Abraham Lincoln ran in 1860. Despite the moderate political rhetoric of Lincoln, who pledged never to interfere with slavery where it already existed, most white southerners viewed the Republican victory as a sign of abolitionist triumph. Secession and Civil War ensued. Union victory in the war led to northern and Republican dominance of the national government for most of the rest of the nineteenth century.

Seward, William

Seward held a variety of important positions during the mid-nineteenth century, including governor of New York, U.S. senator, and secretary of state. Born in New York in 1801, he graduated from Union College in New York and practiced law in his home state. Taking an interest in politics, he gravitated toward the Whig Party and won election as governor, serving from 1839 to 1843. In 1849, Seward earned a seat in the U.S. Senate, where he quickly made a name for himself as a forceful opponent of slavery and slaveholding interests. In stirring speeches, Seward championed the notion that a "higher law" prevented the spread of slavery to the West and that an "irrepressible conflict" would ensue between the slave states and the free states. He argued a few important cases before the Supreme Court, including *Genesee Chief v. Fitzhugh* (1852) and *Jones v. Van Zandt* (1847), and as a senator he bitterly attacked the Court's ruling in *Dred Scott v. Sandford* (1857). From the floor of the Senate, Seward portrayed the justices and President James Buchanan as coconspirators in a Democratic plot to subvert the Constitution and spread slavery throughout the land. Seward was a candidate for the Republican nomination for the presidency in 1860. (Taney later remarked that if Seward had won the White House he would have refused to administer the oath of office.) Seward went on to serve as secretary of state under President Lincoln, and in this position he skillfully prevented European powers from recognizing the Confederacy. Seward remained secretary of state under President Andrew Johnson and succeeded in negotiating the purchase of Alaska. He died in 1872.

Tariff

A tariff is a tax levied on imports, which serves to discourage the entry of such goods into the country. For much of the nineteenth century, the tariff issue was among the most important in American politics. In general, Democrats, southerners, and agriculturalists favored low tariffs, whereas Whigs, northerners, and industrial interests wanted high tariffs. Low tariffs ensured that consumers would pay low prices for manufactured goods imported into the United States and helped keep low the likelihood that other nations would impose protective tariffs against U.S. products. Southern cotton interests in particular wanted to be able to ship their product overseas for the European market. Northern industrialists, in contrast, wanted to keep cheap imported goods out of the United States in order to protect domestic markets for their products. This would allow U.S. industry to develop and thrive. The Nullification Crisis of 1828–1832 constituted the greatest political battle over tariff rates, as South Carolina attempted to declare a federal law increasing the tariff to be null and void. *See also Nullification Crisis.*

Webster, Daniel

One of the most important national political and legal figures of the early nineteenth century, Daniel Webster served as a congressman, a senator, and secretary of state. Born in 1782 in Salisbury (now Franklin), New Hampshire, Webster graduated from Dartmouth College in 1801, studied law, and later practiced in Boscawen and Portsmouth, New Hampshire. In 1812 he won election to the U.S. House of Representatives as a Federalist and served two terms. Defeated for reelection in 1816, he moved to Boston and again won a seat in Congress. He served in the House from 1823 to 1827 and won a seat in the Senate from Massachusetts in 1826. As a senator for nearly two decades (1827–1841, 1845–1850), Webster became a Whig after the decline of the Federalist Party and soon emerged as the nation's foremost spokesman for economic development and national unity. He served as secretary of state under Presidents William Henry Harrison, John Tyler, and Millard Fillmore (1841–1843, 1845–1850) at a time when that office often propelled its occupants to the presidency. Sectional division over slavery, however, prevented Webster from ever attaining the nation's highest office. As a lawyer, Webster argued 249 cases before the U.S. Supreme Court. Most of these came during the Marshall era, a period during which the justices were sympathetic to Webster's nationalist views. He did not fare as well during the Taney era. He argued unsuccessfully, for example, in *Charles River Bridge v. Warren Bridge* (1837), that the Charles River Bridge Company's charter granted them exclusive rights to operate a bridge over the river, and he failed to convince the justices in *Groves v. Slaughter* (1841) that congressional power over commerce was exclusive. Still, his arguments won the day in the *Passenger Cases* (1849), in which a 5–4 majority struck down state laws regulating and taxing immigrants. Webster died in 1852.

Whig Party

The Whig Party emerged during the 1830s as the opposition party to the administration of President Andrew Jackson. In particular, Whigs decried Jackson's expansion of the powers of his office, including his use of the "spoils system" and his repeated exercise of the presidential veto. Some Whigs of the more aristocratic sort thought that Jackson went too far in catering to the wishes of the people and championing liberty at the expense of established authority. For their part, Whigs looked favorably on the use of governmental power to promote economic development and carry out moral reform. They thus tended to favor internal improvements—the use of government funds for public projects such as roads, bridges, canals, and railroads—and reform movements such as temperance. Whigs achieved minimal electoral success. Only two Whig presidential candidates—William Henry Harrison in 1840 and Zachary Taylor in 1848—succeeded in winning the nation's highest office. The party's most prominent spokesmen, Henry Clay and Daniel Webster, were unsuccessful in their own quests for the presidency. By the middle of the 1850s, the Whig Party had faded from the scene, and many of its adherents became Know-Nothings and, later, Republicans. *See also Know-Nothing Party; National Republicans; Republican Party.*

Wilmot Proviso

Introduced in the U.S. House of Representatives in 1846 by Democrat David Wilmot, of Pennsylvania, the proviso was intended to prevent the spread of slavery to any of the new territories won by the United States in its war with Mexico. Although Wilmot's proposal never passed, it immediately alerted southerners to the threat of national interference with the institution of slavery. It led John C. Calhoun, of South Carolina, to speak of the need for a southern confederacy and to organize a meeting of representatives of the southern states in Nashville in 1850. Although in the short term the crisis involving the introduction of the proviso was resolved with the Compromise of 1850, the long-term issue remained: What was the extent of the national government's power over slavery, either in new territories or where slavery already existed? This question continued to polarize the country along sectional lines throughout the 1850s and eventually led to the Civil War.

Excerpts from Landmark Decisions

Original spelling and punctuation have been retained. Words in brackets have been inserted by the author.

Charles River Bridge Company v. Warren Bridge Company, 36 U.S. 420 (1837)

Chief Justice TANEY delivered the opinion of the Court.

The questions involved in this case are of the gravest character, and the court have given to them the most anxious and deliberate consideration. The value of the right claimed by the plaintiffs is large in amount; and many persons may no doubt be seriously affected in their pecuniary interests by any decision which the court may pronounce; and the questions which have been raised as to the power of the several States, in relation to the corporations they have charted, are pregnant with important consequences; not only to the individuals who are concerned in the corporate franchises, but to the communities in which they exist. The court are fully sensible that it is their duty, in exercising the high powers conferred on them by the constitution of the United States, to deal with these great and extensive interests with the utmost caution; guarding, as far as they have the power to do so, the rights of property, and at the same time carefully abstaining from any encroachment on the rights reserved to the States.

Borrowing, as we have done, our system of jurisprudence from the English law; and having adopted, in every other case, civil and criminal, its rules for the construction of statutes; is there any thing in our local situation, or in the nature of our political institutions, which should lead us to depart from the principle where corporations are concerned? Are we to apply to acts of incorporation, a rule of construction differing from that of the English law, and, by implication, make the terms of a charter in one of the States, more unfavorable to the public, than upon an act of parliament, framed in the same words, would be sanctioned in an English court? Can any good reasons be assigned for excepting this particular class of cases from the operation of the general principle; and for introducing a new and adverse rule of construction in favor of corporations, while we adopt and adhere to the rules of construction known to the English common law, in every other case, without exception? We think not; and it would present a singular spectacle, if, while the courts in England are restraining, within the strictest limits, the spirit of monopoly, and exclusive privileges in nature of monopolies, and confining corporations to the privileges plainly given to them in their charter; the courts of this country should be found enlarging these privileges by implication; and construing a statute more unfavorably to the public, and to the rights of the community, than would be done in a case in an English court of justice.

But we are not now left to determine, for the first time, the rules by which public grants are to be construed in this country. . . . [T]he case most analogous to this, and in which the question came more directly before the court, is the case *The Providence Bank v. Billings*. . . .

It may, perhaps, be said, that in the case of *The Providence Bank*, this court were speaking of the taxing power; which is of vital importance to the very existence of every government. But the object and end of all government is to promote the happiness and prosperity of the community by which it is established; and it can never be assumed, that the government intended to diminish its power of accomplishing the end for which it was created. And in a country like ours, free, active, and enterprising, continually advancing in numbers and wealth, new channels of communication are daily found necessary, both for travel and trade; and are essential to the comfort, convenience, and prosperity of the people. A State ought never to be presumed to surrender this power, because, like the taxing power, the whole community have an interest in preserving it undiminished. And when a corporation alleges, that a State has surrendered for seventy years, its power of improvement and public accommodation, in a great and important line of travel, along which a vast number of its citizens must daily pass; the community have a right to insist, in the language of this court above quoted, "that its abandonment ought not to be presumed, in a case, in which the deliberate purpose of the State to abandon it does not appear." The continued existence of a government would be of no great value, if by implications and presumptions, it was disarmed of the powers necessary to accomplish the ends of its creation; and the functions it was designed to perform, transferred to the hands of privileged corporations. The rule of construction announced by the court, was not confined to the taxing power; nor is it so limited in the opinion delivered. On the contrary, it was distinctly placed on the ground that the interests of the community were concerned in preserving, undiminished, the power then in question; and whenever any power of the State is said to be surrendered or diminished, whether it be the taxing power or any other affecting the public interest, the same principle applies, and the rule of construction must be the same. No one will question that the interests of the great body of the people of the State, would, in this instance, be affected by the surrender of this great line of travel to a single corporation, with the right to exact toll, and exclude competition for seventy years. While the rights of private property are sacredly guarded, we must not forget that the community also have rights, and that the happiness and well being of every citizen depends on their faithful preservation.

Adopting the rule of construction above stated as the settled one, we proceed to apply it to the charter of 1785, to the proprietors of the Charles River Bridge. This act of incorporation is in the usual form, and the privileges such as are commonly given to corporations of that kind. It confers on them the ordinary faculties of a corporation, for the purpose of building the bridge; and establishes certain rates of toll, which the company are authorized to take. This is the whole grant. There is no exclusive privilege given to them over the waters of Charles River, above or below their bridge. No right to erect another bridge themselves, nor to prevent other persons from erecting one. No engagement from the State that another shall not be erected; and no undertaking not to sanction competition, nor to make improvements that may diminish the amount of its income. Upon all these subjects the charter is silent; and nothing is said in it about a line of travel, so much insisted on in the argument, in which they are to have exclusive privileges. No words are used, from which an intention to grant any of these rights can be inferred. If the plaintiff is entitled to them, it must be implied, simply, from the nature of the grant; and cannot be inferred from the words by which the grant is made.

The relative position of the Warren Bridge has already been described. It does not interrupt the passage over the Charles River Bridge, nor make the way to it or from it less convenient. None of the faculties or franchises granted to that corporation have been revoked by the legislature, and its right to take the tolls granted by the charter remains unaltered. In short, all the franchises and rights of property enumerated in the charter, and there mentioned to have been granted to it, remain unimpaired. But its income is destroyed by the Warren Bridge; which, being free, draws off the passengers and property which would have gone over it, and renders their franchise of no value. This is the gist of the complaint. For it is not pretended that the erection of the Warren Bridge would have done them any injury, or in any degree affected their right of property, if it had not diminished the amount of their tolls. In order then to entitle themselves to relief, it is necessary to show that the legislature contracted not to do the act of which they complain, and that they impaired, or, in other words, violated that contract by the erection of the Warren Bridge.

The inquiry then is, Does the charter contain such a contract on the part of the State? Is there any such stipulation to be found in that instrument? It must be admitted on all hands that there is none,—no words that even relate to another bridge, or to the diminution of their tolls, or to the line of travel. If a contract on that subject can be gathered from the charter, it must be by implication, and cannot be found in the words used. Can such an agreement be implied? The rule of construction before stated is an answer to the question. In charters of this description, no rights are taken from the public, or given to the corporation, beyond those which the words of the charter, by their natural and proper construction, purport to convey. There are no words which import such a contract as the plaintiffs in error contend for, and none can be implied; and the same answer must be given to them that was given by this court to the Providence Bank. The whole community are interested in this inquiry, and they have a right to require that the power of promoting their comfort and convenience, and of advancing the public prosperity, by providing safe, convenient, and cheap ways for the transportation of produce and the purposes of travel, shall not be construed to have been surrendered or diminished by the State, unless it shall appear by plain words that it was intended to be done. . . .

Can the legislature be presumed to have taken upon themselves an implied obligation, contrary to its own acts and declarations contained in the same law? It would be difficult to find a case justifying such an implication, even between individuals; still less will it be found where sovereign rights are concerned, and where the interests of a whole community would be deeply affected by such an implication. It would, indeed, be a strong exertion of judicial power, acting upon its own views of what justice required, and the parties ought to have done, to raise, by a sort of judicial coercion, an implied contract, and infer from it the nature of the very instrument in which the legislature appear to have taken pains to use words which disavow and repudiate any intention, on the part of the State, to make such a contract.

Indeed, the practice and usage of almost every State in the Union, old enough to have commenced the work of internal improvements, is opposed to the doctrine contended for on the part of the plaintiffs in error. Turnpike roads have been made in succession on the same line of travel; the later one interfering materially with the profits of the first. These corporations have, in some instances, been utterly ruined by the introduction of newer and better modes of transportation and travelling. In some cases, railroads have rendered the turnpike roads on the same line of travel so entirely useless, that the franchise of the turnpike corporation is not worth preserving. Yet in none of these cases have the corporation supposed that their privileges were invaded, or any contract violated on the part of the State. Amid the multitude of cases which have occurred, and have been daily occurring for the last forty or fifty years, this is the first instance in which such an implied contract has been contended for, and this court called upon to infer it from an ordinary act of incorporation, containing nothing more than the usual stipulations and provisions to be found in every such law. The absence of any such controversy, when there must have been so many occasions to give rise to it, proves that neither States, nor individuals, nor corporations, ever imagined that such a contract could be implied from such charters. It shows that the men who voted for these laws, never imagined that they were forming such a contract; and if we maintain that they have made it, we must create it by a legal fiction, in opposition to the truth of the fact, and the obvious intention of the party. We cannot deal thus with the rights reserved to the States, and by legal intendments and mere technical reasoning, take away from them any portion of that power over their own internal police and improvement, which is so necessary to their well being and prosperity.

And what would be the fruits of this doctrine of implied contracts on the part of the States, and of property in a line of travel by a corporation, if it should now be sanctioned by this court? To what results would it lead us? If it is to be found in the charter to this bridge, the same process of reasoning must discover it in the various acts which have been passed, within the last forty years, for turnpike companies. And what is to be the extent of the privileges of exclusion on the different sides of the road? The counsel who have so ably argued this case, have not attempted to define it by any certain boundaries. How far must the new improvement be distant from the old one? How near may you approach without invading its rights in the privileged line? If this court should establish the principles now contended for, what is to become of the numerous railroads established on the same line of travel with turnpike companies; and which have rendered the franchises of the turnpike corporations of no value? Let it once be understood that such charters carry with them these implied contracts, and give this unknown and undefined property in a line of traveling, and you will soon find the old turnpike corporations awakening from their sleep, and calling upon this court to put down the improvements which have taken their place. The millions of property which have been invested in railroads and canals, upon lines of travel which had been before occupied by turnpike corporations, will be put in jeopardy. We shall be thrown back to the improvements of the last century, and obliged to stand still, until the claims of the old turnpike corporations shall be satisfied, and they shall consent to permit these States to avail themselves of the lights of modern science, and to partake of the benefit of those improvements which are now adding to the wealth and prosperity, and the convenience and comfort of every other part of the civilized world. Nor is this all. This court will find itself compelled to fix, by some arbitrary rule, the width of this new kind of property in a line of travel; for if such a right of property exists, we have no lights to guide us in marking out its extent, unless, indeed, we resort to the old feudal grants, and to the exclusive rights of ferries, by prescription, between towns; and are prepared to decide that when a turnpike road from one town to another had been made, no railroad or canal, between these two points, could afterwards be established. This court are not prepared to sanction principles which must lead to such results. . . .

Justice STORY dissenting.

. . . It is a well known rule in the construction of private grants, if the meaning of the words be doubtful, to construe them most strongly against the grantor.

In the case of a legislative grant, there is no ground to impute surprise, imposition or mistake to the same extent as in a mere private grant of the crown. The words are the words of the legislature, upon solemn deliberation, and examination, and debate. Their purport is presumed to be well known, and the public interests are watched, and guarded by all the varieties of local, personal and professional jealousy; as well as by the untiring zeal of numbers, devoted to the public service.

It should also be constantly kept in mind, that in construing this charter, we are not construing a statute involving political powers and sovereignty, . . . We are construing a grant of the legislature, which though in the form of a statute, is still but a solemn contract. In such a case, the true course is to ascertain the sense of the parties from the terms of the instrument; and that once ascertained, to give it full effect. Lord Coke, indeed, recommends this as the best rule, even in respect to royal grants. "The best exposition (says he) of the king's charter is, upon the consideration of the whole charter, to expound the charter by the charter itself; every material part thereof (being) explained according to the true and genuine sense, which is the best method." . . .

But with a view to induce the Court to withdraw from all the common rules of reasonable and liberal interpretation in favour of grants, we have been told at the argument, that this very charter is a restriction upon the legislative power; that it is in derogation of the rights and interests of the state, and the people; that it tends to promote monopolies, and exclusive privileges; and that it will interpose an insuperable barrier to the progress of improvement. Now, upon every one of these propositions, which are assumed, and not proved, I entertain a directly opposite opinion; and, if I did not, I am not prepared to admit the conclusion for which they are adduced. If the legislature has made a grant, which involves any or all of these consequences, it is not for courts of justice to overturn the plain sense of the grant, because it has been improvidently or injuriously made.

But I deny the very ground work of the argument. This charter is not (as I have already said) any restriction upon the legislative power; unless it be true that because the legislature cannot grant again what it has already granted, the legislative power is restricted. If so, then every grant of the public land is a restriction upon that power; a doctrine, that has never yet been established, nor (as far as I know) ever contended for. Every grant of a franchise is, so far as that grant extends, necessarily exclusive; and cannot be resumed, or interfered with. All the learned judges in the state court admitted, that the franchise of Charles River Bridge, whatever it be, could not be resumed, or interfered with. The legislature could not recall its grant, or destroy it. It is a contract, whose obligation cannot be constitutionally impaired. In this respect, it does not differ from a grant of lands. In each case, the particular land, or the particular franchise, is withdrawn from the legislative operation. The identical land, or the identical franchise, cannot be regranted, or avoided by a new grant. But the legislative power remains unrestricted. The subject matter only (I repeat it) has passed from the hands of the government. If the legislature should order a government debt to be paid by a sale of the public stock, and it is so paid, the legislative power over the funds of the government remains unrestricted, although it has ceased over the particular stock, which has been thus sold. For the present, I pass over all further consideration of this topic, as it will necessarily come again under review, in examining an objection of a more broad and comprehensive nature.

Then, again, how is it established that this is a grant in derogation of the rights and interests of the people? No individual citizen has any right to build a bridge over navigable waters; and consequently he is deprived of no right, when a grant is made to any other persons for that purpose. Whether it promotes or injures the particular interest of an individual citizen, constitutes no ground for judicial or legislative interference, beyond what his own rights justify. When, then, it is said, that such a grant is in derogation of the rights and interests of the people, we must understand that reference is had to the rights and interests common to the whole people, as such, (such as the right of navigation,) or belonging to them as a political body; or, in other words, the rights and interests of the state. Now, I cannot understand how any grant of a franchise is a derogation from the rights of the people of the state, any more than a grant of public land. The right, in each case, is gone to the extent of the thing granted, and so far may be said to derogate from, that is to say, to lessen the rights of the people, or of the state. But that is not the sense in which the argument is pressed; for, by derogation, is here meant an injurious or mischievous detraction from the sovereign rights of the state. On the other hand, there can be no derogation from the rights of the people, as such, except it applies to rights common there before; which the building of a bridge over navigable waters certainly is not. If it had been said that the grant of this bridge was in derogation of the common right of navigating the Charles River, by reason of its obstructing, pro tanto, a free and open passage, the ground would have been intelligible. So, if it had been an exclusive grant of the navigation of that stream. But, if at the same time, equivalent public rights of a different nature, but of greater public accommodation and use, had been obtained; it could hardly have been said, in a correct sense, that there was any derogation from the rights of the people, or the rights of the state. It would be a mere exchange of one public right for another.

Then, again, as to the grant being against the interests of the people. I know not how that is established; and certainly it is not to be assumed. It will hardly be contended that every grant of the government is injurious to the interests of the people; or that every grant of a franchise must necessarily be so. The erection of a bridge may be of the highest utility to the people. It may essentially promote the public convenience, and aid the public interests, and protect the public property. And if no persons can be found willing to undertake such a work, unless they receive in return the exclusive privilege of erecting it, and taking toll; surely it cannot be said, as of course, that such a grant, under such circumstances, is, per se, against the interests of the people. Whether the grant of a franchise is, or is not, on the whole, promotive of the public interests; is a question of fact and judgment, upon which different minds may entertain different opinions. It is not to be judicially assumed to be injurious, and then the grant to be reasoned down. It is a matter exclusively confided to the sober consideration of the legislature; which is invested with full discretion, and possesses ample means to decide it. For myself, meaning to speak with all due deference for others, I know of no power or authority confided to the judicial department, to rejudge the decisions of the legislature upon such a subject. It has an exclusive right to make the grant, and to decide whether it be, or be not, for the public interests. It is to be presumed, if the grant is made, that it is made from a high sense of public duty, to promote the public welfare, and to establish the public prosperity. In this very case, the legislature has, upon the very face of the act, made a solemn declaration as to the motive for passing it; that—"The erecting of a bridge over Charles River, &c., will be of great public utility."

What court of justice is invested with authority to gainsay this declaration? To strike it out of the act, and reason upon the other words, as if it were not there? To pronounce that a grant is against the interests of the people, which the legislature has declared to be of great utility to the people? It seems to me to be our duty to interpret laws, and not to wander into speculations upon their policy. And where, I may ask, is the proof that Charles River Bridge has been against the interests of the people? The record contains no such proof; and it is, therefore, a just presumption that it does not exist.

Again, it is argued that the present grant is a grant of a monopoly, and of exclusive privileges; and therefore to be construed by the most narrow mode of interpretation. The sixth article of the bill of rights of Massachusetts has been supposed to support the objection; "No man, nor corporation, or association of men, have any other title to obtain advantages or particular and exclusive privileges distinct from those of the community, than what arises from the consideration of services rendered to the public; and this title being in nature neither hereditary nor transmissive to children, or descendants, or relations by blood, the idea of a man born a magistrate, lawgiver, or judge, is absurd and unnatural." Now, it is plain, that taking this whole clause together, it is not an inhibition of all legislative grants of exclusive privileges; but a promulgation of the reasons why there should be no hereditary magistrates, legislators, or judges. But it admits, by necessary implication, the right to grant exclusive privileges for public services, without ascertaining of what nature those services may be. It might be sufficient to say, that all the learned judges in the state court, admitted that the grant of an exclusive right to take toll at a ferry, or a bridge, or a turnpike, is not a monopoly which is deemed odious in law; nor one of the particular and exclusive privileges, distinct from those of the community, which are reprobated in the bill of rights. All that was asserted by the judges, opposed to a liberal interpretation of this grant, was, that it tended to promote monopolies. . . .

No sound lawyer will, I presume, assert that the grant of a right to erect a bridge over a navigable stream, is a grant of a common right. Before such grant, had all the citizens of the state a right to erect bridges over navigable streams? Certainly they had not; and, therefore, the grant was no restriction of any common right. It was neither a monopoly; nor, in a legal sense, had it any tendency to a monopoly. It took from no citizen what he possessed before; and had no tendency to take it from him. It took, indeed, from the legislature the power of granting the same identical privilege or franchise to any other persons. But this made it no more a monopoly, than the grant of the public stock or funds of a state for a valuable consideration. Even in cases of monopolies, strictly so called, if the nature of the grant be such that it is for the public good, as in cases of patents for inventions, the rule has always been to give them a favourable construction in support of the patent . . .

But it has been argued, and the argument has been pressed in every form which ingenuity could suggest, that if grants of this nature are to be construed liberally, as conferring any exclusive rights on the grantees, it will interpose an effectual barrier against all general improvements of the country. For myself, I profess not to feel the cogency of this argument; either in its general application to the grant of franchises, or in its special application to the present grant. This is a subject upon which different minds may well arrive at different conclusions, both as to policy and principle. Men may, and will, complexionally differ upon topics of this sort, according to their natural and acquired habits of speculation and opinion. For my own part, I can conceive of no surer plan to arrest all public improvements, founded on private capital and enterprise, than to make the outlay of that capital uncertain, and questionable both as to security, and as to productiveness. No man will hazard his capital in any enterprise, in which, if there be a loss, it must be borne exclusively by himself; and if there be success, he has not the slightest security of enjoying the rewards of that success for a single moment. If the government means to invite its citizens to enlarge the public comforts and conveniences, to establish bridges, or turnpikes, or canals, or railroads, there must be some pledge, that the property will be safe; that the enjoyment will be co-extensive with the grant: and that success will not be the signal of a general combination to overthrow its rights, and to take away its profits. The very agitation of a question of this sort, is sufficient to alarm every stockholder in every public enterprise of this sort, throughout the whole country. Already, in my native state, the legislature has found it necessary expressly to concede the exclusive privilege here contended against; in order to insure the accomplishment of a rail road for the benefit of the public. And yet, we are told, that all such exclusive grants are to the detriment of the public.

But if there were any foundation for the argument itself in a general view, it would totally fail in its application to the present case. Here, the grant, however exclusive, is but for a short and limited period, more than two-thirds of which have already elapsed; and, when it is gone, the whole property and franchise are to revert to the state. The legislature exercised a wholesome foresight on the subject; and within a reasonable period it will have an unrestricted authority to do whatever it may choose, in the appropriation of the bridge and its tolls. There is not, then, under any fair aspect of the case, the slightest reason to presume that public improvements either can, or will, be injuriously retarded by a liberal construction of the present grant.

I have thus endeavoured to answer, and I think I have successfully answered all the arguments, (which indeed run into each other) adduced to justify a strict construction of the present charter. I go further, and maintain not only, that it is not a case for strict construction; but that the charter upon its very face, by its terms, and for its professed objects, demands from the Court, upon undeniable principles of law, a favourable construction for the grantees. In the first place, the legislature has declared, that the erecting of the bridge will be of great public utility; and this exposition of its own motives for the grant, requires the Court to give a liberal interpretation, in order to promote, and not to destroy an enterprise of great public utility. In the next place, the grant is a contract for a valuable consideration, and a full and adequate consideration. The proprietors are to lay out a large sum of money, (and in those times it was a very large outlay of capital,) in erecting a bridge; they are to keep it in repair during the whole period of forty years; they are to surrender it in good repair at the end of that period to the state, as its own property; they are to pay, during the whole period, an annuity of two hundred pounds to Harvard college; and they are to incur other heavy expenses and burthens, for the public accommodation. In return for all these charges, they are entitled to no more than the receipt of the tolls during the forty years, for their reimbursement of capital, interest and expenses. With all this they are to take upon themselves the chances of success; and if the enterprise fails, the loss is exclusively their own. Nor let any man imagine, that there was not, at the time when this charter was granted, much solid ground for doubting success. . . .

This is not all. It is well known, historically, that this was the very first bridge ever constructed in New England, over navigable tide waters so near the sea. The rigours of our climate, the dangers from sudden thaws and freezing, and the obstructions from ice in a rapid current, were deemed by many persons to be insuperable obstacles to the success of such a project. It was believed, that the bridge would scarcely stand a single severe winter. And I myself am old enough to know, that in regard to other arms of the sea, at much later periods, the same doubts have had a strong and depressing influence upon public enterprises. If Charles River Bridge had been carried away during the first or second season after its erection, it is far from being certain, that up to this moment another bridge, upon such an arm of the sea, would ever have been erected in Massachusetts. I state these things which are of public notoriety, to repel the notion that the legislature was surprised into an incautious grant, or that the reward was more than adequate to the perils. There was a full and adequate consideration, in a pecuniary sense, for the charter. But, in a more general sense, the erection of the bridge, as a matter of accommodation, has been incalculably beneficial to the public. Unless, therefore, we are wholly to disregard the declarations of the legislature, and the objects of the charter, and the historical facts of the times; and indulge in mere private speculations of profit and loss by our present lights and experience; it seems to me, that the Court is bound to come to the interpretation of this charter, with a persuasion that it was granted in furtherance, and not in derogation of the public good.

But I do not insist upon any extraordinary liberality in interpreting this charter. All I contend for is that it shall receive a fair and reasonable interpretation; so as to carry into effect the legislative intention, and secure to the grantees a just security for their privileges. I might, indeed, well have spared myself any investigation of the principles upon which royal and legislative grants are ordinarily to be construed; for this Court has itself furnished an unequivocal rule for interpreting all public contracts. The present grant is confessedly a contract . . .

The legislature understood itself to be granting a boon; and not making a bargain, or asking a favour. It was liberal, because it meant to be just, in a case of acknowledged hazard, and of honourable enterprise, very beneficial to the public. To suppose, that the plaintiffs meant to surrender their present valuable and exclusive right of franchise for thirty-four remaining years, and to put it in the power of the legislature, the next day, or the next year, to erect a bridge, toll or free, which by its contiguity should ruin theirs, or take away all their profits; is a supposition, in my judgment, truly extravagant, and without a scintilla of evidence to support it. The burdens of maintaining the bridge were to remain; the payment of the annuity to Harvard college was to remain: and yet, upon this supposition, the extension of the term of their charter, granted in the shape of a bounty, would amount to a right to destroy the franchise the next day, or the next hour, at the pleasure of the legislature. I cannot perceive, upon what ground such an implication can be made; an implication, not arising from any words or intent expressed on the face of the act, or fairly inferrible from its purposes; and wholly repugnant to the avowed objects of the grant, which are to confer a benefit, and not to impose an oppressive burden, or create a ruinous competition.

Upon the whole, my judgment is, that the act of the legislature of Massachusetts granting the charter of Warren Bridge, is an act impairing the obligation of the prior contract and grant to the proprietors of Charles River Bridge; and, by the constitution of the United States, it is, therefore, utterly void. . . .

Dred Scott v. Sandford, 60 U.S. 393 (1857)

Chief Justice TANEY delivered the opinion of the Court.

. . . The question is simply this: Can a negro, whose ancestors were imported into this country, and sold as slaves, become a member of the political community formed and brought into existence by the Constitution of the United States, and as such become entitled to all the rights, and privileges, and immunities, guarantied by that instrument to the citizen? One of which rights is the privilege of suing in a court of the United States in the cases specified in the Constitution. . . .

The words "people of the United States" and "citizens" are synonymous terms, and mean the same thing. They both describe political body who . . . form the sovereignty, and who hold the power and conduct the Government through their representatives. . . . The question before us is, whether the class of persons described in the plea in abatement compose a portion of this people, and are constituent members of this sovereignty? We think they are not, and that they are not included, and were not intended to be included, under the word "citizens" in the Constitution, and can therefore claim none of the rights and privileges which that instrument provides for and secures to citizens of the United States. On the contrary, they were at that time considered as a subordinate and inferior class of beings, who had been subjugated by the dominant race, and, whether emancipated or not, yet remained subject to their authority, and had no rights or privileges but such as those who held the power and the Government might choose to grant them.

It is not the province of the court to decide upon the justice or injustice, the policy or impolicy, of these laws. The decision of that question belonged . . . to those who formed the sovereignty and framed the Constitution. The duty of the court is, to interpret the instrument they have framed, with the best lights we can obtain on the subject, and to administer it as we find it, according to its true intent and meaning when it was adopted.

In discussing this question, we must not confound the rights of citizenship which a State may confer within its own limits, and the rights of citizenship as a member of the Union. It does not by any means follow, because he has all the rights and privileges of a citizen of a State, that he must be a citizen of the United States. He may have all of the rights and privileges of the citizen of a State, and yet not be entitled to the rights and privileges of a citizen in any other State. For, previous to the adoption of the Constitution of the United States, every State had the undoubted right to confer on whomsoever it pleased the character of citizen, and to endow him with all its rights. But this character of course was confined to the boundaries of the State, and gave him no rights or privileges in other States beyond those secured to him by the laws of nations and the comity of States. Nor have the several States surrendered the power of conferring these rights and privileges by adopting the Constitution of the United States. Each State may still confer them upon an alien, or any one it thinks proper, or upon any class or description of persons; yet he would not be a citizen in the sense in which that word is used in the Constitution of the United States, nor entitled to sue as such in one of its courts, nor to the privileges and immunities of a citizen in the other States. The rights which he would acquire would be restricted to the

State which gave them. The Constitution has conferred on Congress the right to establish an uniform rule of naturalization, and this right is evidently exclusive, and has always been held by this court to be so. Consequently, no State, since the adoption of the Constitution, can by naturalizing an alien invest him with the rights and privileges secured to a citizen of a State under the Federal Government, although, so far as the State alone was concerned, he would undoubtedly be entitled to the rights of a citizen, and clothed with all the rights and immunities which the Constitution and laws of the State attached to that character.

It is very clear, therefore, that no State can, by any act or law of its own, introduce a new member into the political community created by the Constitution of the United States. It cannot make him a member of this community by making him a member of its own. . . .

The question then arises, whether the provisions of the Constitution, in relation to the personal rights and privileges to which the citizen of a State should be entitled, embraced the negro African race . . . made free in any State; and to put it in the power of a single State to make him a citizen of the United States, and endue him with the full rights of citizenship in every other State without their consent? Does the Constitution of the United States act upon him whenever he shall be made free under the laws of a State, and raised there to the rank of a citizen, and immediately clothe him with all the privileges of a citizen in every other State, and in its own courts?

The court think the affirmative of these propositions cannot be maintained. And if it cannot, [Dred Scott] could not be a citizen of the State of Missouri, within the meaning of the Constitution of the United States, and consequently, was not entitled to sue in its courts.

It is true, every person, and every class and description of persons, who were at the time of the adoption of the Constitution recognized as citizens in the several States, became also citizens of this new political body; but none other; it was formed by them, and for them and their posterity, but for no one else. . . .

It becomes necessary, therefore, to determine who were citizens of the several States when the Constitution was adopted.

[T]he legislation and histories of the times, and the language used in the Declaration of Independence, show, that neither the class of persons who had been imported as slaves, nor their descendants, whether they had become free or not, were then acknowledged as a part of the people, nor intended to be included in the general words used in that memorable instrument.

It is difficult at this day to realize the state of public opinion in relation to that unfortunate race, which prevailed in the civilized and enlightened portions of the world at the time of the Declaration of Independence, and when the Constitution of the United States was framed and adopted.

They had for more than a century before been regarded as beings of an inferior order, and altogether unfit to associate with the white race, either in social or political relations; and so far inferior, that they had no rights which the white man was bound to respect; and that the negro might justly and lawfully be reduced to slavery. . . . He was bought and sold, and treated as an ordinary article of merchandise and traffic, whenever a profit could be made by it. This opinion was at that time fixed and universal in the civilized portion of the white race. It was regarded as an axiom in morals as well as in politics, which no one thought of disputing, or supposed to be open to dispute; and men in every grade and position in society daily and habitually acted upon it in their private pursuits, as well as in matters of public concern, without doubting for a moment the correctness of this opinion. . . .

The legislation of the different colonies furnishes positive and indisputable proof of this fact.

The province of Maryland, in 1717, passed a law declaring "that if any free negro or mulatto intermarry with any white woman, or if any white man shall intermarry with any negro or mulatto woman, such negro or mulatto shall become a slave during life, excepting mulattoes born of white women, who, for such intermarriage, shall only become servants for seven years. . . ."

The other colonial law to which we refer was passed by Massachusetts in 1705. It is entitled "An act for the better preventing of a spurious and mixed issue," &c.; and it provides, that "if any negro or mulatto shall presume to smite or strike any person of the English or other Christian nation, such negro or mulatto shall be severely whipped. . . ."

[T]hese laws . . . show, too plainly to be misunderstood, the degraded condition of this unhappy race. They were still in force when the Revolution began, and are a faithful index to the state of feeling towards the class of persons of whom they speak, and of the position they occupied throughout the thirteen colonies, in the eyes and thoughts of the men who framed the Declaration of Independence and established the State Constitutions and Governments. They show that a perpetual and impassable barrier was intended to be erected between the white race and the one which they had reduced to slavery, and governed as subjects with absolute and despotic power, and which they then looked upon as so far below them in the scale of created beings, that intermarriages between white persons and negroes or mulattoes were regarded as unnatural and immoral, and punished as crimes, not only in the parties, but in the person who joined them in marriage. And no distinction in this respect was made between the free negro or mulatto and the slave, but this stigma, of the deepest degradation, was fixed upon the whole race. . . .

The language of the Declaration of Independence is equally conclusive:

> We hold these truths to be self-evident: that all men are created equal; that they are endowed by their Creator with certain unalienable rights; that among them is life,

> liberty, and the pursuit of happiness; that to secure these rights, Governments are instituted, deriving their just powers from the consent of the governed.

The general words above quoted would seem to embrace the whole human family, and if they were used in a similar instrument at this day would be so understood. But it is too clear for dispute, that the enslaved African race were not intended to be included, and formed no part of the people who framed and adopted this declaration; for if the language, as understood in that day, would embrace them, the conduct of the distinguished men who framed the Declaration of Independence would have been utterly and flagrantly inconsistent with the principles they asserted; and instead of the sympathy of mankind, to which they so confidently appeared, they would have deserved and received universal rebuke and reprobation.

Yet the men who framed this declaration were great men—high in literary acquirements—high in their sense of honor, and incapable of asserting principles inconsistent with those on which they were acting. They perfectly understood the meaning of the language they used, and how it would be understood by others; and they knew that it would not in any part of the civilized world be supposed to embrace the negro race, which, by common consent, had been excluded from civilized Governments and the family of nations, and doomed to slavery. They spoke and acted according to the then established doctrines and principles, and in the ordinary language of the day, no one misunderstood them. The unhappy black race were separated from the white by indelible marks, and laws long before established, and were never thought of or spoken of except as property, and when the claims of the owner or the profit of the trader were supposed to need protection.

This state of public opinion had undergone no change when the Constitution was adopted, as is equally evident from its provisions and language. . . .

[There] are two clauses in the Constitution which point directly and specifically to the negro race as a separate class of persons, and show clearly that they were not regarded as a portion of the people or citizens of the Government then formed.

One of these clauses reserves to each of the thirteen States the right to import slaves until the year 1808. . . . And by the other provision the States pledge themselves to each other to maintain the right of property of the master, by delivering up to him any slave who may have escaped from his service, and be found within their respective territories. . . . And these two provisions show, conclusively, that neither the description of persons therein referred to, nor their descendants, were embraced in any of the other provisions of the Constitution; for certainly these two clauses were not intended to confer on them or their posterity the blessings of liberty, or any of the personal rights so carefully provided for the citizen. . . .

And we may here again refer, in support of this proposition, to the plain and unequivocal language of the laws of the several States, some passed after the Declaration of Independence and before the Constitution was adopted, and some since the Government went into operation.

[The] . . . laws of the present slaveholding States . . . are full of provisions in relation to this class [and] . . . have continued to treat them as an inferior class, and to subject them to strict police regulations, drawing a broad line of distinction between the citizen and the slave races, and legislating in relation to them upon the same principle which prevailed at the time of the Declaration of Independence. As related to these States, it is too plain for argument, that they have never been regarded as a part of the people or citizens of the State, nor supposed to possess any political rights which the dominant race might not withhold or grant at their pleasure. . . .

And if we turn to the legislation of the States where slavery had worn out, or measures taken for its speedy abolition, we shall find the same opinions and principles equally fixed and equally acted upon.

Thus, [a] Massachusetts . . . Law of 1786 . . . forbids the marriage of any white person with any negro, Indian, or mulatto . . . and declares all such marriages absolutely null and void, and degrades thus the unhappy issue of the marriage by fixing upon it the stain of bastardy. . . .

And again, in 1833, Connecticut passed another law, which made it penal to set up or establish any school in that State for the instruction of persons of the African race not inhabitants of the State, or to instruct or teach in any such school or institution, or board or harbor for that purpose, any such person, without the previous consent in writing of the civil authority of the town in which such school or institution might be. . . .

By the laws of New Hampshire . . . no one was permitted to be enrolled in the militia of the State, but free white citizens; and the same provision is found in a subsequent collection of the laws, made in 1855. Nothing could more strongly mark the entire repudiation of the African race. . . . [W]hy are the African race, born in the State, not permitted to share in one of the highest duties of the citizen? The answer is obvious; he is not, by the institutions and laws of the State, numbered among its people. He forms no part of the sovereignty of the State, and is not therefore called on to uphold and defend it. . . .

The legislation of the States therefore shows, in a manner not to be mistaken, the inferior and subject condition of that race at the time the Constitution was adopted, and long afterwards, . . . and it is hardly consistent with the respect due to these States, to suppose that they regarded at that time, as fellow-citizens and members of the sovereignty, a class of beings whom they had thus stigmatized; . . . and upon whom they had impressed such deep and enduring marks of inferiority and degradation; or, that when they met in convention to form the Constitution, they looked upon them as a portion of their constituents, or designed to include them in the provisions so carefully inserted for the security and protection of the liberties and rights of their citizens. . . .

It is impossible, it would seem, to believe that the great men of the slaveholding States, who took so large a share in framing the Constitution of the United States, and exercised so much influence in procuring its adoption, could have been so forgetful or regardless of their own safety and the safety of those who trusted and confided in them. . . .

To all this mass of proof we have still to add, that Congress has repeatedly legislated upon the same construction of the Constitution that we have given. . . .

The first of these acts is the naturalization law . . . [of] March 26, 1790, [which] confines the right of becoming citizens *"to aliens being free white persons."* . . .

Another of the early laws of which we have spoken, is the first militia law, which was passed in 1792, at the first session of the second Congress. The language of this law is equally plain and significant. . . . It directs that every "free able-bodied white male citizen" shall be enrolled in the militia. The word *white* is evidently used to exclude the African race, and the word *citizen* to exclude unnaturalized foreigners; the latter forming no part of the sovereignty, owing it no allegiance, and therefore under no obligation to defend it. The African race, however, born in the country, did owe allegiance to the Government, whether they were slave or free; but it is repudiated, and rejected from the duties and obligations of citizenship in marked language.

The third act to which we have alluded is even still more decisive; it was passed as late as 1813, and it provides: "That from and after the termination of the war in which the United States are now engaged with Great Britain, it shall not be lawful to employ, on board of any public or private vessels of the United States, any person or persons except citizens of the United States, *or* persons of color, natives of the United States."

Here the line of distinction is drawn in express words. Persons of color, in the judgment of Congress, were not included in the word *citizens*, and they are described as another and different class of persons, and authorized to be employed, if born in the United States. . . .

No one, we presume, supposes that any change in public opinion or feeling, in relation to this unfortunate race, in the civilized nations of Europe or in this country, should induce the court to give to the words of the Constitution a more liberal construction in their favor than they were intended to bear when the instrument was framed and adopted. Such an argument would be altogether inadmissible in any tribunal called on to interpret it. . . .

And upon a full and careful consideration of the subject, the court is of opinion, that, . . . Dred Scott was not a citizen of Missouri within the meaning of the Constitution of the United States, and not entitled as such to sue in its courts; and consequently, that the Circuit Court had no jurisdiction of the case, and that the judgement on the plea in abatement is erroneous. . . .

It appears affirmatively on the record that he is not a citizen, and consequently his suit against Sandford was not a suit between citizens of different States, and the court had no authority to pass any judgment between the parties. The suit ought, in this view of it, to have been dismissed by the Circuit Court, and its judgment in favor of Sandford is erroneous, and must be reversed.

It is true that the result either way, by dismissal or by a judgment for the defendant, makes very little, if any, difference in a pecuniary or personal point of view to either party. But the fact that the result would be very nearly the same to the parties in either form of judgment, would not justify this court in sanctioning an error in the judgment which is patent on the record, and which, if sanctioned, might be drawn into precedent, and lead to serious mischief and injustice in some future suit.

We proceed, therefore, to inquire whether the facts relied on by the plaintiff entitled him to his freedom. . . .

In considering this part of the controversy, two questions arise: 1. Was he, together with his family, free in Missouri by reason of the stay in the territory of the United States . . . ? And 2. If they were not, is Scott himself free by reason of his removal to Rock Island, in the State of Illinois, as stated in the above admissions?

We proceed to examine the first question.

The act of Congress [the Missouri Compromise], upon which the plaintiff relies, declares that slavery and involuntary servitude, except as a punishment for crime, shall be forever prohibited in all that part of the territory ceded by France, under the name of Louisiana, which lies north of thirty-six degrees thirty minutes north latitude, and not included within the limits of Missouri. [But] . . . [was Congress] authorized to pass this law under any of the powers granted to it by the Constitution; for if the authority is not given by that instrument, it is the duty of this court to declare it void and inoperative, and incapable of conferring freedom upon any one who is held as a slave under the laws of any one of the States.

The counsel for the plaintiff [Dred Scott] has laid much stress upon that article in the Constitution which confers on Congress the power "to dispose of and make all needful rules and regulations respecting the territory or other property belonging to the United States;" but, in the judgment of the court, that provision has no bearing on the present controversy, and the power there given . . . was intended to be confined, to the territory which at that time belonged to, or was claimed by, the United States, and was within their boundaries as settled by the treaty with Great Britain, and can have no influence upon a territory afterwards acquired from a foreign Governments. It was a special provision for a known and particular territory, and to meet a present emergency, and nothing more. . . .

The . . . clause . . . does not speak of *any* territory, nor of *Territories*, but uses language which, according to its legitimate meaning, points to a particular thing. The power is given in relation only to *the* territory of the United States—that is, to a territory then in existence, and then known or claimed as the territory of the United

States. [It] . . . gives the power which was necessarily associated with the disposition and sale of the lands—that is, the power of making needful rules and regulations respecting the territory. . . .

Whether, therefore, we take the particular clause in question, by itself, or in connection with the other provisions of the Constitution, we think it clear, that it applies only to the particular territory of which we have spoken, and cannot, by any just rule of interpretation, be extended to territory which the new Government might afterwards obtain from a foreign nation. Consequently, the power which Congress may have lawfully exercised in this Territory . . . can furnish no justification and no argument to support a similar exercise of power over territory afterwards acquired by the Federal Government. We put aside, therefore, any argument, drawn from precedents, showing the extent of the power which the General Government exercised over slavery in this Territory, as altogether inapplicable to the case before us. . . .

But the power of Congress over the person or property of a citizen [is] regulated and plainly defined by the Constitution itself. And when the Territory becomes a part of the United States, the Federal Government enters . . . upon it with its powers over the citizen strictly defined, and limited by the Constitution. . . . It has no power of any kind beyond it; and it cannot, when it enters a Territory of the United States, put off its character, and assume discretionary or despotic powers which the Constitution has denied to it. . . . [A]nd the Federal Government can exercise no power over his person or property, beyond what that instrument confers, nor lawfully deny any right which it has reserved. . . .

For example, no one, we presume, will contend that Congress can make any law in a Territory respecting the establishment of religion, or the free exercise thereof, or abridging the freedom of speech or of the press, or the right of the people of the Territory peaceably to assemble, and to petition the Government for the redress of grievances.

Nor can Congress deny to the people the right to keep and bear arms, nor the right to trial by jury, nor compel any one to be a witness against himself in a criminal proceeding.

These powers, and others, in relation to rights of person, which it is not necessary here to enumerate, are, in express and positive terms, denied to the General Government; and the rights of private property have been guarded with equal care. Thus the rights of property are united with the rights of person, and placed on the same ground by the fifth amendment to the Constitution, which provides that no person shall be deprived of life, liberty, and property without due process of law. And an act of Congress which deprives a citizen of the United States of his liberty or property, merely because he came himself or brought his property into a particular Territory of the United States and who had committed no offence against the laws, could hardly be dignified with the name of due process of law. . . .

The powers over person and property of which we speak are not only not granted to Congress, but are in express terms denied, and they are forbidden to exercise them. And this prohibition . . . extend[s] to the whole territory over which the Constitution gives it power to legislate. . . . It is a total absence of power everywhere within the dominion of the United States, and places the citizens of a Territory, so far as these rights are concerned, on the same footing with citizens of the States, and guards them as firmly and plainly against any inroads which the General Government might attempt under the plea of implied or incidental powers. And if Congress itself cannot do this—if it is beyond the powers conferred on the Federal Government—it will be admitted, we presume, that it could not authorize a Territorial Government to exercise them. It could confer no power on any local Government, established by its authority, to violate the provisions of the Constitution. . . .

Now, as we have already said . . . the right of property in a slave is distinctly and expressly affirmed in the Constitution. The right to traffic in it, like an ordinary article of merchandise and property, was guarantied to the citizens of the United States, in every State that might desire it, for twenty years. And the Government in express terms is pledged to protect it in all future time, if the slave escapes from his owner. This is done in plain words—too plain to be misunderstood. And no word can be found in the Constitution which gives Congress a greater power over slave property, or which entitles property of that kind to less protection than property of any other description. The only power conferred is the power coupled with the duty of guarding and protecting the owner in his rights.

Upon these considerations, it is the opinion of the court that the act of Congress which prohibited a citizen from holding and owning property of this kind in the territory . . . is not warranted by the Constitution, and is therefore void; and that neither Dred Scott himself, nor any of his family, were made free by being carried into this territory; even if they had been carried there by the owner, with the intention of becoming a permanent resident.

But there is another point in the case which depends on State power and State law. And it is contended, on the part of the plaintiff, that he is made free by being taken to Rock Island, in the State of Illinois, independently of his residence in the territory of the United States; and being so made free, he was not again reduced to a state of slavery by being brought back to Missouri.

Our notice of this part of the case will be very brief; for the principle on which it depends was decided in this court, upon much consideration, in the case of *Strader et al. v. Graham.* In that case, the slaves had been taken from Kentucky to Ohio, with the consent of the owner, and afterwards brought back to Kentucky. And this court held that their *status* or condition, as free or slave, depended upon the laws of Kentucky, when they were brought back into that State, and not of Ohio; and that this court had no jurisdiction to revise the judgment of a State court upon its own laws.

This was the point directly before the court, and the decision that this court had no jurisdiction turned upon it, as will be seen by the report of the case.

So in this case. As Scott was a slave when taken into the State of Illinois by his owner, and was there held as such, and brought back in that character, his *status*, as free or slave, depended on the laws of Missouri, and not of Illinois.

Upon the whole, therefore, it is the judgment of this court, that it appears by the record before us that the plaintiff in error is not a citizen of Missouri, in the sense in which that word is used in the Constitution; and that the Circuit Court of the United States, for that reason, had no jurisdiction in the case, and could give no judgment in it. Its judgment for the defendant must, consequently, be reversed, and a mandate issued, directing the suit to be dismissed for want of jurisdiction.

Justice CURTIS dissenting.

[The] . . .question is, whether any person of African descent, whose ancestors were sold as slaves in the United States, can be a citizen of the United States. If any such person can be a citizen, this plaintiff has the right to the judgment of the court . . . ; for no cause is shown why he is not so, except his descent and the slavery of his ancestors.

The first section of the second article of the Constitution uses the language, "a citizen of the United States at the time of the adoption of the Constitution." One mode of approaching this question is, to inquire who were citizens of the United States at the time of the adoption of the Constitution.

To determine whether any free persons, descended from Africans held in slavery, were citizens of the United States . . . at the time of the adoption of the Constitution of the United States, it is only necessary to know whether any such persons were citizens of either of the States under the Confederation, at the time of the adoption of the Constitution.

Of this there can be no doubt. At the time of the ratification of the Articles of Confederation, all free native-born inhabitants of the States of New Hampshire, Massachusetts, New York, New Jersey, and North Carolina, though descended from African slaves, were not only citizens of those States, but such of them as had the other necessary qualifications possessed the franchise of electors, on equal terms with other citizens. . . .

[In Massachusetts] . . . persons of color, descended from African slaves, were by [the 1780 state] Constitution made citizens of the State; and such of them as have had the necessary qualifications, have held and exercised the elective franchise, as citizens, from that time to the present.

The [1784] Constitution of New Hampshire conferred the elective franchise upon "every inhabitant of the State having the necessary qualifications," of which color or descent was not one.

The Constitution of New York gave the right to vote to "every male inhabitant . . ." making no discrimination between free colored persons and others. . . .

That of New Jersey, to "all inhabitants of this colony, of full age, who are worth £50 proclamation money, clear estate."

New York, by its Constitution of 1820, required colored persons to have some qualifications as prerequisites for voting, which white persons need not possess. And New Jersey, by its present Constitution, restricts the right to vote to white male citizens. But these changes can have no other effect upon the present inquiry, except to show, that before they were made, no such restrictions existed; and colored in common with white persons, were not only citizens of those States, but entitled to the elective franchise on the same qualifications as white persons, as they now are in New Hampshire and Massachusetts. . . . And . . . no argument can obscure, that in some of the original thirteen States, free colored persons, before and at the time of the formation of the Constitution, were citizens of those States.

The fourth of the fundamental articles of the Confederation was as follows: "The free inhabitants of each of these States, paupers, vagabonds, and fugitives from justice, excepted, shall be entitled to all the privileges and immunities of free citizens in the several States."

The fact that free persons of color were citizens of some of the several States, and the consequence, that this fourth article of the Confederation would have the effect to confer on such persons the privileges and immunities of general citizenship, were not only known to those who framed and adopted those articles, but the evidence is decisive, that the fourth article was intended to have that effect, and that more restricted language, which would have excluded such persons, was deliberately and purposely rejected.

On the 25th of June, 1778 . . . the delegates from South Carolina moved to amend this fourth article, by inserting after the word "free," and before the word "inhabitants," the word "white," so that the privileges and immunities of general citizenship would be secured only to white persons. Two States voted for the amendment, eight States against it, and the vote of one State was divided. The language of the article stood unchanged, and both by its terms of inclusion, "free inhabitants," and the strong implication from its terms of exclusion, "paupers, vagabonds, and fugitives from justice," who alone were excepted, it is clear, that under the Confederation, and at the time of the adoption of the Constitution, free colored persons of African descent might be, and, by reason of their citizenship in certain States, were entitled to the privileges and immunities of general citizenship of the United States.

Did the Constitution of the United States deprive them or their descendants of citizenship?

That Constitution was ordained and established by the people of the United States, through the action, in each State, of those persons who were qualified by its laws to act thereon, in behalf of themselves and all other citizens of that State. In some of the States, as we have seen, colored persons were among those qualified by law to act on this subject. These colored persons were not only included in the body of "the people of the United States," by whom the Constitution was ordained and established, but in at least five of the States they had the power to act, and doubtless did act, by their suffrages, upon the question of its adoption. It would be strange, if we were to find in that instrument anything which deprived of their citizenship any part of the people of the United States who were among those by whom it was established.

I can find nothing in the Constitution which, *propio vigore* [by its own force], deprives of their citizenship any class of persons who were citizens of the United States at the time of its adoption, or who should be native-born citizens of the states after its adoption; nor any power enabling Congress to disfranchise persons born on the soil of any State, and entitled to citenship of such State by its Constitution and laws. And my opinion is, that, under the Constitution of the United States, every free person born on the soil of a State, who is a citizen of that State by force of its Constitution or laws, is also a citizen of the United States.

Undoubtedly . . . it is a principle of public law, recognized by the Constitution itself, that birth on the soil of a country both creates the duties and confers the rights of citizenship. . . .

It has been often asserted that the Constitution was made exclusively by and for the white race. It has already been shown that in five of the thirteen original States, colored persons then possessed the elective franchise, and were among those by whom the Constitution was ordained and established. If so, it is not true, in point of fact, that the Constitution was made exclusively by the white race. And that it was made exclusively for the white race is, in my opinion, not only an assumption not warranted by anything in the Constitution, but contradicted by its opening declaration, that it was ordained and established by the people of the United States, for themselves and their posterity.

And as free colored persons were then citizens of at least five States, and so in every sense part of the people of the United States, they were among those for whom and whose posterity the Constitution was ordained and established. . . .

The truth is, that citizenship, under the Constitution of the United States, is not dependent on the possession of any particular political or even of all civil rights; and any attempt so to define it must lead to error. To what citizens the elective franchise shall be confided, is a question to be determined by each State, in accordance with its own views of the necessities or expediencies of its condition. What civil rights shall be enjoyed by its citizens, and whether all shall enjoy the same, or how they may be gained or lost, are to be determined in the same way. . . .

It has sometimes been urged that colored persons are shown not to be citizens of the United States by the fact that the naturalization laws apply only to white persons. But whether a person born in the United States be or be not a citizen, cannot depend on laws which refer only to aliens, and do not affect the status of persons born in the United States. The utmost effect which can be attributed to them is, to show that Congress has not deemed it expedient generally to apply the rule to colored aliens. That they might do so, if thought fit, is clear. The Constitution has not excluded them.

The conclusions at which I have arrived on this part of the case are:

First. That the free native-born citizens of each State are citizens of the United States.

Second. That as free colored persons born within some of the States are citizens of those States, such persons are also citizens of the United States.

Third. That every such citizen, residing in any State, has the right to sue and is liable to be sued in the Federal courts, as a citizen of that State in which he resides.

Fourth. That as the plea to the jurisdiction in this case shows no facts, except that the plaintiff was of African descent, and his ancestors were sold as slaves, and as these facts are not inconsistent with his citizenship of the United States, and his residence in the State of Missouri, the plea to the jurisdiction was bad, and judgment of the Circuit Court overruling it was correct.

I dissent, therefore, from that part of the opinion of the majority of the court, in which it is held that a person of African descent cannot be a citizen of the United States; and I regret I must go further, and dissent both from what I deem their assumption of authority to examine the constitutionality of the act of Congress commonly called the Missouri compromise act. . . .

The general question may be stated to be, whether the plaintiff's status, as a slave, was so changed by his residence within that territory, that he was not a slave in the State of Missouri, at the time this action was brought.

[If] the acts of Congress on this subject are valid, the law of the Territory of Wisconsin, within whose limits the residence of the plaintiff and his wife, and their marriage and the birth of one or both of their children, took place, . . . is a law operating directly on the status of the slave. [The Missouri Compromise] enacted that, within this Territory, "slavery and involuntary servitude, otherwise than in the punishment of crimes, whereof the parties shall have been duly convicted, shall be, and is hereby, forever prohibited. . . ."

It becomes necessary, therefore, to inquire whether the operation of the laws of the Territory of Wisconsin upon the status of the plaintiff was or was not such an operation as these principles of international law require other States to recognise and allow effect to. . . .

The material facts agreed, bearing on this part of the case, are, that Dr. Emerson, the plaintiffs master, resided about two years at the military post of Fort Snelling. . . .

On what ground can it be denied that all valid laws of the United States, constitutionally enacted by Congress for the government of the Territory, rightfully extended over an officer of the United States and his servant who went into the Territory to remain there for an indefinite length of time, to take part in its civil or military affairs? They were not foreigners, coming from abroad. Dr. Emerson was a citizen of the country which had exclusive jurisdiction over the Territory; and not only a citizen, but he went there in a public capacity, in the service of the same sovereignty which made the laws. . . . Whether the laws now in question were constitutionally enacted, I repeat once more, is a separate question. But, assuming that they were, . . . I consider that no other State or country could question the rightful power of the United States so to legislate, or, consistently with the settled rules of international law, could refuse to recognise the effects of such legislation upon the status of their officers and servants, as valid everywhere.

This alone would, in my apprehension, be sufficient to decide this question.

But there are other facts stated on the record which should not be passed over. It is agreed that, in the year 1836, the plaintiff, while residing in the Territory, was married, with the consent of Dr. Emerson, to Harriet. . . . And the inquiry is, whether, after the marriage of the plaintiff in the Territory, with the consent of Dr. Emerson, any other State or Country can, consistently with the settled rules of international law, refuse to recognise and treat him as a free man, when suing for the liberty of himself, his wife, and the children of that marriage.

If the laws of Congress governing the Territory of Wisconsin were constitutional and valid laws, there can be no doubt these parties were capable of contracting a lawful marriage, attended with all the usual civil rights and obligations of that condition. In that Territory they were absolutely free persons, having full capacity to enter into the civil contract of marriage.

It is a principle of international law, settled beyond controversy in England and America, that a marriage, valid by the law of the place where it was contracted, and not in fraud of the law of any other place, is valid everywhere. . . .

What, then, shall we say of the consent of the master, that the slave may contract a lawful marriage, attended with all the civil rights and duties which belong to that relation; that he may enter into a relation which none but a free man can assume—a relation which involves not only the rights and duties of the slave, but those of the other party to the contract, and of their descendants to the remotest generation? In my judgment, there can be no more effectual abandonment of the legal rights of a master over his slave, than by the consent of the master that the slave should enter into a contract of marriage, in a free State, attended by all the civil rights and obligations which belong to that condition. . . .

To avoid misapprehension on this important and difficult subject, I will state, distinctly, the conclusions at which I have arrived. They are:

First. The rules of international law respecting the emancipation of slaves, by the rightful operation of the laws of another State or country upon the status of the slave, while resident in such foreign State or country, are part of the common law of Missouri, and have not been abrogated by any statute law of that State.

Second. The laws of the United States, constitutionally enacted, which operated directly on and changed the status of a slave coming into the Territory of Wisconsin with his master, who went thither to reside for an indefinite length of time, in the performance of his duties as an officer of the United States, had a rightful operation on the status of the slave, and it is in conformity with the rules of international law that this change of status should be recognised everywhere.

Third. The laws of the United States, in operation in the Territory of Wisconsin at the time of the plaintiffs residence there, did act directly on the status of the plaintiff, and change his status to that of a free man.

Fourth. The plaintiff and his wife were capable of contracting, and, with the consent of Dr. Emerson, did contract a marriage in that Territory, valid under its laws; and the validity of this marriage cannot be questioned in Missouri, save by showing that it was in fraud of the laws of that State, or of some right derived from them; which cannot be shown in this case, because the master consented to it.

Fifth. That the consent of the master that his slave, residing in a country which does not tolerate slavery, may enter into a lawful contract of marriage, attended with the civil rights and duties which belong to that condition, is an effectual act of emancipation. And the law does not enable Dr. Emerson, or any one claiming under him, to assert a title to the married persons as slaves, and thus destroy the obligation of the contract of marriage, and bastardize their issue, and reduce them to slavery. . . .

I have thus far assumed, merely for the purpose of the argument, that the laws of the United States, respecting slavery in this Territory, were constitutionally enacted by Congress. It remains to inquire whether they are constitutional and binding laws.

No reason has been suggested why any reluctance should have been felt, by the framers of the Constitution, to apply [the Territories Clause] to all the territory which might belong to the United States, or why any distinction should have been made, founded on the accidental circumstance of the dates of the cessions; a circumstance in no way material as respects the necessity for rules and regulations, or the propriety of conferring on the Congress power to make them. And if we look at the course of the debates in the Convention on this article, we shall find that the then unceded lands, so far from having been left out of view in adopting this article, constituted, in the minds of members, a subject of even paramount importance. . . .

There is not, in my judgment, anything in the language, the history, or the subject-matter of this article, which restricts its operation to territory owned by the United States when the Constitution was adopted.

I construe [the territories] clause, therefore, as if it had read, Congress shall have power to make all needful rules and regulations respecting those tracts of country, out of the limits of the several States, which the United States have acquired, or may hereafter acquire, by cessions, as well of the jurisdiction as of the soil, so far as the soil may be the property of the party making the cession, at the time of making it. . . .

But it is insisted, that whatever other powers Congress may have respecting the territory of the United States, the subject of negro slavery forms an exception. The Constitution declares that Congress shall have power to make "all needful rules and regulations" respecting the territory belonging to the United States.

The assertion is, though the Constitution says all, it does not mean all—though it says all, without qualification, it means all except such as allow or prohibit slavery. It cannot be doubted that it is incumbent on those who would thus introduce an exception not found in the language of the instrument, to exhibit some solid and satisfactory reason, drawn from the subject-matter or the purposes and objects of the clause, the context, or from other provisions of the Constitution, showing that the words employed in this clause are not to be understood according to their clear, plain, and natural signification. . . .

A practical construction, nearly contemporaneous with the adoption of the Constitution, and continued by repeated instances through a long series of years, may always influence, and in doubtful cases should determine, the judicial mind, on a question of the interpretation of the Constitution. . . .

It has already been stated, that after the Government of the United States was organized under the Constitution, the temporary Government of the Territory northwest of the river Ohio could no longer exist, save under the powers conferred on Congress by the Constitution. . . . And, accordingly, an act was passed on the 7th day of August, 1789 [reenacting the substance of the Northwest Ordinance, including the prohibition of slavery].

Here is an explicit declaration of the will of the first Congress, of which fourteen members, including Mr. Madison, had been members of the Convention which framed the Constitution, that the ordinance, one article of which prohibited slavery, "should continue to have full effect." Gen. Washington, who signed this bill, as President, was the President of that Convention. . . .

I consider the passage of this law to have been an assertion by the first Congress of the power of the United States to prohibit slavery within this part of the territory of the United States; for it clearly shows that slavery was thereafter to be prohibited there, and it could be prohibited only by an exertion of the power of the United States, under the Constitution; no other power being capable of operating within that territory after the Constitution took effect. . . .

It appears, however, from what has taken place at the bar, that notwithstanding the language of the Constitution, and the long line of legislative and executive precedents under it, three different and opposite views are taken of the power of Congress respecting slavery in the Territories.

One is, that though Congress can make a regulation prohibiting slavery in a Territory, they cannot make a regulation allowing it; another is, that it can neither be established nor prohibited by Congress, but that the people of a Territory, when organized by Congress, can establish or prohibit slavery; while the third is, that the Constitution itself secures to every citizen who holds slaves, under the laws of any State, the indefeasible right to carry them into any Territory, and there hold them as property.

No particular clause of the Constitution has been referred to at the bar in support of either of these views. The first seems to be rested upon general considerations concerning the social and moral evils of slavery, its relations to republican Governments, its inconsistency with the Declaration of Independence and with natural right.

The second is drawn from considerations equally general, concerning the right of self-government, and the nature of the political institutions which have been established by the people of the United States.

While the third is said to rest upon the equal right of all citizens to go with their property upon the public domain, and the inequality of a regulation which would admit the property of some and exclude the property of other citizens; and, inasmuch as slaves are chiefly held by citizens of those particular States where slavery is established, it is insisted that a regulation excluding slavery from a Territory operates, practically, to make an unjust discrimination between citizens of different States, in respect to their use and enjoyment of the territory of the United States.

With the weight of either of these considerations, when presented to Congress to influence its action, this court has no concern. One or the other may be justly entitled to guide or control the legislative judgment upon what is a needful regulation. The question here is, whether they are sufficient to authorize this court to insert into this clause of the Constitution an exception of the exclusion or allowance of slavery, not found therein, nor in any other part of that instrument. To engraft on any instrument a substantive exception not found in it, must be admitted to be a matter attended with great difficulty. And the difficulty increases with the importance of the instrument, and the magnitude and complexity of the interests involved in its construction. To allow this to be done with the Constitution, upon reasons purely political, renders its judicial interpretation impossible—because judicial tribunals, as such, cannot decide upon political considerations. Political reasons have not the requisite certainty to afford rules of judicial interpretation. They are different in different men. They are different in the same men at different times. And when a strict interpretation of the Constitution, according to the fixed rules which govern the interpretation of laws, is abandoned, and the theoretical opinions of individuals are allowed to control its meaning, we have no longer a Constitution; we are under the government of individual men, who for the time being have power to declare what the Constitution is, according to their own views of what it ought to mean. When such a method of interpretation of the Constitution obtains, in place of a republican Government, with limited and defined powers, we have a Government which is merely an exponent of the will of Congress; or what, in my opinion, would not be preferable, an exponent of the individual political opinions of the members of this court.

If it can be shown, by anything in the Constitution itself, that when it confers on Congress the power to make all needful rules and regulations respecting the territory belonging to the United States, the exclusion or the allowance of slavery was excepted; or if anything in the history of this provision tends to show that such an exception was intended by those who framed and adopted the Constitution to be introduced into it, I hold it to be my duty carefully to consider, and to allow just weight to such considerations in interpreting the positive text of the Constitution. But where the Constitution has said all needful rules and regulations, I must find something more than theoretical reasoning to induce me to say it did not mean all . . .

[But the opinion of the Court suggests that the slavery prohibition in the Missouri Compromise violates] that clause in the fifth article of the amendments of the Constitution which declares that no person shall be deprived of his life, liberty, or property, without due process of law. . . .

Slavery, being contrary to natural right, is created only by municipal law. This is not only plain in itself, and agreed by all writers on the subject, but is inferable from the Constitution, and has been explicitly declared by this court. The Constitution refers to slaves as "persons held to service in one State, under the laws thereof." Nothing can more clearly describe a status created by municipal law. In *Prigg v. Pennsylvania*, this court said: "The state of slavery is deemed to be a mere municipal regulation, founded on and limited to the range of territorial laws." In *Rankin v. Lydia*, the Supreme Court of Appeals of Kentucky said: "Slavery is sanctioned by the laws of this State, and the right to hold them under our municipal regulations is unquestionable. But we view this as a right existing by positive law of a municipal character, without foundation in the law of nature or the unwritten common law." I am not acquainted with any case or writer questioning the correctness of this doctrine.

Nor, in my judgment, will the position, that a prohibition to bring slaves into a Territory deprives any one of his property without due process of law, bear examination. . . .

Besides, if the prohibition upon all persons . . . to bring slaves into a Territory, and a declaration that if brought they shall be free, deprives citizens of their property without due process of law, what shall we say of the legislation of many of the slaveholding States which have enacted the same prohibition? As early as October, 1778, a law was passed in Virginia, that thereafter no slave should be imported into that Commonwealth by sea or by land, and that every slave who should be imported should become free. . . . I am not aware that such laws, though they exist in many States, were ever supposed to be in conflict with the principle of Magna Charta. . . . It was certainly understood by the Convention which framed the Constitution, and has been so understood ever since, that, under the power to regulate commerce, Congress could prohibit the importation of slaves; and the exercise of the power was restrained till 1808. A citizen of the United States owns slaves in Cuba, and brings them to the United States, where they are set free by the legislation of Congress. Does this legislation deprive him of his property without due process of law? If so, what becomes of the laws prohibiting the slave trade? If not, how can a similar regulation respecting a Territory violate the fifth amendment of the Constitution? . . .

In my opinion, the judgment of the Circuit Court should be reversed, and the cause remanded for a new trial.

Chronology

1828 November 4 Andrew Jackson elected president.

1829 March 4 President Andrew Jackson inaugurated.

March 6 President Jackson nominates John McLean to replace Justice Robert Trimble

November 26 Justice Bushrod Washington dies.

1830 January 4 President Jackson nominates Henry Baldwin to replace Justice Bushrod Washington.

January 11 Justice John McLean takes his seat on the Supreme Court.

January 18 Justice Henry Baldwin takes his seat on the Supreme Court.

May 28 Congress passes Indian Removal Act, which authorizes President Jackson to begin removal of Native Americans from the Southeastern United States.

1831 January 1 William Lloyd Garrison publishes the first issue of the abolitionist newspaper, *The Liberator*, which calls for an immediate and unconditional end to slavery.

June 21 President Jackson appoints Roger B. Taney U.S. Attorney General.

August 22 Slave preacher Nat Turner leads bloodiest slave revolt in U.S. history in Southampton County, Virginia.

1832 July 10 President Jackson vetoes bill rechartering the Second Bank of the United States.

1832, *cont.* November 6 President Jackson elected to a second term.

November 24 South Carolina passes Ordinance of Nullification, which declares the federal tariff null and void.

1833 March 1 Congress enacts Compromise of 1833, which resolves the Nullification Crisis by gradually lowering the federal tariff over the next decade.

March 4 President Jackson inaugurated for second term.

September 23 President Jackson appoints Taney U.S. Secretary of the Treasury while Congress is in recess. Secretary of Treasury Taney begins withdrawal of federal government deposits from National Bank.

1834 June 24 Senate refuses to confirm Taney's appointment as Secretary of Treasury

August 4 Justice William Johnson dies.

1835 January 6 President Jackson nominates James Wayne to replace Justice William Johnson.

January 14 Justice Gabriel Duval dies.

January 14 Justice James Wayne takes his seat on the Supreme Court.

January 15 President Jackson nominates Roger Taney to replace Justice Gabriel Duval.

March 3 Senate postpones vote on Taney's nomination to the Supreme Court.

July 6 Chief Justice John Marshall dies.

December 28 President Jackson nominates Taney to replace Chief Justice Marshall.

December 28 President Jackson nominates Philip P. Barbour to replace Justice Gabriel Duval.

1836 March 15 Senate confirms nomination of Taney as chief justice.

March 28 Roger B. Taney takes his seat on the Supreme Court.

May 12 Philip P. Barbour takes his seat on the Supreme Court

November 1 Martin Van Buren elected president.

1837 February 11 *Briscoe v. Bank of the Commonwealth of Kentucky* (36 U.S. 257)

February 12 *Charles River Bridge v. Warren Bridge* (36 U.S. 420)

February 16 *New York v. Miln* (36 U.S. 102)

March 3 Congress passes Judiciary Act of 1837, which adds two federal judicial circuits and expands the size of the Court from seven to nine members. President Jackson nominates John Catron to fill one of the new seats on the Supreme Court.

March 4 Martin Van Buren inaugurated as president.

May 1 John Catron takes his seat on the Supreme Court.

September 18 President Van Buren nominates John McKinley to fill a new seat on the Supreme Court.

1838 January 9 Justice John McKinley takes his seat on the Supreme Court.

March 12 *Kendall v. United States ex rel. Stokes* (37 U.S. 254)

1839 March 9 *Bank of Augusta v. Earle* (38 U.S. 519)

1840 November 3 William Henry Harrison elected president.

1841 February 25 Justice Philip P. Barbour dies.

February 26 President Van Buren nominates Peter V. Daniel to replace Justice Philip P. Barbour.

1841, *cont.* March 2 Justice Peter V. Daniel takes his seat on the Supreme Court.

March 4 William Henry Harrison inaugurated as president.

March 9 *United States v. The Amistad* (40 U.S. 518)

March 10 *Groves v. Slaughter* (40 U.S. 449)

April 4 President William Henry Harrison dies. John Tyler assumes the presidency.

1842 January 25 *Swift v. Tyson* (41 U.S. 1)

March 1 *Prigg v. Pennsylvania* (41 U.S. 539)

1843 February 23 *Bronson v. Kinzie* (42 U.S. 311)

December 18 Justice Smith Thompson dies.

1844 February 4 President John Tyler nominates Samuel Nelson to replace Justice Smith Thompson.

February 27 Justice Samuel Nelson takes his seat on the Supreme Court.

March 7 *Louisville Railroad Company v. Letson* (43 U.S. 497)

April 21 Justice Henry Baldwin dies.

November 5 James K. Polk elected president.

1845 March 4 President James K. Polk inaugurated.

September 10 Justice Joseph Story dies.

December 23 President Polk nominates Levi Woodbury to replace Justice Joseph Story.

1846 January 3 Justice Levi Woodbury takes his seat on the Supreme Court.

May 13 United States declares war on Mexico.

August 3 President Polk nominates Robert Cooper Grier to replace Justice Henry Baldwin.

August 8 Congressman David Wilmot introduces the Wilmot Proviso.

August 10 Justice Robert Cooper Grier takes his seat on the Supreme Court.

1847 March 2 *Waring v. Clark* (46 U.S. 441)

March 5 *Jones v. Van Zandt* (46 U.S. 215)

March 6 *License Cases* (*Thurlow v. Massachusetts; Fletcher v. Rhode Island; Peirce v. New Hampshire*) [46 U.S. 504]

1848 January 31 *West River Bridge v. Dix* (47 U.S. 507)

March 6 *Planters' Bank of Mississippi v. Sharp* (47 U.S. 301)

March 7 *New Jersey Steam Navigation Co. v. Merchants' Bank of Boston* (47 U.S. 344)

March 10 Senate ratifies Treaty of Guadalupe Hidalgo, which ends the Mexican-American War and provides for U.S. acquisition of present-day American Southwest for $15 million.

November 7 Zachary Taylor elected president.

1849 January 3 *Luther v. Borden* (48 U.S. 1)

February 7 *Passenger Cases* (*Smith v. Turner, Norris v. Boston*) [48 U.S. 283]

March 4 President Zachary Taylor inaugurated.

1850 July 9 President Taylor dies. Vice President Millard Fillmore assumes the presidency.

September 17 Compromise of 1850 enacted into law.

1851 January 6 *Strader v. Graham* (51 U.S. 82)

September 4 Justice Levi Woodbury dies.

September 22 President Millard Fillmore nominates Benjamin R. Curtis to replace Justice Levi Woodbury.

October 10 Justice Benjamin R. Curtis takes his seat on the Supreme Court.

1852 February 20 *Genesee Chief v. Fitzhugh* (53 U.S. 443)

March 2 *Cooley v. Board of Wardens* (53 U.S. 299)

July 19 Justice John McKinley dies.

November 2 Franklin Pierce elected president.

1853 March 4 President Franklin Pierce inaugurated.

March 22 President Franklin Pierce nominates John A. Campbell to replace Justice John McKinley.

April 11 Justice John A. Campbell takes his seat on the Supreme Court.

1854 May 8 *Marshall v. Baltimore and Ohio Railroad Company* (57 U.S. 314)

May 24 *Piqua Branch of the State Bank of Ohio v. Knoop* (57 U.S. 369)

May 24 *Ohio Life Insurance and Trust Company v. DeBolt* (57 U.S. 416)

May 30 Kansas Nebraska Act, opening the two territories to slavery on the basis of popular sovereignty, becomes law.

1856 April 8 *Dodge v. Woolsey* (59 U.S. 331)

November 4 James Buchanan elected president.

1857 March 4 President James Buchanan inaugurated.

March 6 *Dred Scott v. Sandford* (60 U.S. 393)

September 30 Justice Benjamin Curtis resigns.

December 9 President Buchanan nominates Nathan Clifford to replace Benjamin Curtis.

1858 January 21 Justice Nathan Clifford takes his seat on the Supreme Court.

1859 March 7 *Ableman v. Booth* (62 U.S. 506)

October 16 Abolitionist John Brown leads raid on U.S. arsenal at Harper's Ferry, Virginia.

1860 May 31 Justice Peter V. Daniel dies.

November 6 Abraham Lincoln elected president.

December 20 South Carolina is first of eleven states to secede from the Union.

1861 February 18 Jefferson Davis inaugurated as president of the Confederate States of America.

March 4 President Abraham Lincoln inaugurated.

March 14 *Kentucky v. Dennison* (65 U.S. 66)

April 4 Justice John McLean dies.

April 12 First shots of Civil War are fired at Fort Sumter, South Carolina.

April 26 Justice John A. Campbell resigns his seat on the Supreme Court.

April 27 President Lincoln suspends the writ of habeas corpus in Maryland.

May 28 *Ex parte Merryman* (17 Fed. Cas. 144 [No. 9487] [C.C.D. Md. 1861])

June 8 Tennessee is last of eleven states to secede from the Union.

1862 January 22 President Lincoln nominates Noah H. Swayne to replace John McLean.

1862, *cont.* January 27 Justice Noah H. Swayne takes his seat on the Supreme Court.

July 16 President Lincoln nominates Samuel F. Miller to replace Peter V. Daniel.

December 1 President Lincoln nominates David Davis to replace John A. Campbell.

1863 January 1 Emancipation Proclamation declares slaves in Confederate-held areas to be forever free.

March 10 *The Prize Cases* (67 U.S. 635)

July 13 New York City Draft Riots begin and last for five days.

July 4 Confederates surrender to Union forces at Vicksburg, Mississippi. Union regains control of Mississippi River.

July 5 Confederates surrender to Union forces at Gettysburg, Pennsylvania. Confederate attempt to invade the North is unsuccessful.

1864 October 12 Chief Justice Roger B. Taney dies.

November 8 President Lincoln elected to a second term.

December 6 President Lincoln nominates Salmon P. Chase to replace Roger B. Taney.

December 15 Chief Justice Chase takes his seat on the Supreme Court.

1865 February 23 Congress refuses to appropriate money for a bust of Taney.

March 4 President Lincoln inaugurated for second term.

April 9 Civil War ends with Gen. Robert E. Lee's surrender at Appomattox Court House, Virginia.

April 14 President Abraham Lincoln is assassinated. Vice President Andrew Johnson assumes the presidency.

Table of Cases

Ableman v. Booth, 62 U.S. 506 (1859)
Baker v. Carr, 369 U.S. 186 (1962)
Bank of Augusta v. Earle, 38 U.S. 519 (1839)
Bank of the United States v. Deveaux, 9 U.S. 61 (1809)
Bank of the United States v. Primrose, 38 U.S. 519 (1839)
Briscoe v. Bank of the Commonwealth of Kentucky, 36 U.S. 257 (1837)
Bronson v. Kinzie, 42 U.S. 311 (1843)
Brown v. Maryland, 25 U.S. 419 (1827)
Carpenter v. United States (1863), unreported
Charles River Bridge v. Warren Bridge, 36 U.S. 420 (1837)
Christ's Church Hospital v. County of Philadelphia, 65 U.S. 300 (1861)
The Circassian, 69 U.S. 135 (1865)
Cohens v. Virginia, 19 U.S. 264 (1821)
Commercial and Railroad Bank of Vicksburg v. Slocumb, 39 U.S. 60 (1840)
Commonwealth v. Aves, 35 Mass. 193 (1836)
Cook v. Moffat, 46 U.S. 295 (1847)
Cooley v. Board of Wardens, 53 U.S. 299 (1852)
Craig v. Missouri, 29 U.S. 410 (1830)
Cummings v. Missouri, 71 U.S. 277 (1867)
Dartmouth College v. Woodward, 17 U.S. 518 (1819)
Dobbins v. Erie County, 41 U.S. 435 (1842)
Dodge v. Woolsey, 59 U.S. 331 (1855)
Dred Scott v. Sandford, 60 U.S. 393 (1857)
Ex parte Crane, 30 U.S. 190 (1831)
Ex parte Garland, 71 U.S. 333 (1867)
Ex parte Merryman, 17 Fed. Cas. 144 (1861)
Ex parte Milligan, 71 U.S. 2 (1866)
Ex parte Vallandigham, 68 U.S. 243 (1864)
Fairfax's Devisee v. Hunter's Lessee, 11 U.S. 603 (1813)
Fletcher v. Peck, 10 U.S. 87 (1810)

Fletcher v. Rhode Island, 46 U.S. 504 (1847)
Foster and Elam v. Neilson, 27 U.S. (1829)
Gelpke v. Dubuque, 68 U.S. 175 (1864)
Genesee Chief v. Fitzhugh, 53 U.S. 443 (1852)
Gibbons v. Ogden, 22 U.S. 1 (1824)
Groves v. Slaughter, 40 U.S. 449 (1841)
Holmes v. Jennison, 39 U.S. 540 (1840)
Hotchkiss v. Greenwood, 52 U.S. 248 (1851)
Jackson v. Steamboat Magnolia, 61 U.S. 296 (1858)
Jones v. Van Zandt, 46 U.S. 215 (1847)
Kendall v. United States ex rel. Stokes, 37 U.S. 524 (1838)
Kentucky v. Dennison, 65 U.S. 66 (1861)
Lafayette Insurance v. French, 59 U.S. 404 (1856)
License Cases, 46 U.S. 504 (1847)
Louisville Railroad Company v. Letson, 43 U.S. 497 (1844)
Luther v. Borden, 48 U.S. 1 (1849)
Marbury v. Madison, 5 U.S. 137 (1803)
Marshall v. Baltimore and Ohio Railroad Company, 57 U.S. 314 (1854)
Martin v. Hunter's Lessee, 14 U.S. 304 (1816)
McCulloch v. Maryland, 17 U.S. 316 (1819)
Moore v. Illinois, 55 U.S. 13 (1852)
New Jersey Steam Navigation Co. v. Merchants Bank, 47 U.S. 344 (1848)
New Orleans and Carrollton Railroad v. Earle, 38 U.S. 519 (1839)
New York v. Miln, 36 U.S. 102 (1837)
Norris v. Boston, 48 U.S. 283 (1849)
Ogden v. Saunders, 25 U.S. 213 (1827)
Ohio Life Insurance and Trust Co. v. DeBolt, 57 U.S. 416 (1854)
Passenger Cases, 48 U.S. 283 (1849)
Peirce v. New Hampshire, 46 U.S. 504 (1847)
Pennsylvania v. Wheeling and Belmont Bridge Company, 54 U.S. 518 (1852)
Piqua Branch of the State Bank of Ohio v. Knoop, 57 U.S. 369 (1854)
Planters' Bank of Mississippi v. Sharp, 47 U.S. 301 (1848)
Prigg v. Pennsylvania, 41 U.S. 539 (1842)
Prize Cases, 67 U.S. 635 (1863)
Providence Bank v. Billings, 29 U.S. 514 (1830)
Renner v. Bank of Columbia, 22 U.S. 581 (1824)
Rhode Island v. Massachusetts, 37 U.S. 657 (1838)
Richmond, Fredericksburg, and Potomac Railroad Company v. Louisa Railroad Company, 54 U.S. 71 (1852)
Rowan v. Runnels, 46 U.S. 134 (1847)

Rundle v. Delaware and Raritan Canal Company, 55 U.S. 80 (1853)
Searight v. Stokes, 44 U.S. 151, (1845)
Seymour v. McCormick, 60 U.S. 96 (1857)
Slaughterhouse Cases, 83 U.S. 36 (1873)
Smith v. Turner, 48 U.S. 283 (1849)
State v. Foreman, 16 Tenn. 256 (1835)
Steamboat New World v. King, 57 U.S. 469 (1854)
Strader v. Graham, 51 U.S. 82 (1851)
Swift v. Tyson, 41 U.S. 1 (1842)
Test Oath Cases, 71 U.S. 277 (1867), 71 U.S. 333 (1867)
The Thomas Jefferson, 23 U.S. 428 (1825)
Thurlow v. Massachusetts, 46 U.S. 504 (1847)
United States v. Amistad, 40 U.S. 518 (1841)
United States v. Greathouse, 26 F. Cas. 18 (1863)
United States v. Hanway, 26 F. Cas. 105 (1851)
United States v. Nixon, 418 U.S. 683 (1974)
Van Metre v. Mitchell, 28 F. Cas. 1036 (1847)
Waring v. Clarke, 46 U.S. 441 (1847)
West River Bridge v. Dix, 47 U.S. 507 (1848)
Worcester v. Georgia, 31 U.S. 515 (1832)

Glossary

admiralty An area of law that pertains to maritime commerce and navigation, to business transacted at sea, to ships and shipping, to the transportation of persons and property by sea, and to marine affairs in general.

affirm An appellate court ruling that upholds the judgment of a lower court—that the judgment of the lower court is correct and should stand.

appeal A process by which a final judgment of a lower court ruling is reviewed by a higher court.

appellant The party who seeks review of a lower court ruling before a higher court; the party dissatisfied with a lower court ruling who appeals the case to a superior court for review.

appellate jurisdiction Authority of a superior court to review decisions of inferior courts. Appellate jurisdiction empowers a higher court to conduct such a review and affirm, modify, or reverse the lower court's decision. Appellate jurisdiction is conveyed through constitutional or statutory mandate. Federal appellate jurisdiction is granted by Article III of the U.S. Constitution, which confers on the Supreme Court such jurisdiction "both as to law and fact, with such exceptions and under such regulations as the Congress shall make."

appellee The party that prevails in a lower court and against whom an appeal of the judgment is sought; in some situations called a "respondent."

bill of attainder An act of a legislature that inflicts punishment on persons supposedly guilty of high crimes, without any conviction in a normal judicial proceeding. Bills of attainder are specifically banned in Article I, Sections 9 and 10 of the U.S. Constitution.

case A general term for an action, cause, suit, or controversy, at law.

civil rights Positive acts of government designed to protect persons against arbitrary and discriminatory treatment by government or individuals. Civil rights guarantees may be found in constitutions but more frequently are provided in statutes.

comity Legal principle that prompts a court to defer to the exercise of jurisdiction by another court. Comity is a rule of judicial courtesy rather than a firm requirement of law, and it suggests that a court that first asserts jurisdiction will not undergo interference by another court without its consent.

Commerce Clause A provision found in Article I, Section 8 of the U.S. Constitution. The clause empowers Congress to "regulate commerce with foreign nations, and among the several states, and with the Indian tribes."

common law A body of principles that derive their authority from court judgments that are grounded in common customs and usages. Common law consists of principles that do not have their origin in statute and, as such, is distinct from law created by legislative enactments.

concurring opinion An opinion by a judge that agrees with the decision of the majority but disagrees with the majority's rationale—that is, the judge has arrived at the same conclusion but for different reasons.

conference A meeting of Supreme Court justices in which the justices conduct all business associated with deciding cases. It is in conferences that the Supreme Court determines which cases will be reviewed, discusses the merits of cases after oral argument, and decides by vote which party to a case will prevail. Conferences are closed to all but the justices.

Contract Clause Article I, Section 10 of the U.S. Constitution forbids any state from passing a "law impairing the obligation of contracts."

defendant The party who is sued in a civil action or charged in a criminal case; the party responding to a civil complaint. A defendant in a criminal case is the person or persons formally accused of criminal conduct.

dissenting opinion An opinion written by a judge who disagrees with the result reached by the majority.

diversity jurisdiction Authority conveyed by Article III of the U.S. Constitution empowering federal courts to hear civil actions involving parties from different states.

Due Process Clause Government procedures that follow principles of essential or fundamental fairness. Provisions designed to ensure that laws will be reasonable both in substance and in means of implementation are contained in two clauses of the U.S. Constitution. The Fifth Amendment prohibits deprivation of "life, liberty, or property, without due process of law." It sets a limit on arbitrary and unreasonable actions by the federal government. The Fourteenth Amendment contains parallel language aimed at the states. Due process requires that actions of government occur through ordered and regularized processes.

ex parte Latin for "only one side"; done for, in behalf of, or on the application of one party only.

ex post facto law A law that is passed after the occurrence of a fact or the commission of an act and thus changes the legal consequences of the fact or deed. Article I, Sections 9 and 10 of the U.S. Constitution prohibit the passage of such laws.

executive order A regulation issued by the president, a state governor, or some other executive authority for the purpose of giving effect to a constitutional or statutory provision. An executive order has the force of law and is one means by which the executive branch implements laws.

federalism A political system in which a number of sovereign political units join together, forming a larger political unit that has authority to act on behalf on the whole. A federal system or federation preserves the political integrity of all the entities comprised in the federation. Federal systems are regarded as "weak" if the central government has control over very few policy questions and "strong" if the central government possesses authority over most significant policy issues. Authority that is not exclusively assigned may be shared by the two levels and exercised concurrently. Powers not assigned to the national government are "reserved" for the states by the Tenth Amendment.

Fugitive Slave Clause Article IV, Section 2 of the U.S. Constitution provided that "no Person held to Service or Labour in one State, under the Laws thereof, escaping into another, shall, in Consequence of any Law or Regulation therein, be discharged from such Service or Labour, but shall be delivered up on Claim of the Party to whom such Service or Labour may be due." This clause provided that escaped slaves be returned to their masters. In 1793 Congress passed a fugitive slave law to implement the clause, and a revised fugitive slave law was enacted in 1850.

Guarantee Clause Article IV, section 4 of the U.S. Constitution provides that the national government shall guarantee to each state a "republican form of government"—that is, a government by representatives chosen by the people. A republic is distinguished from a pure democracy, in which the people make policy decisions themselves rather than through elected representatives.

habeas corpus Latin for "you have the body." Habeas corpus was a procedure in English law designed to prevent the improper detention of prisoners. The habeas process forced jailers to bring a detained person before a judge who would examine the justification for his or her detention. If the court found that the person was being improperly held, it could order the prisoner's release by issuing a writ of habeas corpus.

implied power Authority that is possessed by inference from expressed provisions of a constitution or statute. The intention is not manifested by explicit and direct words. The meaning is gathered by necessary deduction. Implied power is not conveyed by explicit language but rather by implication or necessary deduction from circumstances, general language, or the conduct of parties.

indictment A written accusation presented by a grand jury to a court, charging that a person has done some act or omission that by law is a punishable offense.

in re Latin for "in the matter of." The usual manner of entitling a judicial proceeding in which there are no adversary parties as such, but some issue requiring judicial action.

judicial review The power of a court to examine the actions of the legislative and executive branches with the possibility that those actions could be declared unconstitutional. The power of judicial review was discussed extensively at the Constitutional Convention of 1787, but it was not included in the Constitution as an expressly delegated judicial function. The Supreme Court first asserted the power of judicial review in *Marbury v. Madison*, 5 U.S. 137 (1803).

judicial self-restraint A view of appellate court decision making that minimizes the extent to which judges apply their personal views to the legal judgments they render. Judicial self-restraint holds that courts should defer to the policy judgments made by the elected branches of government.

jurisdiction Jurisdiction defines the boundaries within which a particular court may exercise judicial power; it defines the power of a court to hear and decide cases. The jurisdiction of federal courts is provided in Article III of the U.S. Constitution in the case of the Supreme Court, and in acts of Congress in the case of the lower federal courts. Federal judicial power may extend to classes of cases defined in terms of substance and party as well as to cases in law and equity stemming directly from the federal Constitution, federal statutes, treaties, or those cases falling into the admiralty and maritime category. Federal judicial power also extends to cases involving specified parties. Regardless of the substance of the case, federal jurisdiction includes actions to which the federal government itself is a party, between two or more states, between a state and a citizen of another state, between citizens of different states, between a state and an alien, between a citizen of a state and an alien, and in which foreign ambassadors are involved. State constitutions and statutes define the jurisdiction of state courts.

jurisprudence A legal philosophy or the science of law. A term used to refer to the course or direction of judicial rulings. Jurisprudence draws on philosophical thought, historical and political analysis, sociological and behavioral evidence, and legal experience; it is grounded in the view that ideas about law evolve from critical thinking in a number of disciplines. Jurisprudence enables people to understand how law has ordered both social institutions and individual conduct.

justiciable A justiciable matter is one that may be appropriate for a court to hear and decide.

litigant A party to a lawsuit.

mandamus Latin for "we command." A writ issued by a court of superior jurisdiction to an inferior court or governmental official commanding the performance of an official act.

martial law Military government established over a civilian population during an emergency. Under martial law, military decrees supersede civilian laws, and military tribunals replace civil courts. Martial law can be invoked by the president when necessary for the security of the nation. State governors, as commanders in chief of state militias, may declare martial law during an emergency occasioned by internal disorders or natural disasters.

motion A request made to a court for a certain ruling or action.

obiter dictum Latin for "a remark by the way." *Dicta* are statements contained in a court's opinion that are incidental to the disposition of the case. *Obiter dicta* often are directed to issues on which no formal arguments have been heard, and hence the positions represented in *dicta* are not binding on later cases.

Opinion of the Court The statement of a court that expresses the *ratio decidendi,* or the reasoning on which a decision is based. The opinion summarizes the principles of law that apply in a given case and represents the views of the majority of a court's members. When the opinion of a court reflects the views of less than a majority of its members, it is called a plurality opinion.

order A written command issued by a judge.

original jurisdiction The authority of a court to hear and decide a legal question before any other court. Original jurisdiction typically is vested with trial courts rather than appellate courts, although Article III of the U.S. Constitution extends very limited original jurisdiction to the U.S. Supreme Court. Trial courts are assigned specific original jurisdiction defined in terms of subject matter or party.

petitioner A party seeking relief in court.

plaintiff The party who brings a legal action to court for resolution or remedy.

police power Authority that empowers government to regulate private behavior in the interest of public health, safety, and general welfare. In the American constitutional system, police power resides with the state governments and not the federal government. The police power enables states and their respective local units of government to enact and enforce policies deemed appropriate to serve the public good. It is a comprehensive power, and the states have substantial discretion for its exercise. It is limited by various provisions of the U.S. Constitution and state constitutions, however, and must conform to the requirements of due process.

political question An issue that is not justiciable or that is not appropriate for judicial determination. A political question is one in which the substance of an issue is primarily political or involves a matter directed toward either the legislative or the executive branch by constitutional language. The political question doctrine is sometimes invoked by the Supreme Court not because the Court is without power or jurisdiction but because the Court adjudges the question inappropriate for judicial response. In the Court's view, to intervene or respond in such a case would be to encroach on the functions and prerogatives of one of the other two branches of government.

remand To send a case back to an inferior court for additional action. Appellate courts send cases back to lower courts with instructions to correct a specified error.

respondent The party against whom a legal action is filed.

reverse An action by an appellate court setting aside or changing a decision of a lower court. The opposite of affirm.

right A power or privilege to which a person is entitled. A right is legally conveyed by constitutions, statutes, or common law. A right may be absolute, such as one's right to believe, or it may be conditional, so that, for example, the acting out of one's beliefs will not injure other members of a political community.

separation of powers The principle of dividing the powers of government among several coordinate branches to prevent excessive concentration of power. The principle of separation of powers is designed to limit abusive exercise of governmental authority by partitioning power and assigning it to several locations. The distribution of powers embodied in the U.S. Constitution functionally distinguishes between government and people and between legislative, executive, and judicial branches. Although the Constitution creates three separate branches of government, it also assigns overlapping responsibilities, which makes the branches interdependent through the operation of a system of checks and balances.

Slave Trade Clause Article I, Section 9 of the U.S. Constitution provides that "the

Migration or Importation of such Persons as any of the States now existing shall think proper to admit, shall not be prohibited by the Congress prior to the Year one thousand eight hundred and eight, but a Tax or duty may be imposed on such Importation, not exceeding ten dollars for each person." This meant that Congress could pass a law ending the importation of African slaves in the year 1808. Congress passed such a law at that time, and the legal importation of slaves came to an end.

sovereignty The supreme power of a state or independent nation free from external interference. Sovereignty is exercised by government, which has exclusive and absolute jurisdiction within its geographical boundaries.

standing The requirement that a real dispute exist between the prospective parties in a lawsuit before it can be heard by a court. As a result, courts typically are unable to respond to hypothetical questions. If a party does not have standing to sue, the matter is not justiciable.

stare decisis Latin for "let the decision stand." Stare decisis holds that once a principle of law is established for a particular fact or situation, courts should adhere to that principle in similar cases in the future. The case in which the rule of law is established is called a precedent. Stare decisis creates and maintains stability and predictability in the law. Precedents may be modified or abandoned if circumstances require, but the expectation is that rules from previously adjudicated cases will prevail.

Tenth Amendment A provision added to the U.S. Constitution in 1791 that retains or "reserves" to the states powers that the Constitution has not assigned to the federal government. The Tenth Amendment has frequently been invoked to limit the actions of the federal government.

Three-Fifths Clause Article I, Section 2 of the U.S. Constitution provided that representatives in the U.S. House of Representatives be apportioned among the states on the basis of population. The total population of a state would include "the whole Number of free Persons, including those bound to Service for a Term of Years, and excluding Indians not taxed, three fifths of all other Persons." This meant that three-fifths of the slave population would be counted for the purposes of apportioning representatives. The Fourteenth Amendment of the Constitution specifically overruled this clause.

writ A written order of a court commanding the recipient to perform certain specified acts.

Annotated Bibliography

Published Primary Sources

Baldwin, Henry. "A General View of the Origin and Nature of the Constitution and Government of the United States, Deduced from the Political History and Conditions of the Colonies and States, from 1774 until 1788, and the Decisions of the Supreme Court of the United States, Together with Opinions in the Cased Decided at January Term 1837, Arising on the Restraints on the Powers of the States." Philadelphia: n.p., 1837.

This is an exposition of Justice Baldwin's opinions in a series of cases that he published separately from the other justices' opinions.

Curtis, Benjamin R. A Memoir of Benjamin Robbins Curtis. 2 vols. Boston: Little, Brown, and Company, 1879.

Includes not only Curtis's memoirs but also letters and other materials related to his life and work.

Tyler, Samuel, ed. *Memoir of Roger Brooke Taney, LL.D., Chief Justice of the Supreme Court of the United States*. Baltimore: John Murphy and Company, 1872.

Although overtly apologetic in tone, Tyler's memoir provides valuable insight into Taney's life and judicial career.

"The Unjust Judge: A Memorial of Roger Brooke Taney, Late Chief Justice of the United States." New York: Baker and Godwin, 1865.

This essay is the most important and vitriolic of the post–Civil War attacks on Taney.

Secondary Sources

Books

Abraham, Henry J. Justices, Presidents, and Senators: A History of the U.S. Supreme Court Appointments from Washington to Clinton, 4th ed. Lanham, MD: Rowman and Littlefield, 1999.

This reference work is the best place to begin when examining the politics of any appointment to the Supreme Court.

Baxter, Maurice. Daniel Webster and the Supreme Court. Amherst: University of Massachusetts Press, 1966.

This classic study illustrates Webster's greatness as a lawyer and his profound influence in shaping early nineteenth-century constitutional doctrine.

———. *Henry Clay the Lawyer.* Lexington: University Press of Kentucky, 2000.

This slim volume is a splendid overview of Clay's contributions to America's constitutional past.

Currie, David P. The Constitution in the Supreme Court: The First Hundred Years, 1789–1888. Chicago: University of Chicago Press, 1985.

This book surveys the Court's major constitutional decisions during the nineteenth century.

Dunne, Gerald T. Justice Joseph Story and the Rise of the Supreme Court. New York: Simon and Schuster, 1970.

A fine treatment of one of the most important members of the Taney Court.

Ely, James W., Jr. The Guardian of Every Other Right: A Constitutional History of Property Rights. New York: Oxford University Press, 1992.

This brief survey of the history of property rights includes summaries of many of the Taney Court's most important decisions in this area.

Epstein, Lee, et al. The Supreme Court Compendium: Data, Decisions, and Developments. Washington, DC: Congressional Quarterly, Inc., 1994.

This reference volume includes qualitative and quantitative information about the justices as well as patterns in their decision making.

Fehrenbacher, Don E. The Dred Scott Case: Its Significance in American Law and Politics. New York: Oxford University Press, 1978.

By far the best comprehensive study of a single case, this book will remain the authoritative work on *Dred Scott* for many years to come.

Finkelman, Paul. Dred Scott v. Sandford: A Brief History with Documents. Boston: Bedford Books, 1997.

This volume includes a very insightful overview essay on the case as well as the opinions of all of the justices.

Frank, John P. Justice Daniel Dissenting: A Biography of Peter V. Daniel, 1784–1860. New York: Augustus M. Kelley, 1970.

The only biography of the intriguing Justice Daniel.

Frankfurter, Felix. The Commerce Clause Under Marshall, Taney, and Waite. Chapel Hill: University of North Carolina, 1937.

This classic study takes a highly favorable view of Taney's commerce power decisions as well as Taney's overall judicial record.

Friedman, Leon, and Fred L. Israel. The Justices of the United States Supreme Court, 1789–1969: Their Lives and Major Opinions. 5 Vols. New York: Chelsea House, 1969.

The first and second volumes of this multivolume set are a treasure trove of information about the Taney era justices and their major decisions.

Hall, Kermit L., ed. The Oxford Companion to the Supreme Court of the United States. New York: Oxford University Press, 1992.

The best single-volume reference on the Supreme Court and its history; includes brief sketches all of the justices and major decisions of the Court.

———. The Oxford Guide to Supreme Court Decisions. New York: Oxford University Press, 1999.

This guide includes brief descriptions of all the major opinions of the Court.

Horwitz, Morton J. The Transformation of American Law, 1790–1860. Cambridge, MA: Harvard University Press, 1977.

A landmark of American legal history, this book includes a discussion of a few of the Taney Court's important decisions regarding contracts.

Huebner, Timothy S. The Southern Judicial Tradition: State Judges and Sectional Distinctiveness, 1790–1890. Athens: University of Georgia Press, 1999.

This collective biographical portrait of six nineteenth century southern state judges contains a chapter on Justice Catron's life and work.

Hyman, Harold M., and William M. Wiecek. Equal Justice Under Law: Constitutional Development, 1835–1875. New York: Harper and Row, 1982.

This book includes a balanced and insightful discussion of the work of Taney and his colleagues, with particular emphasis on the slavery issue before the Supreme Court.

Irons, Peter. A People's History of the Supreme Court. New York: Penguin Books, 1999.

An engaging account of the Court's history; includes a handful of chapters about the Taney era, particularly on slavery and the *Dred Scott* decision.

Kutler, Stanley I. Privilege and Creative Destruction: The Charles River Bridge Case. Baltimore: Johns Hopkins University Press, 1971.

The only comprehensive study of this landmark case, Kutler's work remains useful and insightful.

Levy, Beryl Harold. Our Constitution: Tool or Testament? Port Washington, NY: Kennikat Press, 1941; reprint edition, 1965.

This work includes a chapter on Taney that casts him in a very favorable light.

Lawrence, Alexander A. James Moore Wayne, Southern Unionist. Chapel Hill: University of North Carolina Press, 1943.

The only biography of Wayne, this work devotes more attention to Wayne's life than to his major opinions.

Lewis, Walker. Without Fear or Favor: A Biography of Chief Justice Roger B. Taney. Boston: Houghton Mifflin Company, 1965.

A sympathetic biography of the chief justice, this work covers the most important episodes in Taney's career.

Mendelson, Wallace. "Chief Justice Taney: Jacksonian Judge," University of Pittsburgh Law Review 12 (1950–1951): 381–393.

As the title suggests, this article seeks to explain Taney's life and work in the context of his association with Jackson.

Newmyer, R. Kent. Supreme Court Justice Joseph Story: Statesman of the Old Republic. Chapel Hill: University of North Carolina Press, 1985.

This brilliant biography is not only the best treatment of Story, it also offers insights into the other justices and the Taney era in general.

———. The Supreme Court Under Marshall and Taney. Arlington Heights, IL: Harlan Davidson, 1968.

This compact account of the Court's history under Marshall and Taney is the best succinct overview of the Taney years.

Palmer, B. W. Marshall and Taney: Statesmen of the Law. New York: Russell and Russell, 1939; reprint edition, 1966.

This work includes interpretive essays about the two towering figures in nineteenth-century U.S. constitutional history.

Saunders, Robert. John Archibald Campbell: Southern Moderate, 1811–1889. Tuscaloosa: University of Alabama Press, 1997.

The only recent scholarly study of Campbell, this book is a fine overview of the justice's life and work.

Schwartz, Bernard. A History of the Supreme Court. New York: Oxford University Press, 1993.

This survey of the Court's history includes a few chapters on the Taney era, including a chapter devoted exclusively to *Dred Scott.*

Semonche, John E. Keeping the Faith: A Cultural History of the U.S. Supreme Court. Lanham, MD: Rowman and Littlefield.

This unique interpretation of the Court and its history offers insights into a few of the Taney Court's major decisions.

Silver, David M. Lincoln's Supreme Court. Urbana: University of Illinois Press, 1957.

Although now nearly a half century old, this work stands as the authoritative study of the justices, their decisions, and the politics surrounding the Court during the Civil War era.

Smith, Charles W., Jr. Roger B. Taney: Jacksonian Jurist. Chapel Hill: University of North Carolina Press, 1936.

This brief biography provides a sympathetic portrayal of Taney's judicial work.

Steiner, Bernard. Life of Roger Brooke Taney, Chief Justice of the U.S. Supreme Court. Westport, CT: Greenwood Press, 1970; originally published in 1922.

The first attempt to write a comprehensive biography of Taney.

Swisher, Carl B. *Roger B. Taney.* New York: Macmillan, 1936.

Despite its age and its admiring tone, this biography is still the most compelling and comprehensive account of Taney's life and work.

———. History of the Supreme Court of the United States, vol. 6, The Taney Period, 1836–1864. New York: Macmillan, 1974.

By far the best and most comprehensive history of the Supreme Court under Taney, this volume includes information on the justices, the major decisions of the era, and the inner workings of the Court.

Urofsky, Melvin I., ed. The Supreme Court Justices: A Biographical Dictionary. New York: Garland Publishing, 1987.

This collection contains useful biographical sketches of the justices.

Warren, Charles. The Supreme Court in United States History, vol. 2, 1836–1918. Boston: Little, Brown, and Company, 1928.

This work is still the best survey of most of the major decisions of the Taney Court.

Weisenburger, F. P. The Life of John McLean: A Politician on the United States Supreme Court. Columbus: Ohio State University Press, 1937.

Although dated, this is the only biographical study of Justice McLean.

Wiecek, William M. The Guarantee Clause of the U.S. Constitution. Ithaca, NY: Cornell University Press, 1972.

This is the best treatment of the Guarantee Clause and the Court's landmark decision in *Luther v. Borden.*

Wiecek, William M. Liberty Under Law: The Supreme Court in American Life. Baltimore: Johns Hopkins University Press, 1988.

A brief history of the Court, this book contains a few chapters on the Taney Era.

Articles

Burnette, Lawrence, Jr. "Peter V. Daniel: Agrarian Justice." Virginia Magazine of History and Biography 62 (1954): 289–305.

This engaging article is one of the few scholarly treatments of an often overlooked member of the Taney Court.

Conron, Michael A. "Law, Politics, and Chief Justice Taney: A Reconsideration of the Luther v. Borden Decision." American Journal of Legal History 11 (1967): 377–388.

This essay offers a distinctive interpretive twist on the landmark case.

Chandler, Walter. "The Centenary of Associate Justice John Catron of the United States Supreme Court." Tennessee Law Review 15 (1937): 32–51.

This essay is still one of the best overviews of Justice Catron's career on the Supreme Court.

Finkelman, Paul. "'Hooted Down the Page of History': Reconsidering the Greatness of Chief Justice Taney." Journal of Supreme Court History (1994): 83–102.

This insightful and forcefully argued article takes a dim view of Taney's judicial record.

———. "Prigg v. Pennsylvania and Northern State Courts: Anti-Slavery Use of a Pro-Slavery Decision." Civil War History 25 (1979): 5–35.

An insightful essay in which Finkelman makes the point that *Prigg* was more proslavery than is often admitted in the scholarship on the case.

"From Judicial Grant to Legislative Power: The Admiralty Clause in the Nineteenth Century." Harvard Law Review 67 (1954): 1214–1237.

A nice overview of the Court's early and mid–nineteenth century admiralty decisions.

Gass, Edmund C. "The Constitutional Opinions of Justice John Catron." East Tennessee Historical Society Publications (1936): 54–73.

A survey of Catron's major constitutional opinions.

Harris, Robert J. "Chief Justice Taney: Prophet of Reform and Reaction." Vanderbilt Law Review 10 (1956–57): 227–257.

An overview of Taney's major constitutional opinions emphasizing Taney's contributions to the doctrine of police power and the notion of federalism.

Hicks, Jimmie. "Associate Justice John McKinley: A Sketch." Alabama Review 18 (1965): 227–233.

One of only a few treatments of Justice McKinley.

Hughes, Charles Evans. "Roger Brooke Taney." American Bar Association Journal 17 (December 1931): 785–790.

Hughes's important essay stands as one of the landmarks in Taney's early-twentieth-century rehabilitation.

Jordan, Christine. "Justice John Campbell: Last of the Jacksonians." Supreme Court Historical Society Yearbook (1980): 78–88.

A helpful, brief treatment of an important yet often overlooked member of the Court.

Kahn, Michael A. "The Appointment of John McLean to the Supreme Court: Practical Presidential Politics in the Jacksonian Era." Journal of Supreme Court History (1993): 59–72.

This essay is one of the few in-depth studies of the appointment of a justice during the Taney period.

Leach, Richard H. "Benjamin Robbins Curtis: Judicial Misfit." New England Quarterly 25 (1952): 507–524.

One of the few assessments of Curtis's Supreme Court career.

Schmidhauser, John R. "Judicial Behavior and the Sectional Crisis of 1837–1860." Journal of Politics 23 (1961): 615–640.

Offering a unique interpretation, Schmidhauser places the justices of the Taney Court era firmly in the context of the sectional dispute.

Spector, Robert M. "Lincoln and Taney: A Study in Constitutional Polarization." American Journal of Legal History 15 (1971): 199–214.

This essay shows the extent to which Lincoln and Taney embodied the constitutional conflicts of the Civil War.

Stern, Robert L. "Chief Justice Taney and the Shadow of Dred Scott." Journal of Supreme Court History (1992): 39–52.

An overview of Taney's judicial career, with a particular emphasis on *Dred Scott.*

Streichler, Stuart A. "Justice Curtis's Dissent in the Dred Scott Case: An Interpretive Study." Hastings Constitutional Law Quarterly 24 (1997): 509–544.

Streichler's essay clearly explicates Justice Curtis's significant dissenting opinion in *Dred Scott.*

Taylor, M. Flavia. "The Political and Civil Career of Henry Baldwin, 1799–1830." Western Pennsylvania Historical Magazine 24 (1941): 37–50.

This is the only scholarly treatment of Baldwin's career to date.

Winitsky, Marvin Laurence. "Roger B. Taney: A Historiographical Inquiry." Maryland Historical Magazine 69 (1974): 1–26.

An insightful survey of how historians have treated Taney, invaluable for understanding the chief justice's ever-changing reputation.

Internet Resources

The Internet has become a useful tool for researching the U.S. Supreme Court. Many Web sites include information about the Court, including some that have most or all of the opinions published in the *United States Reports.* Because information about the pre–Civil War Supreme Court is still relatively scarce on the Web, the books and articles listed above remain the best place to begin when researching the Taney period.

www.findlaw.com

This site includes federal and state case law and statutes. Although its historical case database is incomplete, it does provide the texts of many opinions from the Taney era.

www.lexis-nexis.com

A subscription database, Lexis-Nexis is the best site for accessing the complete decisions of the U.S. Supreme Court, including those from the Taney period.

http://oyez.itcs.northwestern.edu/oyez/frontpage

This site contains basic biographical data on all of the justices of the U.S. Supreme Court, their pictures, and a list of the Court's major decisions.

http://www.supremecourt.us.gov

This site provides an overview of the U.S. Supreme Court as an institution, including information about the Court's traditions, procedures, rules, docket, and calendar. Particularly useful for students of the Taney era are a "case citation finder" and a list of decision dates for most of the Court's nineteenth-century opinions.

Index

About the Author

Timothy S. Huebner is associate professor of history at Rhodes College in Memphis, Tennessee.

www.ingramcontent.com/pod-product-compliance
Ingram Content Group UK Ltd.
Pitfield, Milton Keynes, MK11 3LW, UK
UKHW050946290926
15470UKWH00005B/1664